Flower Hunters

Flower Hunters

MARY GRIBBIN & JOHN GRIBBIN

OXFORD
UNIVERSITY PRESS

OXFORD
UNIVERSITY PRESS

Great Clarendon Street, Oxford OX2 6DP

Oxford University Press is a department of the University of Oxford.
It furthers the University's objective of excellence in research, scholarship,
and education by publishing worldwide in

Oxford New York

Auckland Cape Town Dar es Salaam Hong Kong Karachi
Kuala Lumpur Madrid Melbourne Mexico City Nairobi
New Delhi Shanghai Taipei Toronto

With offices in

Argentina Austria Brazil Chile Czech Republic France Greece
Guatemala Hungary Italy Japan Poland Portugal Singapore
South Korea Switzerland Thailand Turkey Ukraine Vietnam

Oxford is a registered trade mark of Oxford University Press
in the UK and in certain other countries

Published in the United States
by Oxford University Press Inc., New York

British Library Cataloguing in Publication Data

Data available

Library of Congress Cataloging in Publication Data

Data available

Typeset by SPI Publisher Services, Pondicherry, India
Printed in Great Britain
on acid-free paper by
Clays Ltd, St Ives plc

ISBN 978-0-19-280718-2

1

ACKNOWLEDGEMENTS

W E WOULD LIKE to thank the following people and institutions for help in finding information about the botanists whose lives and work we describe in this book: Biblioteca Apostolica Vaticana; Bibliothèque nationale de France; Catharina Blomberg; Cambridge University Library; Charles Denoon; Eleanor Gallucci; Ben Gribbin; Jon Gribbin; Mark Hindmarsh; Jardin des Plantes, Paris; the library of King's College, London; Linnaean Society; Manchester Museum; Middleton Hall Trust; Public Record Office, Kew; Ray Society; Peter and Susan Rogan; Bernard Rondeau; Royal Botanical Gardens, Kew; Royal Geographical Society; Royal Horticultural Society; Royal Society; Trinity College, Dublin. Latha Menon of Oxford University Press suggested significant improvements in the presentation.

Financial support was provided by the Alfred C. Munger Foundation, and the University of Sussex continues to provide us with a base from which to work. We would also like to thank the staff at Southlands canteen for providing a quiet corner and cups of tea when needed.

Mary Gribbin
John Gribbin

April 2007

CONTENTS

LIST OF ILLUSTRATIONS

INTRODUCTION

B OTANY MAY SEEM like a safe, stay-at-home occupation, like stamp collecting. But that certainly was not the case for many adventurous botanists from the middle of the seventeenth century to the end of the nineteenth century. Where, after all, did the plants that are now so familiar in Europe come from? From the Douglas-fir and the monkey puzzle tree to orchids and azaleas, they were found in distant regions of the globe by intrepid botanist explorers who travelled on foot or horseback through wild and often unexplored country, up previously unclimbed mountains and through almost impenetrable jungle, often encountering hostility from the locals, overcoming hunger and disease to send back the fruits of their labours. Why is tea grown in India? How did quinine get to be produced in industrial quantities to alleviate the scourge of malaria? All thanks to the botanical explorers, men driven by their thirst for knowledge (and in some cases profit) to an extent that often made them outcasts from polite society.

Think of Charles Darwin on the famous voyage of the *Beagle*, of the reason why Botany Bay in Australia got its name, or the origins of the blue poppy. And if you still think botany is a 'soft' science, think of its importance to the development of science. For the obvious reason that, like astronomy, botany can be investigated in some detail using the unaided human senses, the study of plants was at the forefront of the scientific revolution of the seventeenth century, which was the key factor in shaping the modern world. The botanical discoveries made then only seem obvious to us now because familiarity has bred contempt—just as it is 'obvious' to us that the Earth goes round the Sun, although this was a revolutionary idea at the beginning of the seventeenth century.

Our story involves the overlapping lives of eleven botanical explorers, from the early eighteenth century to the early twentieth century. But the 'pre-history' of these adventures begins with John Ray, a seventeenth-century botanist who can be regarded as the botanical equivalent of his contemporary Isaac Newton. He did more than anyone else to lay the foundations for the scientific study of the world of plants, and it would be remiss of us not to include him, if only as the Prologue to our main story. Rising from his childhood as the son of a blacksmith to become a Fellow of Trinity College, Cambridge, Ray established the modern concept of species, spelling out that one species is 'never born from the seed of another species'. He was also a pioneer plant hunter travelling for three years throughout Europe on a botanical odyssey—small beer, perhaps, compared with the travels of some of his successors, but at the time an unprecedented journey of scientific discovery.

The Swede Carl Linnaeus, chronologically the first of our 'First XI' botanical explorers, took Ray's ideas forward into the eighteenth century. An obsessive who made lists of everything and governed his life by strict routine, he wrote of himself that he could not 'understand anything that is not systematically ordered'. This passion for order led him to develop the idea of using the differences between the reproductive parts of flowering plants as a means of cataloguing and classifying them. Linnaeus gave each species a two-word Latin name, and disciplined this idea into a precise and systematic method of identification.

Linnaeus ran his university field trips like some sort of good-natured botanical boot camp full of order and expected obedience. He didn't travel much himself and told exaggerated tales about his limited experience of botanical exploration. But none of this prevented him from being a popular and inspirational teacher who encouraged his students to travel the world to seek out new plants. They were the first generation of global botanist explorers, and many of them paid with their lives for their discoveries.

As the world was opened up to Europeans by voyagers such as Captain James Cook, botanists sailed with them. Joseph Banks, often described as the father of plant explorers and one of the most influential scientists of his time, was the botanist on Cook's first voyage around the world. Banks decided not to travel with Cook on his second circumnavigation mainly because his grand ideas of personal luggage led him to fall out with the Admiralty. Instead his place as botanical explorer was taken by Francis Masson, a gardener who was the first plant collector to be sent out from Kew. A quiet, unassuming man from Aberdeen, Masson was jolted into a life of adventure in South Africa, narrowly escaping death many times. Circumstances led him to travel with a botanist from the Linnean School in Sweden, Carl Peter Thunberg. The modest, quietly spoken Masson was probably one of the few people who could stand living with Thunberg, who was a loud and incorrigibly conceited know-all. But this odd couple made a good team in braving the dangers and privations of the wilds of South Africa—floods, inhospitable terrain and inhabitants, as well as the unexpected dangers of hippopotamus pits.

David Douglas also had a passionate interest in botany from early childhood. Born in Scone, Scotland he served a seven-year apprenticeship in the gardens of Scone Place, impressing everyone with his quick wit and determination to learn. Exploring in the north-west of North America, Douglas suffered many alarming incidents, mainly due to crushingly bad luck, which seemed to dog him wherever he went. But with a relentless determination to get through and do the job Douglas persevered, took time out to climb mountains just for the fun of it, and eventually returned to England the hard way—on foot across the continent to the eastern seaboard of Canada before embarking on a ship. Sadly he is probably equally well remembered for coming to a dramatically sticky end. While on an expedition to the

Sandwich Islands in 1834 he fell into a covered pit that had been dug to trap animals and was gored to death by a bullock already caught in the same trap.

The puzzle about Richard Spruce is why he *didn't* die in the jungles of South America. A Yorkshireman who had a brief career as a schoolmaster before giving up on grounds of chronic ill-health, he dedicated his life to botany. He collected first in the Pyrenees in 1845–6 and from 1849 until 1864 in South America. He scraped a subsistence living from the modest profits made by botanical specimens sent back to Britain. Battling against rats, vampire bats, scorpions, armies of viciously stinging ants, disease, and even a plot to kill him, Spruce made flower and fern discoveries which opened up South America. His great achievement was collecting seeds of the plant from which quinine is produced, but even for this he was paid scarcely enough by the British Government to cover his living expenses. His health completely ruined, he did at least make it back to Scotland, where he lived out his remaining years on a modest pension in a tiny cottage.

Just one woman makes our team—the extraordinary Marianne North, who visited almost every continent and many islands in the Pacific and Atlantic Oceans in search of flowers, not so much as a collector but as a skilled painter, who has left us a beautiful, and scientifically valuable, record of the plants she saw. Her adventures were less dramatic than those of David Douglas or Richard Spruce, but for a Victorian woman no less remarkable in their way.

Spruce made a major contribution to human health by getting quinine out of South America; Robert Fortune made a major contribution to human happiness by getting tea out of China. He spent nineteen years exploring the East, becoming one of the first Britons to speak fluent Chinese. He travelled widely throughout China, often in disguise, through regions officially closed to Westerners. Attacked by pirates, dismayed by the living conditions he had to face, and suffering from tropical fevers, he managed, despite the protective secretiveness of the Chinese, to transfer nearly 25,000 young tea plants, more than

15,000 seedlings, and eight Chinese growers from China to the foot-hills of the Himalayas and Ceylon for the East India Company. By the end of the nineteenth century, tea was India's main export.

But the man who found out most about the plants of the Himalaya was Joseph Hooker. He served his apprenticeship as a naval surgeon and botanist on the last great expedition by sail into Antarctic waters, under Captain James Ross. But he made his name with his travels through India, trekking up from the foothills of the Himalaya to the high passes, which led to his discovery of spectacular rhododendron trees and exquisite magnolias. He travelled to Sikkim and Tibet, where the volatile political situation coupled with the terrible weather and harsh terrain sorely tested his strength and determination. During his journey to the area around Kanchenjunga, a starting party of over 50 'servants' dwindled to fifteen local porters as conditions became increasingly bad. In his eyes, the magnificent rhododendrons he saw were alone enough to justify the hardship, and he collected seed from twenty-five different species to send back to Kew—it was Hooker who was largely responsible for the Victorians' mania for rhododendrons.

Joseph Banks circled the globe with Cook in a sailing ship. Joseph Hooker came home from India by steamship. Our story is mostly about the adventures of the botanists who explored the globe between those eras, before travel became easy. We have had to be selective, and could not include all of those botanists and all of their adventures. We have chosen to tell the story more or less chronologically, from the time of Ray in the seventeenth century up to the twentieth century, picking subjects whose lives mostly overlap (or nearly overlap) in time, to span the best part of four centuries. So our 'First XI' is first chronologically as much as anything, which rules out such pioneers as Ernest 'Chinese' Wilson or George Forrest, whose botanizing took place mostly in the twentieth century.

Like any such list, our choice is also to some extent subjective, and there is one inclusion and one omission in particular that deserve comment. Carl Linnaeus didn't really do much exploring in his own right; but he had such an influence both on other plant hunters and on botany in general that we could not exclude him. On the other hand, you will find little here about Charles Darwin (1809–82), even though he was a botanical explorer of the first rank, simply because his story has been told so often already and we hope to offer something less familiar. Even so, it was difficult to narrow our choice down to eleven, and had we had space to include a 'twelfth man' it would certainly have been Alfred Russel Wallace (1823–1913), Darwin's contemporary and the independent co-discoverer of the principle of evolution by natural selection, who was active as a botanical explorer in both South America and the Far East. Happily, though, he does come into the story to some extent in our final chapters.

But the scene for our story is set by the tale of John Ray, who lived in times that were revolutionary in more ways than one.

JOHN RAY

(1627–1705)

J OHN RAY WAS well aware that he lived through, and participated in, a profound revolution in the way people interacted with nature. In the preface to his synopsis of British plants, published in 1690, he gave thanks to God that he had been born in a time when the traditional dependence on the teaching of Aristotle had given way to the new philosophy, based on experiment and observation of the real world, that we now call science. He picked out as examples of the success of this new experimental philosophy the work of Robert Boyle in investigating the properties of air, the invention of the telescope and microscope, and William Harvey's discovery of the circulation of the blood—all examples which still highlight today what exciting times Ray lived in. The other landmark we might hightlight was the foundation of the Royal Society, in 1660.

Ray was the son of Roger Ray, the blacksmith in the village of Black Notley, near Braintree in Essex. John Ray's mother, Elizabeth, was also an important and respected member of the community, a healer who was an expert in folk medicine and the use of herbs to treat ailments. John was born on 29 November 1627; he had one brother, Roger, who was three years his senior, and a sister, Elizabeth, who was 2 when John was born. Roger would die, probably of smallpox, at the age of 8; but apart from the record of their births and in Roger's case death, we know nothing else about the siblings. Ray must have stood out as an unusually bright boy among his schoolmates, and his academic talents were recognized by the Vicar of Braintree, a Samuel Collins, who had graduated from Trinity College, Cambridge, in 1600, and maintained his links with the university. Under the influence of Collins, Ray was admitted to Trinity on 12 May 1644, when he was in his seventeenth year—a huge step for a village blacksmith's son. He was a little old to be starting at university in those days, and registered with the status of 'sizar', a poor student who was excused fees in exchange for acting as a servant for a more wealthy student. But something—there is no record of what—went wrong with the arrangement, and on 28 June Ray transferred to Catharine Hall,[1] entirely through the good offices of Collins.

In 1631, a Thomas Hobbes of Gray's Inn (not 'the' Thomas Hobbes) had left a bequest to be administered by the Vicar of Braintree which provided in part for the support of poor scholars at the University of Cambridge, specifying that the students should be chosen by the Vicar, and suggesting as preference that they be educated at Catharine Hall or Emmanuel College. So Ray made the transfer, with one minor hiccup. In the records at Catharine Hall he was entered as 'Wray a scholar'. Spelling was fairly free and easy in those days, and although Ray had always been Ray up until then, he made no objection and would be known as Wray until 1670, when he reverted to the spelling favoured by his father. We shall stick to Ray, for consistency.

Although Cambridge was in the Parliamentary sphere of influence during the Civil War, and was not directly affected by the violence of the times, the alliance between Parliament and the Scots under the Solemn League and Covenant, which occurred in the year Ray went up to Cambridge, would cause problems for many of the university's members. At the start of the troubles most members of the university, which was still very much a religious establishment, leaned towards

Puritanism, but also felt a loyalty to the Crown; this led to the expulsion of many senior members who refused to swear to the Solemn League and Covenant, and their replacement. Ray himself might best be described as a puritan with a small 'p'. He had no time for the ostentatious trappings and ceremonies of the Anglican church that had been inherited from Catholicism, but he wasn't the sort of person to go round cutting people's heads off if they didn't agree with him. He was deeply religious, and took formal vows and oaths seriously; but as a very junior member of the university in the 1640s, these changes went on over his head.

Ray made a solid start at Catharine Hall, and quickly gained a reputation as a brilliant student; but he found the college old-fashioned and backward in its teaching, which harked back to the Liberal Arts of antiquity. In 1646, a year after his first tutor, Daniel Duckfield, died, Ray, with his reputation as a scholar now established, and Collins's continuing influence to help, transferred back to Trinity as a sizar. There he found that 'the politer arts and sciences were principally minded and cultivated'. Trinity was more amenable to the new idea of studying the world through experiment and observation rather than regarding Aristotle as the last word, and Ray found a kindred spirit there in his contemporary Isaac Barrow, born in 1630, who also transferred to Trinity in 1646, after two years at Peterhouse. Barrow is best remembered today as the first Lucasian Professor of Mathematics in Cambridge, appointed in 1663, who taught Isaac Newton and was succeeded by him in 1669; he later became Master of Trinity.

The two students spurred each other on, mastering the Classics (Greek, Latin, and Hebrew) and mathematics; but there was nothing that we would now call science in the curriculum. They graduated together in 1648, and in 1649, Ray's twenty-second year, they were both elected as junior Fellows of Trinity College. Ray later became a senior Fellow, but the exact date of that election is not known. Because the colleges were religious foundations, part of the traditional process involved a new Fellow seeking ordination. But at the time Ray was elected to his Fellowship, bishops had been abolished by the Commonwealth, and the official view of Trinity College, along with many other institutions, was that if there were no bishops around to do the ordaining, nobody could be ordained. Ray let the matter rest, and progressed through the college hierarchy for the next decade without taking holy orders. He was appointed Lecturer in Greek in 1651, Lecturer in Mathematics in 1653, Lecturer in Humanities in 1655, and Lecturer in Greek (once again) the following year.

Ray seems to have taken up the study of the natural world, together with a circle of friends that he had acquired as an undergraduate, almost immediately after graduating, at the end of the 1640s. His conversion into a naturalist—in particular, into a botanist—followed an illness. In the Preface to his catalogue of English plants, Ray tells us that he suffered an illness in his early twenties, and was advised to take long walks and ride in the fresh air while recovering. The illness seems to have been as much a mental breakdown as physical, and may have been a result of overwork and the strain of seeking election to his Fellowship, which would place the convalescence in 1649 or 1650. By the autumn of 1654, the activities of Ray and his friends had become such a notable part of the Cambridge scene that Barrow referred to them light-heartedly in an Oration at Trinity:

At what time, I ask you, since the foundation of the University has a murderous curiosity wrought savageries of death and dismemberment against so many dogs, fishes, birds in order to notify you of the structure and functions of the parts of animals? A most innocent cruelty! An easily excusable ferocity! What am I to say of the history of plants, a subject eagerly explored by your freshmen? Men have hardly struck their roots in the seed plots of the Muses before they are able to recognise and name all the plants that grow wild in the fields or cultivated in gardens—plants most of which Dioscorides[2] himself if he were still alive would fail to identify.

The reason why even the first-year students at Trinity in the mid-1650s were able to identify the plants and flowers around Cambridge was that they were being taught (unofficially; none of this was part of their formal education) by Ray, who, finding nobody able to teach him, had investigated the flora for himself.

Many of these followers of Ray were young gentlemen, the sons of landed gentry, who had a natural, if dilettante, interest in country matters. But a few of the young men that Ray met around this time, including Francis Willughby and Philip Skippon, took his efforts to understand the natural world much more seriously; Willughby, in particular, would soon play a major part in changing the course of Ray's life.

Ray's father died in 1656, leaving the widowed Elizabeth Ray on her own—there is no mention of John's sister, and the presumption is she had also died some time earlier. Thanks to his Fellowship at Trinity, John Ray was able to pay for a new house to be built for her at Black Notley, where she lived in reasonable comfort on a modest income from the rent on a small plot of land. Ray had only himself to support from now on, which would become an important factor in the 1660s.

By this time, having been forced to teach himself about the plants of the region for lack of any authority on which to draw, Ray had started work on what would become his *Cambridge Catalogue* of plants.[3] The book wouldn't be published until 1660, because Ray, as he explained in the Preface, had to start from scratch:

I had first to become familiar with the literature, to compare the plants that I found with the pictures, and when there seemed to be a resemblance to go fully into the descriptions. Gaining skill by experience, I enquired of any unknown plant to what tribe and family it belonged or could be assigned: this taught me to notice points of similarity and saved a vast deal of labour. Then the desire arose to help others in their difficulties. I was eager to make progress myself: I wanted to entice my friends to share my pursuits: so the idea of the *Catalogue* was formed.

The result was the first truly scientific attempt at classifying plants, which Ray dedicated to 'the true philosophers whose concern is not so much to know what authors think as to gaze with their own eyes on the nature of things and to listen with their own ears to [nature's] voice'. This way of thinking was at the heart of the scientific revolution, and very much in the spirit of the Royal Society, which had its own formal beginning at a meeting held in London[4] the year the *Cambridge Catalogue* was published.

In the *Catalogue*, Ray first discussed the state of knowledge before his work, giving credit to his predecessors in the world of botanical classification and reviewing their achievements—he was a master at this kind of preliminary survey. He clarified existing descriptions of plants, sorting out a confusion of synonyms, and from his own observations he gave details about morphology, flowering times, whether the plants were annual or perennial, and, echoing his mother's skills, their medicinal uses. He gave both English and Latin names, and information about the habitats the plants preferred. Just as importantly, he eschewed the astrological and alchemical speculations of his predecessors and many of his contemporaries, and stuck to the facts.

By the time the *Cambridge Catalogue* was published, Ray was already making plans for a much more ambitious work, a complete *Flora* of Britain. But even this would be only part of a much wider scheme hatched in collaboration with Willughby—a complete description of the plant and animal worlds. Such a grandiose scheme could never have been put into practice by a blacksmith's son from Essex. He simply didn't have the resources to carry it through. But Willughby did have the requisite resources, connections, and aristocratic background, and his imagination had been fired by Ray's enthusiasm.

Willughby was the only son of Sir Francis Willughby of Middleton Hall in Warwickshire, who also had estates in Nottinghamshire. Sir Francis was married to Lady Cassandra, the daughter of Thomas Ridgeway, the first Earl of Londonderry. His son, who had been born in 1635, was one of those conscientious wealthy men with a sense of duty and responsibility, diligently carrying out the affairs of their estates, and sometimes the affairs of State. He was also eager to help the older man, by now his friend, in his botanical adventures, and he had the financial resources to put their ideas into practice.

In the summer of 1658, Ray made a journey across England and into Wales studying plants and their habitats. He learned of the death of Oliver Cromwell, who was succeeded by his son Richard, while on these travels. In 1659, Ray stayed in Cambridge working on the *Catalogue*, but in the long vacation of 1660, now accompanied by Willughby, he went on a tour of the north of England, even venturing across the sea to the Isle of Man, and into Scotland. This was a key event in the lives of both men. Their plan, hatched on the expedition and made feasible by Willughby's wealth, became to bring order to nature by classifying every living thing according to its own properties and its relationship to other living things. This expansion of the geographical and scientific range of Ray's investigation of the natural world took place, however, against a background of political change in the country at large that also swept through Cambridge.

When the Master of Trinity died in 1659, his successor, appointed by Richard Cromwell at the specific request of the Fellows of the college, was John Wilkins, the Warden of Wadham College in Oxford. During the Parliamentary interregnum, Wilkins had been instrumental in gathering together in Oxford a group of experimental philosophers—including Robert Boyle, Robert Hooke, Christopher Wren, and Ray's former Cambridge contemporary Thomas Millington—who laid the foundations of organized science in England; after the Restoration, many of these men moved to London, and helped to found the Royal Society.

With the Restoration, Wilkins and many other senior members of the university (indeed, both universities), seen as Parliamentary sympathizers, were ejected, and many of the older men who had been ejected by Parliament were recalled while the old ways were re-established. Ray's position was complicated by two facts. First, although the governing body of Trinity College had decided in 1658 that it would be legal for

Fellows to be ordained after all, Ray had not yet taken that step. He seems to have regarded his convictions as a matter between himself and God, and did not see that being ordained ought to make any difference either to his convictions or to his right to minister; indeed, he often preached in the college chapel without having been ordained. With the Restoration, it was assumed by most of his colleagues at Trinity that Ray would continue to decline ordination, and would lose his fellowship; but many hoped that he might be persuaded to stay. The second complication was that at the time all this was happening Ray was away on his tour of the north with Willughby, and wasn't in Cambridge to discuss the possibilities.

Ray's first inclination was to accept the inevitable, as is shown in letters he wrote in the autumn of 1660. In one, he commented: 'I am at present resolved to discontinue from the college so soon as I shall have made even my accounts therewith . . . If I do concoct this subscription, it will be certainly contrary to my inclinations, and purely out of fear.' But Ray was by now an important member of the college community. In 1658 he had been appointed Junior Dean, and in 1659 Steward, as well as being a respected Tutor and Lecturer. His colleagues were eager for him to stay, and persuaded him that the rituals he disliked so strongly were part of the price to pay for a reformed and united church in a peaceful and settled society. This was, in essence, the whole reason for the Restoration; he allowed himself to be convinced, and was ordained in December 1660. But like so many people, his hopes would be dashed by the unreliability of Charles II.

In 1661, the year Isaac Newton went up to Trinity, Ray settled down to his duties in Cambridge. In the summer, he went on another expedition to the north, accompanied by Philip Skippon and a single servant (Skippon's, of course).

The seeds for their European adventure may have been sown in conversations between Ray and Willughby on their expedition of 1660, but they would flower in 1662, a year after the second expedition to the north. During the Easter vacation of 1662, Ray travelled south, staying with friends in Sussex, and during what would turn out to be his last term in Cambridge he continued to explore the locality, and to discover plants that he had never seen before. This may have been a conscious farewell to the region, because by then Parliament had already discussed what became known as the Act of Uniformity, although it had not yet come into force.[5] The Act would impose the rites and ceremonies of the Book of Common Prayer as standard practice in the established Church of England, and require ordination by bishops for all ministers. But there was another requirement of the Act, which would come into force on St Bartholomew's Day, 24 August. This harked back to the Civil War, and the Solemn League and Covenant.

Charles II insisted not only that the oath taken by Covenanters was unlawful and that nobody was bound by it, but also that all clerics and holders of university posts had to formally declare that they agreed with this. Ray had never sworn the Covenanter's oath, but he deeply believed that an oath was a commitment in the eyes of God, whatever the reason why it was sworn, and that nobody, not even a king, could make it otherwise. He knew that he would never declare the oath of allegiance to the Covenant unlawful, and that therefore he would be ejected from all his posts in Cambridge on 24 August. After that date, in spite of his ordination, he would be regarded as a nonconformist, and be disbarred from any official post involving holy orders. But in his own eyes, he would still be a priest, and in his own words, divinity would be his profession, barred from any secular employment by the fact of his ordination. Hardly surprisingly, he left Cambridge early that year, on Ascension Day, 8 May 1662. He travelled through North-amptonshire and via Coventry to Middleton Hall, to meet up not just with Willughby but Skippon as well.

All of the travelling companions got on well together, and as they travelled through Wales and down into the West Country of England the vague scheme of classifying nature, planted in the minds of Willughby and Ray the previous year, grew into a real project in which they planned to travel through Europe, where Ray, now free from his university commitments, would classify the world of plants, while Willughby would concentrate on birds, beasts, fishes, and insects (the term 'insect' at that time meant anything not classified as a bird, beast, or fish). Skippon, with a more dilettante interest, would be their companion in the adventures they planned, and help to finance the expedition. It was also on their travels through Wales and the West Country that Ray and Willughby developed techniques for recording their observations in a scientific manner, so that species could be compared with one another, and began to pay more attention to the conditions in which plants and animals lived naturally.

Ray returned via London to Essex, staying away from Cambridge, with his mother at Black Notley, while the fateful date of 24 August passed. At the end of the month he went to Cambridge for a few days to settle his affairs, then took a temporary post as tutor, one of the few possibilities open to an ordained priest without a parish, at the home of a Thomas Bacon, Friston Hall, near Saxmundham in Suffolk. In March 1663, now aged 35 and with no prospects but a few good friends, Ray left Suffolk and met up with Skippon at Leeds Abbey, in Kent; together, they travelled to Dover, where they joined Willughby and Nathanial Bacon (probably no relation to Thomas Bacon), who had gone up to Trinity in 1653, a year after Willughby, and been one of Ray's students. They sailed on 18 April on an adventure that would last, for Ray and Skippon, for three years.

We know a great deal about the expedition because in 1673 the Royal Society published Ray's account of his travels under the splendid title *Observations Topographical, Moral & Physiological; Made in a Journey Through Part of the Low-Countries, Germany, Italy, and France: with A Catalogue of Plants not Native of England, found Spontaneously growing in those Parts and their Virtues*; Robert Hooke records in his diary buying one of the first copies of the book, on 26 February that year. As the title suggests, the catalogue, which was the important scientific record that Ray and the Royal Society wanted to get into print, was combined, for sound commercial reasons, with an account of the travels likely to appeal to non-scientific readers who would buy the book for the travel story and thereby subsidize the publication of the scientific material. As Ray put it himself in the book, the narrative was included 'considering the paucity of those who delight in studies and enquiries of this nature [the Catalogue]'.

The book is full of information about the places Ray's party passed through—the buildings, forms of government, universities, social customs, geography, and more. It is a surprisingly good read, at least in parts, with many highlights which are fascinating historically both because of the light they shed on a period from our past and because of the light they shed on how strange many of the people and places Ray encountered were to him. Passing through what is now Belgium (then a province of Spain), he is struck by buried forests 'found in places which five hundred years ago were sea', and struggles to combine this evidence of antiquity with the then accepted biblical chronology of the Earth:

digging ten or twenty Ells deep in the Earth, they find whole woods of Trees in which the trunks, Boughs and Leaves do exactly appear, that one may easily distinguish the several kinds of them, and very plainly discern the series of Leaves which have fallen yearly. These subterraneous woods are found in those places which 500 years ago were Sea, and afterwards either left and thrown up by Sea, or gained from it, the Tides being kept of by Walls and Fences. But before the fore-mentioned term of 500 years, there is no memory that these places were part of the Continent...

The Question is, How these Trees come to be buried so deep under ground? To which we may probably answer, that many Ages ago before all Records of Antiquity... these places were part of the firm Land, and covered with Wood; afterwards being undermined and overwhelmed by the violence of the Sea, they continued so long underwater, till the Rivers brought down Earth and Mud enough to cover the trees, fill up thes Shallows, and restore them to firm Land again ... that of old time the bottom of the Sea lay so deep and that that hundred foot thickness of Earth arose from the sediment of those great Rivers which there emptied themselves into the Sea ... is a strange thing considering the novity of the World, the age whereof according to the usual account is not 5600 years.

Ray was very much still in a minority of advanced scientific thinkers when he said that the fossils he saw later on the journey 'were originally the shells or bones of living fishes and other animals bred in the sea'.

The party travelled by boat up the Rhine, then overland through Switzerland to Italy. After visiting Venice they moved on to Padua for the winter, where Ray, not one to waste time in idling even when the season was unsuitable for botanizing, attended lectures in anatomy at the university. Padua was one of the best medical schools (indeed, best universities) in Europe at the time, and the teaching was, of course, in Latin, a language in which Ray was fluent. William Harvey had studied there at the beginning of the seventeenth century; Galileo Galilei spent what he later described as the happiest years of his life as Professor of Mathematics in Padua from 1592 to 1610. So by the time Ray and his colleagues moved on in February 1664 he had gained a thorough grounding in another area of biology.

In February the party left Venice and moved on through northern Italy, collecting all the way and reaching Genoa early in March. There, they were able to continue their journey by sea. In Naples the party divided. Willughby and Bacon stayed in Naples for a while before Willughby moved on to Rome and then back to England via Spain and France. He was back in London in time to present an account of his journey to the meeting of the Royal Society on 4 January 1665.[6] This highlights just how much of the work later credited, thanks to Ray's generosity, to Willughby was actually carried out by Ray, with some assistance from Skippon.

Continuing south largely by sea, in May Ray and Skippon reached Malta, the southernmost point of the expedition. The *Observations* describes not just plants but fossils found on the island, the island breed of dogs (which has since died out), and Ray's encounter with the local insects, 'the very biting or stinging of the gnats being more virulent than in other places: I do not remember that in England a gnat did ever cause a swelling of the skin of my face, but there it left a mark behind it that was not out for a month after'.

Seemingly with few regrets, they soon returned to Sicily, where on 20 May they climbed Mount Etna as far as the snowline. Returning up the western coast of Italy, collecting many plants on their overnight stops, and revisiting Naples, they arrived in Florence, where they stayed for the rest of the summer. At the beginning of September, they moved south to Rome, long after Willughby had left for Spain, where they stayed until 24 January 1665. Ray describes the buildings and archaeology, the wines, and the varieties of fish and meat found in the marketplace. He also made observations of a comet, visible between 20 December and 29 December 1664, and later reported these to the Royal Society.

From Rome, at the end of January Ray and Skippon travelled at a leisurely pace through northern Italy and into Switzerland, arriving in Geneva on 20 April. The winter of 1664–5 was very severe (this was at the beginning of the period known as the Little Ice Age), and Skippon's account of the trip[7] leaves the reader in no doubt that the journey through the mountains was a difficult one; he records that Ray suffered from snow blindness for several days, and that his fingers were too numb to work. At the end of July they started on a roundabout route towards England, via Grenoble, Lyons, Orange, and Avignon to Montpellier. They had intended to continue moving slowly towards England that year, but because of political friction between England and France, on 1 February the French king, Louis XIV, ordered all English nationals to leave France within three months. This hastened their departure from the south of France, but still left enough time in hand for Ray to spend three weeks in Paris in March. There, he visited the Jardin du Roi, the King's botanical gardens, and discussed botany with the French savants.

During the rest of 1666, the year of the Great Fire of London, Ray stayed with friends in Sussex and Essex, and also visited Martin Lister, a botanist he had met in Montpellier, at St John's College in Cambridge. His letters describe how he caught up with his reading, buying books that had been published while he was away, including Hooke's *Micrographia*, volumes by Robert Boyle, and the *Philosophical Transactions* of the Royal Society. In the winter, he settled down at Middleton with Willughby to put their collections in order.

This seems to have kept him busy until June 1667, when he went on another expedition to the west of England with Willughby. In September he suffered a serious illness, affecting his lungs, while staying with his mother at Black Notley, but he recovered in time to attend the Royal Society for his admission as a Fellow on 7 November, three weeks before his fortieth birthday (he had been proposed for election by Wilkins on 31 October).

Ray's position at Middleton Hall was regularized by becoming Willughby's private chaplain, a post which carried more weight when Willughby married an heiress, Emma Barnard, in 1668. She quickly produced three children (Francis, Cassandra, and Thomas), and Ray would be given a role in their upbringing. But in 1669 Willughby was taken ill with a severe fever while on a visit with Ray to Chester, where Wilkins was now Bishop. The effects of the illness lasted well into 1670, the year Ray decided to revert to the original spelling of his name. In spite of an apparent recovery in 1671, Willughby's health declined again in 1672, and he died on 3 July that year. At first, this left Ray well provided for. Willughby left Ray, who was one of the executors of his will, an annuity of £60 a year and charged him with looking after the education of the two sons. With this responsibility, Ray settled at Middleton Hall and began the serious job of preparing the material gathered and already partly organized by himself and Willughby for publication.

But there was a cloud on the horizon. Willughby's widowed mother, Lady Cassandra, was well disposed towards Ray, and regarded him as a family friend rather than a servant. But Emma Willughby disliked him and treated him as a social inferior. Lady Cassandra would not live for ever, so Ray must have known his days at Middleton were numbered. Perhaps with this in mind, in 1673 he married Margaret Oakley, described as a 'gentlewoman' but clearly one without any money, who was probably the governess of the Willughby children. She was just 20, and he was 44. Before proposing, Ray agonized over the possibility of rejection, and made out a list of pros and cons concerning marriage which is curiously similar to the one Charles Darwin made out before proposing to his own future bride, Emma Wedgwood, two centuries later.

Ray's concerns include the fear that Margaret was 'brought up in a different way and not likely to love my prayers' and that any children born to the couple 'will never delight in my company for that I shall be old before they come to years of discretion'. But his fears proved groundless. Margaret accepted his proposal, and they were married on 5 June 1673.

The story of the rest of Ray's life is essentially the story of his books. There were no more expeditions, and Ray concentrated at first on getting the material bequeathed to him by Willughby published. The work on the collections and notes was straightforward enough while Willughby's mother lived and Ray and his wife remained at Middleton. But soon after Lady Cassandra died in 1675, Emma Willughby married a rich and unpleasant man called Josiah Child, whom Ray, seldom one to indulge in name-calling, described as 'sordidly covetous'. Child successfully contested Willughby's will, and had Ray removed from his position of influence over the two boys, although he could not prevent payment of the annuity. Forced to leave Middleton Hall, the Rays moved first to Sutton Coldfield, then, thanks to the generosity of a wealthy friend, Edward Bullock, they were lent the use of Faulkbourne Hall, a house just a few miles from Black Notley. After his mother died in March 1679 at the age of about 78, John and Margaret Ray moved into the house, Dewlands, which he had had built for her. They had the £60 a year annuity from Willughby's bequest, plus some £40 a year from rent on the small parcel of family land—just about enough to make ends meet.

The big personal surprise following the final move to Black Notley must have been the belated arrival of children—twin daughters, Margaret and Mary, born on 12 August 1684, followed by Catharine on 3 April 1687 and Jane on 10 February 1689, completing a set of four girls under the age of five for a man now in his sixty-second year. It's a wonder, and a tribute to his wife, that Ray got any work done at all. In fact, he produced a vast outpouring of books, not just on biological topics, although his later years were marred by serious ill-health, including painful and chronic ulcers on his legs.

Apart from his biological books, Ray published collections of English proverbs, a study of English dialects, and a treatise on religious topics, none of which we have space to discuss here. His first major book, the *Catalogue of English Plants*, was completed during the happy time at Middleton while Willughby was still alive, and is dedicated to him; it was published in 1670. In a remark which echoes Francis Bacon and also reflects the attitude towards science of his contemporaries in the Royal Society, Ray points out that this work is of practical importance: 'It is surely not amiss to spend a whole lifetime [studying plants] if we can discover a medicine or two to alleviate or cure the deadly diseases that afflict us.'

The main scientific interest in the book is that in it Ray gives the first version of what is essentially the modern definition of a species. In his own words, members of one species are 'never born from the seed of another species'. In spelling out the way like begets like (he also presented a paper on these ideas to the Royal Society in 1674), Ray was implicitly rejecting the widely held belief of the time that new species could appear as a result of bizarre matings—to take an extreme example, that a cross between an ordinary pig and a bird might produce a pig covered in feathers.

Ray's first major project after Willughby's death was to complete a study of birds, the *Ornithology*, published by the Royal Society under Willughby's name in 1676. This work was carried out when he still had free access to the material at Middleton Hall; the book was expensively illustrated with engravings of birds, paid for by Willughby's widow. But it was not Willughby's book; it was almost entirely Ray's work, drawing on the collections and notes left by Willughby but using Ray's method of classification.

Although Ray almost immediately moved on to prepare a similar book, also under Willughby's name, about fishes, this turned out to be a lengthy project, not least because of the difficulties that soon arose about his position at Middleton Hall. So while that work was still going on, Ray completed a shorter book about the classification of plants, partly drawing on papers he had sent to the Royal Society. This *Method of Plants* (published in 1682) was his first serious attempt at botanical classification. The most important new idea in the *Method*, which makes Geoffrey Keynes describe it as 'an epoch-making piece of work' of 'profound historical significance', is the division of flowering plants into monocotyledons (which have a single seed leaf on the embryo) and dicotyledons (with two seed leaves). Other important differences between the two kinds of plant concern the structure of veins in their leaves, the nature of their roots, and the structure of their floral parts. Ray also explained the nature of buds for the first time, and divided plants into different groups on the basis of their fruits, flowers, and other parts. But he was so far ahead of his time that the book received little attention and sold poorly.

What became known as 'Willughby's' *History of Fishes* caused Ray a lot more trouble than the *Ornithology*, largely because of the changed circumstances following the remarriage of Willughby's widow. She (or her new husband) declined to make any contribution to the costs of publishing the book, which was, once again, a richly illustrated volume. The Royal Society agreed to publish it only because several patrons undertook to make donations towards the cost. The most generous of these was Samuel Pepys, who was then President of the Royal Society; he contributed £50, which paid the cost of engraving seventy-nine of the 187 plates. The book was published in 1686, but the Royal got carried away and had 500 copies printed, almost exhausting its small reserve of cash.

Meanwhile, Ray had been working on his masterwork, the *History of Plants*, and the first volume of this epic was also published in 1686. But there was one serious flaw with the new project. Because Ray was unable to get sponsors to pay for engravings, and the Royal had run out of money, there were no illustrations in the book. This helps to explain why, although the *History of Plants* was highly regarded among the cognoscenti, it failed to achieve the kind of success achieved by, say, Hooke's *Micrographia* and thereby establish Ray's name alongside those of his contemporaries such as Hooke himself, Halley, and Newton, where it belongs.

One of the reasons Ray gave (in a letter to Hans Sloane) for undertaking this work was:

To facilitate the learning of plants, if need be, without a guide or demonstrator, by so methodizing of them, and giving such certain and obvious characteristic notes of the genera, that it shall not be difficult for any man that shall but attend to them, and the description, to find out infallibly any pl[ant] that shall be offered to him.

His achievement was to succeed in this aim even without the use of illustrations; Ray's 'methodizing' became the established scientific basis of plant classification. The second volume of the book was completed by September 1687 and published the following year; the third and final volume, delayed by Ray's ill-health and by financial difficulties, appeared in 1704, a few months before Ray died, in January 1705, at the age of 77.

Remember that Ray had already established the idea of a species in the modern sense. In his methodizing he extended this to come up with essentially the modern classification, using slightly different terminology from ours. He grouped plants first into what he called 'genera', corresponding to modern orders, then into 'species subalternae' (modern genera) within those groups, and finally into 'species infimae' (our species). He classified many thousands of plants not only in terms of these family relationships, but also in terms of morphology, distribution, and habitat; he described the life cycle of plants, spelling out the detail of processes such as seed germination; and he listed pharmacological uses. He brought order and logic to the investigation of the entire living world, not just plants, and he made the study of both botany and zoology a scientific pursuit.

Although the *History of Plants* was not an immediate commercial success, in 1690 Ray published a little volume, the *Flora of Britain*, which summarized much of his work up to and including the first two volumes of the *History of Plants*. This did sell well, and appeared in a second edition in 1694. It includes, in the Preface, Ray's own comment on the revolution in the way of looking at the world that he had lived through:

I am full of gratitude to God that it was His will for me to be born in this last age when the empty sophistry that usurped the title of philosophy and within my memory dominated the schools has fallen into contempt, and in its place has arisen a philosophy solidly built upon a foundation of experiment...

And in one of his religious works, *Wisdom of God*, published in 1691, he elaborated:

Let it not suffice us to be Book-learned, to read what others have written and take upon trust more Falsehood than Truth: but let us our selves examine things as we have opportunity, and converse with Nature as well as Books. Let us endeavour to promote and increase Knowledge and make new Discoveries not so much distrusting our own Parts or despairing of our own Abilities, as to think that our Industry can add nothing to the Inventions of our Ancestors, or correct any of their mistakes. Let us not think that the bounds of Science are fixed...

This was the message that the scientific revolutionaries of the seventeenth century bequeathed to their successors. The life of the man who would be in some ways Ray's own spiritual heir very nearly overlapped with that of Ray himself. Chronologically the first member of our First XI, Carl Linnaeus was born in 1707, and he certainly never had any distrust of his own parts or despair of his own abilities.

IN THE GARDEN

John Ray's *Historia Plantarum* is a huge work taking up three vast volumes, so planting up a garden containing flowers, trees, and plants listed by him is an easy task. Flowers were grown just for their beauty but much of the garden in John Ray's time was given over to produce that had more practical uses. As well as fruit and vegetables herbs were widely grown both for kitchen and medicinal uses as well as for washing, dying, and 'purifying' both the house and the household linen.

For a more formal garden a popular design of the period was a knot garden, where each section of an ornately designed bed was sectioned off and bordered by low box (buxus) hedges which helped to protect the plants grown within each section from wind and severe cold. Many of the plants grown were popularly believed to be cures or preventatives of disease and many are still in use by herbalists today. John Wesley, the popular preacher, travelled widely evangelizing, and in 1747, barely forty-two years after Ray's death, he collected together many of the 'old wives' tales' of herbal remedies that he found commonly in use as he travelled around Britain. It is almost certain that all of these would have been current during Ray's lifetime and many are still in use for the same purposes to this day.

Borage, Chervil (Sweet Cicely), and Marjoram were thought to improve the spirits, and Thyme tea and Valerian root steeped in tea were thought a good remedy for all types of nervous disorders. John Ray lists St John's Wort, but we can find no reference to its use as a plant to lift melancholy at that time. As well as its more obvious use in cooking, Rosemary was used both as a disinfectant and as a herb to improve memory. Memory could also be boosted, it was thought, by wearing Lavender flowers in a nightcap. Lavender is still commonly used to perfume baths and bedrooms as an aid to restful sleep. Sore limbs would be bathed in an infusion of Mint and Balm or with water in which Comfrey roots had been boiled.

Itching was thought to be relieved by rubbing with the leaves of a Dock plant or by washing in a solution of water and Dock root. Today it is most commonly used to relieve the pain and skin irritation produced by contact with Stinging Nettles. Bruises were commonly eased by an ointment made from butter and Parsley and rheumatic pain and 'ague' were soothed by poultices of onion, Yarrow, Groundsell, Thyme, or Sage. Taking to bed and drinking sweetened Camomile infusions was also recommended. Wormwood, Southern Wood, and Rue eased swollen glands in the neck and tooth-ache was (hopefully!) eased by putting a bruised leaf of Betony up the nose.

Fennel, Coltsfoot, Feverfew, Lungwort (*Pulminaria*), Rue, White Archangel (Dead Nettle), and Pennyroyal were all commonly grown for their medicinal uses. Houses were kept smelling sweet with Fleabane (*Erigeron*), Herb Bennet, Rosemary, and Lavender. Soapwort (*Suponaria*) was used when washing clothes and household linens, and it is still used today to clean old and fragile textiles. Scabious, Clary, Verbena, Crown Imperial, Campion, Cranesbill, Violets, Primroses,

Clove Pinks, Sedum, and Woodbine (Honeysuckle) were all common to gardens of Ray's time, as were Lilies, Roses, and Iris.

The John Ray Memorial Garden in Essex has a mature knot garden filled with plants listed by John Ray as growing in the area of his birth. A further John Ray garden is planned for Black Notley.

1

CARL LINNAEUS

(1707–1778)

L IKE JOHN RAY, Carl Linnaeus was a country boy. He was born on 23 May 1707 in the village of Råshult, in Småland—a poor region in the south-east of Sweden. His mother was just 19 years old, and her husband a 33-year-old curate; the family moved to Stenbrohult, a slightly larger community, in 1708, when Carl's father was appointed pastor there. This was a time of change in Sweden, reflected both in Linnaeus's name and in events in the world at large. The use of family names was just starting to take over from the traditional patronymics, and Linnaeus's paternal grandparents were themselves called Ingemar Bengtsson and Ingrid Ingemarsdotter. By tradition, their son Nils, Carl's father, would have been known as Ingemarsson; but he went to university and became a curate, inventing a family name, Linnaeus, to go with his educated status.[1] The name, according to family legend, was chosen in commemoration of a particularly impressive linden tree that grew near the family farmhouse. But old habits died hard. Carl's father actually signed his name Nils Ingemarsson Linnaeus, and even Carl sometimes used to drop in an 'N', for Nilsson, between the Carl and Linnaeus of his signature; the conversion of patronymics into surnames only became law in Sweden in 1901.

Much more significantly, it was just two years after Carl Linnaeus was born, in 1709, that Sweden was defeated by the Russians under Tsar Peter the Great at Poltava, and as a result lost its Baltic empire. So Carl grew up in a small, religiously orthodox (Lutheran) community in a poor part of a country that had become a European backwater. It was common in that part of the world at that time for parsonships to be essentially inherited, passed on from father to son, or if no son were available, to the husband of the previous incumbent's daughter—as in the case of Linnaeus's father. The particular living at Stenbrohult had been in the family since the time of Carl Linnaeus's great-grandfather's father-in-law, and would be passed on to Carl's younger brother Samuel (he also had three sisters). By tradition, it should have gone to Carl; but he had other ideas.

Nils Linnaeus, the father of Carl and Samuel, was a keen gardener and amateur botanist, who passed on this enthusiasm to his elder son. When he was just 5 years old, Carl had his own bit of garden to tend. After a couple of years being given a very basic education at home by a tutor, he started at the secondary school (Gymnasium) in Växiö in 1717, where he found the experience of working in the classroom much less fun than being outdoors gardening—so much so that he acquired the nickname 'little botanicus'. He neglected his school work so much that the teachers advised Nils that there was no hope of his son following the family tradition and becoming a minister; instead, they suggested he might become a doctor.[2]

This wasn't as bizarre a career choice for a budding botanist then as it might seem now. Understanding plants and their medical uses was a key feature of medicine at the time, as the example of John Ray's mother reminds us. As for the family tradition of religious service, it was also true, of Linnaeus as it had been for Ray, that he regarded the study of nature as God's work. So in 1727 Carl was sent to the University of Lund to begin his formal study of medicine and natural history, with the approval—or at least consent—of his father, but apparently without his mother being aware of the change of plan. In a memoir that he wrote in 1778 following his brother's death, Samuel Linnaeus tells us that Nils kept the decision secret from her for more than a year, since if she had known '[that] Carl was *medicus*, it would have worried her more than if he had changed his religion'.

Lund wasn't much of a university in those days, but Linnaeus tells us in one of his many autobiographical writings (he had a high opinion of his own importance and took care to make sure that posterity would know all about his life) that now that he was studying the things he loved work became fun and he made rapid progress. He lodged in Lund with a local doctor, Kilian Stobaeus, who initially took a dislike to the scruffy but arrogant student. But the doctor soon became impressed by the young man's enthusiasm and ability, and allowed him free access to his library. He also introduced Linnaeus to something he had never seen before—a 'herbarium' consisting of samples of dried plants stuck to sheets of paper. Linnaeus soon began a similar herbarium, which would grow to become one of the great plant collections. After a year in Lund Linnaeus had made such good progress that he was able to move on to the more prestigious University of Uppsala, a few score kilometres north of Stockholm. Presumably, it was at this time that the news of what he was up to was broken to his mother.

Although Uppsala was better than Lund, it was by no means a great university, and its role was still chiefly to educate future clergymen in the basics of Lutheranism. It had uninspiring teachers[3] and a poorly equipped library, which was a particular handicap for a poor student like Linnaeus, who tells us that he had 'no books and no money to buy them'. He depended on gaining access to the private libraries of professors at the university, and on what he could teach himself from the study of plants; he did just enough medical work to keep the authorities satisfied. Carl also struck up a friendship with another medical student with similar botanical interests, Peter (also known as Petrus) Artedi, and they encouraged each other in what must otherwise have been a rather lonely pursuit of knowledge. Artedi was a couple of years older than Linnaeus, and seems to have been a bigger influence on the younger man than Linnaeus would later acknowledge.

The system of passing down jobs from father to son applied as much in the Swedish universities of the day as in the Lutheran church, and one of Linnaeus's teachers at Uppsala, Olof Rudbeck the younger, had inherited his chair from his father, Olof Rudbeck the elder.[4] The older Rudbeck (1630–1702) is widely regarded as one of the most remarkable Swedes of all time. He was the founder of the Uppsala botanic garden and built up in his lifetime a collection of woodblocks illustrating around 11,000 different plants; but these were tragically destroyed in the great Uppsala fire in 1702. He was also a noted anatomist, antiquarian, and botanist, and his memory lives on in the flower Rudbeckia (black-eyed Susan) which was named in honour of both Rudbeck the elder and Rudbeck the younger, commemorating their great services to botany.

Another of the Swedish academic clans was the Celsius family—in this case, Olof Celsius the elder was one of Linnaeus's teachers, and he would duly be succeeded by his son, Olof Celsius the younger. Anders Celsius, of temperature scale fame, was another member of the clan— the nephew of Olof Celsius the elder.[5]

Olof Celsius the elder was also a keen botanist, and provided both financial help and accommodation for Carl for a time; but the young man found an even better niche in the summer of 1730 when Olof Rudbeck the younger, now in his late sixties, took him into his household partly so that Carl could tutor Rudbeck's own three sons, one of them also called Olof. These were not small children, but young men supposedly at an advanced stage of their education; the system was so corrupt that it was regarded simply as a matter of routine that in 1731 Linnaeus actually wrote the doctoral dissertation of 20-year-old Johan Olof Rudbeck, for which he was paid 30 copper dalers, roughly equivalent to 15 English shillings. But there were more important rewards—in the Rudbeck household Linnaeus found 'a pleasing library' in which he could study botanical texts every day. He gave the lectures that Rudbeck couldn't be bothered with while Rudbeck's official assistant, Nils Rosén, was away completing his medical degree in the Netherlands, and was also put in charge of the university's rather neglected botanical garden, which had been established by Olof Rudbeck the elder in the 1650s, but by the 1730s contained only a couple of hundred species. To cap it all, Rudbeck persuaded the authorities to provide Linnaeus with financial support.

The most remarkable feature of Linnaeus's scientific achievements is that much of the work for which he became famous was commenced while he was still a student, beginning with his time in Uppsala, and essentially completed by the time he was 31, before he obtained a formal academic post. In the summer of 1730, Linnaeus worked with Olof Celsius the elder, collecting plants around the region in preparation for the older man's local *Flora*. The work was never published, but it meant that Linnaeus was involved in the classification of the material, for which Celsius used a system based on the ideas of Joseph Tournefort (1656–1708), a French physician and botanist who made his particular mark by defining a genus as a cluster of species; Celsius also took on board some of the ideas from Ray's work, notably his definition of a species. Linnaeus had already been introduced to the work of Tournefort in his final year at the Gymnasium by his tutor Johan Rothman; Rothman also told Linnaeus, then in his twentieth year, about the work of the French botanist Sébastien Vaillant (1669–1722), who promoted the idea that plants reproduced sexually—people like Ray had discussed this in the late seventeenth century, but Vaillant made the case more forcefully and spread the word more widely.

More than anything, working on the project with Celsius put all this in perspective and brought home to Linnaeus the difficulties of all previous classifications, the problems with all existing systems, and the need for a clear and coherent system for classifying plants. There was so much confusion about nomenclature and systems that botanists could often be uncertain about which plant a colleague was referring to. Impressed by Vaillant's approach, when Linnaeus began 'to doubt that Tournefort's [method] was sufficient' and decided to take on the task 'accurately to describe all flowers, to bring them into new classes, reform name and genera, in a completely new way', he decided to do so on the basis of the plants' sexual characteristics.

The strangest thing about Linnaeus as a person, which made him the ideal man for this job, was his obsession with lists. He made lists of his toys as a child, lists of his colleagues at university, and later in life when he owned land he made lists of his cows. He even classified and listed other botanists when he began to write books—in his *Bibliotheca Botanica*, published in 1735, Linnaeus lists botanists down the ages in no fewer than sixteen categories, or classes, somewhat uncharacteristically placing himself in the second rank, below the likes of Tournefort and Vaillant. Linnaeus once commented in a letter to a friend that he could not 'understand anything that is not systematically ordered', and the extremes that he went to suggest that he was so obsessive about classifying and ordering things that today he would be regarded as suffering from a relatively mild version of Asperger's syndrome.

During his student years at Uppsala, Linnaeus was greatly helped by his friendship with Artedi. Artedi left no major mark on science in his own name, not least because in 1735, on his way home on a dark autumn night after a convivial dinner with friends, he fell into a canal in Amsterdam and drowned. But he did leave a mark on Linnaeus. We know from Linnaeus's own writings that the autumn of 1729 was the time when Linnaeus came up with the idea of a sexual system of classification, and we also know that earlier the same year Artedi had compiled a catalogue of the plants in his home parish, which drew on Tournefort's system, but with his own improvements. Linnaeus tells us that Artedi moved on to a classification of the umbellate plants— plants, such as cow parsley, in which the flower stalks form a cluster radiating from a common point. Clearly, the two of them had discussed classification and the need for a new system, and Linnaeus acknowledges the influence of Artedi in his decision to carry out a classification of plants in general. The new classification of umbellates developed by Artedi actually appears in a manuscript of Linnaeus dated 29 July 1730—the same manuscript in which his own sexual system was presented for the first time. It is inconceivable that he had not discussed his own scheme with Artedi, but we shall never know how much input the older man provided.

Around this time Artedi abandoned botany and turned his attention to a study of fish—like Ray and Willughby, the two friends divided up the natural world between them. At the time he died, his *Ichthyologia* was in almost complete manuscript form, and, in a further curious echo of the relationship between Ray and Willughby, Linnaeus saw it into print. The logical structure of the system on which the book is based is so much like the approach used by Linnaeus in his own books that it could have been written by him; in a letter to Haller, Linnaeus says that Artedi has 'established natural classes, natural genera, complete characters, a universal index of synonyms, incomparable descriptions, and unexceptionable specific definitions'. But there is no evidence that Linnaeus completely rewrote the book before publication. We can only conclude from all the evidence that at the very least the two men worked as a team during their years at Uppsala, and it is tempting to speculate that Artedi was, in fact, the team leader. If so, the fact that all of Linnaeus's important work was completed before 1735, and that his later botanical achievements were essentially restricted to reshaping and refining the insights of his formative years, becomes less surprising.

As we have seen, by 1730 Linnaeus was beginning to use the sexual system for classifying plants in his own writings, which were prepared to help him with his duties 'demonstrating' the plants in the botanical garden as Rosén's *locum*. But before we go into the details of his system, we should mention his one major botanical expedition, the hardships of which were much exaggerated in Linnaeus's own auto-biographical writings, so that those accounts provide intriguing insights into his character.

At that time, Lapland, in the north of the Scandinavian Peninsula, was still a remote and mysterious place to most Swedes, let alone other Europeans, and the region's natives, known as the Sami, were considered to be not quite human. Even towards the end of the seventeenth century, in spite of the efforts of Lutheran missionaries, traces of a pagan religion involving spirit worship, a bear cult, and a garbled combination of Viking beliefs and Roman Catholicism still persisted in the north. The old practices were largely stamped out in the 1690s by introducing tithes and compulsory church attendance, with Sami shamans caught (or suspected of) practising the old religion being punished with anything from a fine to torture or being burned at the stake. A popular technique was to hold the victim down and open an artery in his arm, threatening to let him bleed to death unless he promised to give up the old ways. Linnaeus tells us that this approach was 'often successful'.

Rudbeck the younger had visited Lapland in 1695, but in 1702 a fire which burned a large part of Uppsala had destroyed many of the specimens he gathered on that expedition and his other botanical material. In 1732, Linnaeus persuaded the Uppsala Science Society to sponsor him on another expedition to the north, with no written instructions but, apparently, a verbal brief to study the botany and zoology of the region, the people, and the mineral prospects. The contribution towards his expenses provided by the Society was both modest and generous—only 400 copper dalers, but like the widow's mite, just about all the money it had. He set out on horseback in May 1732, the month he turned 25, and returned to Uppsala in October of the same year.

Linnaeus was well equipped for the journey, protected against mosquitoes by leather trousers, knee-high boots, and a hat with netting, and carrying, along with his passport and letters of introduction, pre-folded papers for pressing plants. His writings proudly record these preparations; what they do not record is that he also had maps of Lapland, and a copy of the diary kept by Rudbeck the

younger on his 1695 expedition, whose route Linnaeus largely followed. In truth, he had it easy. He stayed with Swedish homesteaders
and missionaries, he rode on hired horses or in boats rowed by Sami,
and he was guided by friendly Sami who acted as his servants. In his
own accounts, Linnaeus would later present harrowing descriptions of
the hardship he suffered '[walking] by foot through roadless Lapland,
and everywhere with unbelievable work [crawling] around and
[snooping] about for plants', then contradicting this image by making
himself out to be a superman, marching across the rough terrain at
such a pace that the natives could not keep up and 'the Lapps, who are
born to suffer, as birds to fly, moaned that they had never been in such
a state; I pitied them'.

Linnaeus made only three modest efforts to pass beyond the borders of the northern settlements to probe what he later called the
'entirely foreign' lands beyond, where Sami still practised their old
nomadic ways. These mini-expeditions lasted for two, three, and
sixteen days respectively, and geographically speaking he discovered
nothing. He did cover about 3,500 kilometres on his travels overall,
mostly through relatively civilized country on his way to and from
Lapland; but in order to boost his expenses claim he presented his
astonished sponsors with a map showing a meandering route covering
more than twice that distance, including the claim that at one time he
had covered 800 kilometres in four days. Hardly surprisingly, the
society initially refused either to pay anything extra for these imagin-
ary journeys or to publish his account of his travels. In the end, they
scraped up another 40 silver dalers (equivalent to 120 copper dalers),
but stuck with their refusal to endorse his claims by publishing them.
That didn't stop Linnaeus polishing his image as an intrepid botanical
explorer and pioneer. In his own *Flora Lapponica*, published in 1737
and drawing in part (without acknowledgement) on Rudbeck's earlier
studies, he included such wild exaggerations as the claim that at one
time he went without bread for more than four weeks, when in fact he
was never more than four weeks from a settlement, and in a letter to

the Swiss physician and botanist Albrecht von Haller he refers to the 'several years' he spent among the Sami. The *Flora Lapponica* also refers to the 'sky-high mountain overhangs' and among the features of his travels that Linnaeus described in his report to the Uppsala Science Society were the largest mountains in Europe. Linnaeus did travel through the mountain range that forms the spine of the Scandinavian peninsula, but his claim that these 'Alps' were in places 'more than a Swedish mile high' were certainly an exaggeration. A Swedish mile then was about 6.25 English miles (it was redefined in 1889 as exactly 10 km), which would make the mountains Linnaeus described bigger than Everest! Since he brought back no high-altitude plant specimens from his expedition, its likely that he kept to the valleys and the easiest passes on his journey among mountains that were undoubtedly a good deal less than a Swedish mile high.

The crowning glory of the whole fantasy was a 'Sami costume' that Linnaeus assembled from bits and pieces of native dress, some picked up on his journey, some later bought or given to him, in which he posed for his formal portrait. The dress was a mixture of unmatched and inappropriate bits and pieces, including a woman's summer hat, a man's winter clothing, and boots made by the Sami for export but which they never wore themselves. But hey—the southern Swedes, and the Europeans Linnaeus would soon meet on his travels farther south, knew nothing about the Sami and were happy to take his tales, and clothes, at face value. The portraits (several copies of the original were made) were rounded off with the image of a little flowering plant from Lapland, which Linnaeus named *Linnaea borealis* after himself.

Although it is easy to mock Linnaeus's self-aggrandizement, the Lapland journey did broaden his horizons, and he did bring back many valuable specimens. The *Flora Lapponica*, when it eventually appeared in print, would be a worthwhile book which helped to establish Linnaeus's reputation. But the publication of that book still lay five years in the future when he returned to Uppsala and took up his studies again for the winter of 1732–3. Over the summer of 1733, the year his mother died in her mid-forties, and the following winter, with nothing left for him to learn at Uppsala, Linnaeus was based at Falun, in the Dalarna region of Sweden to the north-west of Uppsala, with his friend Claes Sohlberg. Dalarna is popular with tourists today, and the region is sometimes known as Sweden's Lakeland; but in the seventeenth and eighteenth centuries it was important for its mines, producing, among other things, most of Sweden's exports of copper. Linnaeus and Sohlberg studied the mining industry, including the living and working conditions of the miners, as well as the flora and fauna of the region.

The obvious next step for Linnaeus was to travel to the Netherlands to complete his medical degree. He was severely strapped for cash, but had made a good impression on Sohlberg's father, who said that if Linnaeus took Claes with him and acted as a tutor to the younger man, he would be paid 300 copper dalers a year.

After a brief visit to Uppsala, Linnaeus returned to Falun in the summer of 1734, and during the following winter he met and courted Sara Lisa Moraea, proposing to her within a month of their first meeting.[6] She was the 18-year-old daughter of a wealthy physician, and whatever her other attractions the wealth was certainly an important factor to the impoverished Linnaeus. Sara's father encouraged Linnaeus to complete the formalities of his education, which had to involve travelling abroad since at that time Swedish universities could not award medical degrees; Dr Moraea promised that provided Linnaeus spent at least three years studying abroad and then returned as a fully fledged physician he would be allowed to marry Sara; he may well have hoped that the young man's ardour would have cooled by then. The offer of financial support from the Sohlbergs seems to have evaporated, but in February 1735 Linnaeus and Sohlberg left for Holland, travelling via Helsingborg, Lübeck, and Hamburg and arriving in Amsterdam in June. There are occasional references to Sohlberg in the months that followed, but he soon fades from view and seems to have returned to Sweden on his own.

The next three years were the period when Linnaeus's ideas, already sketched out in his mind and in the manuscripts he brought with him, came to fruition. As far as science was concerned, the rest of his life would be an anticlimax, and the publications of his later years would be essentially revisions and restatements of the big ideas of his youth.

Unlike remote, backward Sweden, in the 1730s the Netherlands[7] were at the centre of the scientific and commercial world, the hub of a worldwide empire, with a tradition that every ship that sailed from Dutch ports, whatever its official business, brought back seeds, cuttings, and other botanical specimens from its travels. In the Netherlands Linnaeus would meet with other scientists, communicate easily with colleagues by letter, have ready access to books, and be able to visit other nearby countries such as France and England. At 28 he was in the prime of his life for original thinking, and although he had no official post, that also meant he had no official duties to distract him. He also seems to have been something of a philistine where art was concerned, since his letters make no mention of Rembrandt or Frans Hals, both famous and working in the Netherlands at the time, or even of the flower painters Jan van Huysum and Rachel Ruysch.

But what about the medical degree he had promised his prospective father-in-law he would obtain? That was the least of his problems. Because he had already officially completed his years as a medical student in Uppsala, all that he had to do, following a well-trodden path, was to take an examination and submit a thesis on a medical topic to one of the universities in the Netherlands. Leiden was the best, but required a candidate to spend some time there before submitting a thesis; Harderwijk was respectable, and required only that the candidate pass an examination and submit a satisfactory thesis. Also, their fees were lower than those at Leiden. Linnaeus arrived at Harderwijk on 17 June, took his examination the following day, had the thesis on malaria that he had brought with him from Sweden assessed, and was 'promoted' to become a fully fledged medical practitioner on 23 June. As far as Sara and her father were concerned, all Linnaeus had to do now was spend the next three years away from Sweden and the marriage was on.

Even before he achieved his degree, Linnaeus had begun botanizing. He had arrived in Amsterdam only on 13 June, but had found time before leaving for Harderwijk to stop off at the excellent Amsterdam botanical garden and to introduce himself to Jan Burman, who had been born in the same year as Linnaeus but was already a renowned Dutch botanist with a first-class botanical library. After completing the formalities for the degree, Linnaeus returned to Amsterdam, visited Utrecht briefly, then moved on to Leiden, where he began to attract attention. Always good at pushing himself forward, and with some justified confidence in his own ability, Linnaeus made contact with Hermann Boerhaave (1668–1738), the eminent physician who had been instrumental in making Leiden one of the best medical centres in Europe, and Johann Gronovius (1690–1760), one of the leading botanists of his generation. This was the turning point in Linnaeus's life. Until then, he had just been one of the many Swedish students passing through the Netherlands in order to get a degree.[8] But Boerhaave and Gronovius were impressed by the young man, and by the manuscripts that he showed them—so much so that Gronovius and a young Scottish doctor, Isaac Lawson, arranged for the publication of one of these books, the *Systema naturae*, which duly appeared in print in December 1735. Boerhaave also recommended Linnaeus to Jan Burman, who had previously met Linnaeus only as a casual visitor; now, Burman invited Linnaeus to stay with him in Amsterdam, and, best of all, recommended Linnaeus to the Anglo-Dutch banker George Clifford, a director of the Dutch East India Company. Clifford, a wealthy amateur botanist on good terms with both Burman and Boerhaave, had a large country estate near Haarlem, a botanist's paradise. He employed Linnaeus both as his house physician and to work on cataloguing the botanical specimens. This also gave Linnaeus the opportunity to put in order and publish more of his own manuscripts, which streamed off the presses in the following months.

For Linnaeus it was heaven on earth, like being given the keys to the Garden of Eden. He stayed in the post for two years, from September 1735 to October 1737, based at the estate, de Hartecamp, but making frequent visits to Amsterdam and Leiden. He also travelled, at Clifford's expense, to England, to collect more specimens for the garden. The most important contact he made there was with Johann Dillen (1687–1747), a German-born botanist who had moved to Oxford, where he worked with the ageing Professor of Botany James Sherard, in charge of the botanical garden established by Sherard. Linnaeus also met Hans Sloane, now 76 years old, who had known John Ray well and was at that time President of the Royal Society, having been elected to the post on the death of the previous incumbent, Isaac Newton, in 1727.[9]

In the winter of 1737–8 Linnaeus stayed with Gronovius in Leiden, but he became seriously ill, possibly partly as a result of overwork, around Easter 1738; he had to spend the best part of two months recuperating as a guest of Clifford at de Hartecamp. By then, Linnaeus had become firmly established in the Netherlands, his books were successful, and he was urged to make his permanent home there, with hints that a chair at Utrecht might be his for the asking. But the three years he had planned for were up, and with a bride waiting for him in Sweden Linnaeus was eager to go home. Not so eager, though, that he couldn't take a long route back, setting out in May 1738 for Paris, where his reputation had preceded him.

After a month among the botanists and the botanical gardens, during which time he was elected as a corresponding member (or 'foreign correspondent') of the Academy of Sciences, he left Paris for Le Havre and the boat to Helsingborg. He carried with him fourteen of his own printed books and pamphlets, the core of his contribution to science. But none of this had yet made much impression in his homeland, where the returning Linnaeus was regarded as just another newly qualified doctor back from the Netherlands. After visiting his father in Stenbrohult and his fiancée in Falun, he arrived in

Stockholm to start practising medicine—his only way to make a living—in September 1738. He was 31 years old, and would never travel outside Sweden again; but he would have a profound influence on other Swedish botanical explorers.

Linnaeus's career in medicine was brief, but eventful. Although it was difficult at first for an unknown doctor to build up a practice, through his ability to win friends and influence people Linnaeus managed to wangle an appointment as part-time lecturer on mineralogy and botany at the local mining college. In his private practice, with nothing more salubrious in prospect, he specialized in treating venereal disease, and, thanks to the notorious habits of sailors of the day, this helped him to obtain an appointment as physician for the Admiralty. In October 1738 Linnaeus was elected a member of the Science Society of Uppsala (his creative expense accounting forgiven) and in 1739 he was among the group of scientists who founded the Royal Swedish Academy of Sciences. In his autobiographical memoirs, Linnaeus took care to draw attention to the fact that he was chosen as the first President of the Royal Swedish Academy; what he was careful not to mention was that the honour was decided by drawing lots.

With his status in society growing and his finances on a secure footing, Linnaeus was able to marry Sara Moraea at the farm of her family in June 1739; their first child, a boy also called Carl, would be born in January 1741. At the time of his marriage, Linnaeus wrote to one of the friends he had made in Paris, Bernard de Jussieu—one of several botanical Jussieus[10] and the man who laid out the gardens at Versailles for Louis XV—with characteristic hyperbole:

I have succeeded in obtaining quickly the largest medical clientèle of this town and I have also been appointed titular physician to the admiralty. I have just married the woman whom I wanted for years to marry and who, if I am permitted to speak this way between ourselves, is quite wealthy; I am therefore at last leading a quiet and satisfactory life.

But the medical career would soon be over, and Linnaeus would be putting down on paper what he really thought about making a living treating syphilis.[11] Before we move on to look at his life as an academic—what would prove to be the longest phase of his life—it seems appropriate to look at the work which made his reputation and got him what turned out to be essentially a job for life. Because of the way Linnaeus kept polishing and repackaging his ideas, we won't restrict ourselves to the versions published prior to 1740, but will tell the whole story of his impact on botanical classification before picking up the threads of his life story, and some of his lesser known work.

The value of Linnaeus's classification system wasn't that it was based on the sexual characteristics of flowers. This was an arbitrary choice which didn't really go to the heart of the relationships between species, and it has long since been discarded in favour of other criteria. What mattered was that it was a simple, internally logical, and easily understood system which could be learned with only a little effort. That was what Linnaeus was good at—putting things in order, making lists, and explaining how the system worked. He was not really a scientist in the way that Ray was; he even defined the fundamentals of botany as 'classification and nomenclature', in his book *Philosophia Botanica*. The way Ray developed a classification from the properties of seed leaves and other fundamental criteria proved much more useful (and insightful) in the long term; even in the short term it was taken up by people like Jussieu.[12] But it proved easier to work with Ray's kind of classification when it was adapted to fit the framework created by Linnaeus originally for his sexual system. So both men made important contributions, and you can make your own mind up about which (if either) was the more important.

Linnaeus started out from the concepts of species (which he took from Ray without much acknowledgement) and genus (which he took from Tournefort without much acknowledgement). Just as a genus could be defined as a group, or family, of species which had certain common characteristics, so several genera could be regarded as members of an order with similar characteristics, and so on. Taking this kind of classification with subdivisions from the top down, Linnaeus arbitrarily divided the world of plants into five categories: class, order, genus, species, and variety. This seems to have been in a deliberate attempt to mimic the five philosophical divisions used in classificatory logic, deriving ultimately from Aristotle. In many ways, Linnaeus is best regarded as one of the last natural philosophers—perhaps even the culmination—of the old classical tradition, rather than as a revolutionary pioneer of the new experimental philosophy which came to be known as science. With his love of order, Linnaeus made analogies also with geographical units (kingdom, province, territory, parish, and village) and the military (regiment, company, platoon, squad, and soldier). But his choice of five categories was completely arbitrary and has needed considerable modification. Extending upwards, later biologists would put a category phylum above class, with kingdom at the top. There are also subdivisions of the original categories in modern usage, but in the simplest modern version of the Linnaean classification our own species would be classified as being in the kingdom *animalia*, phylum *chordata*, class *mammalia*, order *primates*, family *hominidae*, genus *homo*, and species *sapiens*. This is actually a particularly interesting classification which caused Linnacus some soul-searching when he extended his system from plants to animals; we shall come back to this later.

The beauty of such a system, to Linnaeus, was that in principle every species (even every variety) could be given a name which specified exactly where it stood in the hierarchy of nature. This would be rather like, to extend his geographical analogy, the way a schoolboy might write his address in the front of an exercise book as '14 The Street, Newtown, Sussex, England, Europe, Earth, The Solar System, The Milky Way, Space, The Universe'. It would be accurate, and contain a lot of information, but it would also take a lot of memorizing and writing down if you used it every time. In early attempts to get round this problem, Linnaeus referred to species by a shortened version of their name and a number corresponding to the place where the full description of the species was given in his books— but field botanists could hardly be expected either to carry a great pile of books around with them, or to remember a somewhat arbitrary list of names and numbers. The binomial system, which is now seen as the key feature of the Linnaean classification and ensured that it swept all other systems aside for centuries, came about almost by accident as a result of the practical need to have a simple version of the classification that could be easily remembered and quickly written down.

The binomial system begins to appear in Linnaeus's writings only at the end of the 1740s, and wasn't finally formalized until 1758. Lisbet Koerner has come up with a neat explanation of why its importance became clear to Linnaeus then. As we shall see, throughout his adult life Linnaeus was concerned about the economic problems of his homeland, and made strenuous, if sometimes misguided, efforts to boost its agriculture and reduce its dependence on imports. At the end of the 1740s, he carried out a project to determine which plants various kinds of domestic animals preferred to eat. The experiment was disarmingly simple. A variety of beasts (cows, pigs, and so on) were set loose to wander the meadows around Uppsala, each with a student diligently following his animal and noting down what they ate—using, of course, quill pens dipped in ink pots carried by the students along with sheaves of paper. As the animal gobbled up the various fodder plants the students had to identify the species and write down the names before the plants were devoured, certainly with no time for looking things up in reference books, even if they had been able to carry them. Clearly, they would have written shortened versions of the names. So, although Koerner herself agrees that this is merely a conjecture, it is no surprise that in the pamphlet describing the results of the study (*Pan Svecicus*, published in 1749) Linnaeus introduces a genuine binomial nomenclature for the first time.

Of course, there must by then have been other indications that the full names were too unwieldy, and numbers too unmemorable, for practical use—as we shall see, by the late 1740s some of Linnaeus's students were travelling on their own voyages of botanical discovery and reporting their findings back to the master. They would have had just as much need of a simple, easily memorized system of nomenclature. The result was that species came to be identified using a two-word system in which the first word (always capitalized) gives the genus, and the second word the species. So we are *Homo sapiens*, the robin redbreast is *Erithacus rubecula*, and the common daisy *Bellis perennis*. Ever the organizer, Linnaeus also set down strict rules about how the Greek or Latin names ought to be chosen, and even set limits on how long the words should be, but these rules need not bother us. What matters is that the binomial classification was established for plants by 1753, with the publication of his book *Species Plantarum*, widely regarded as Linnaeus's crowning achievement. Although the binomial system did not immediately gain universal acceptance, all scientific names used today for plant species date from that publication or later; no earlier names are formally recognized. In 1758, with the publication of the tenth edition of his book *Systema Naturae*, Linnaeus established the equivalent benchmark for zoology—but he never did come up with a single criterion for classifying animals in the way he used sexual characteristics to classify plants.

Apart from the simplicity of the binomial classification, the other reason why Linnaeus's system attracted attention was, of course, its sex appeal. In strictly scientific terminology, Linnaeus's classification scheme wasn't at all racy, and would have been unlikely to rouse adverse criticism on those grounds even in eighteenth-century Europe.[13] For example, in this system plants were divided into classes according to the numbers, length, position, and other properties of their stamens (the male organs, which produce pollen) and classes were divided into orders according to the numbers and other properties of their pistils (the female organs, in which fertilization of the seed takes place). But Linnaeus didn't stop at such a technical description of what was going on. To take one example from his more lurid versions of the story, as early as 1729 he wrote that 'The flowers' leaves...serve as bridal beds which the Creator has so gloriously arranged, adorned with such noble bed curtains, and perfumed with so many soft scents that the bridegroom with his bride might there celebrate their nuptials', and in 1735 he explained that 'The calyx is the bedchamber, the filaments the spermatic vessels, the anthers the testes, the pollen the sperm, the stigma the vulva, the style the vagina'. He also made great play of species in which a single 'bride' had two or more 'husbands'. Love it or hate it, if you were an eighteenth-century botanist, even an amateur with a passing interest in botany, you certainly couldn't ignore Linnaeus's choice of language. The botanist Johann Siegesbeck spoke for many when he called the classification system 'lewd' and 'loathsome harlotry', asking how 'bluebells, lilies and onions could be up to such immorality'; it was widely regarded as unsuitable for women to know about. Linnaeus had the last laugh; he later named the weedy, tiny-flowered plant *siegesbeckia* after his bitter opponent.

But not everyone was so hostile. The British Museum, which was started with the donation of Hans Sloane's collection in 1759, was one of the first institutions to use the Linnaean classification scheme. Although other British institutions were slower to adopt the new scheme, a couple of decades later Erasmus Darwin (1731–1802), the grandfather of Charles and, among many other things, an early advocate of evolutionary ideas,[14] translated Linnaeus into English and wrote a long poem, *The Botanic Garden*. The second part of this, *The Loves of Plants* (published in book form in 1789), spells out the Linnaean system in language that Linnaeus would surely have approved, with technical footnotes that actually take up more room in the book than the poem itself. Here's a flavour of the epic:

> Sweet blooms *Genista* in the myrtle shade,
> And *ten* fond brothers woo the haughty maid.
> *Two* knights before thy fragrant altar bend,

Adored *Melissa*! And *two* squires attend.
Maedia's soft chains *five* suppliant beaux confess,
And hand in hand the laughing belle address;
Alike to all, she bows with wanton air,
Rolls her dark eye, and waves her golden hair.

Hardly surprisingly, Darwin's poem became a huge popular success, even if the *Encyclopaedia Britannica* sniffed that 'obscenity is the very basis of the Linnaean system'.

But we are getting ahead of ourselves. The important point is that the Linnaean system of classes, orders, and so on became the standard and remained so even after the sexual classification was abandoned, and in particular the shorthand binomial version of the classification became the standard scientific way of referring to both plants and animals. Its widespread acceptance was helped by Linnaeus's skills as a popularizer and lecturer, and his determination that science should be accessible; it's time to put that in context by picking up the threads of his life from shortly after his marriage to Sara, at the end of the 1730s.

In February 1840 Olof Rudbeck died. Although Linnaeus hoped that the professorship might come his way, it went, not unreasonably, to Rudbeck's long-time assistant, Nils Rosén. But very soon, the other elderly Professor of Medicine at Uppsala, Lars Roberg, resigned. He seems to have been pushed out by the authorities, who saw Rudbeck's death as an opportunity for something of a fresh start, and in May 1741 Linnaeus was appointed in his place, in the month he turned 34. He wrote to Jussieu with the news, expressing a more jaundiced view of his time in medical practice than in his earlier correspondence:

By God's grace I am now released from the wretched drudgery of a medical practitioner in Stockholm. I have obtained the position I have coveted for so long; the King has appointed me professor of medicine and botany at Uppsala University and so given me back to botany from which I have been sundered all these three years...

In October 1741, with his wife and nine-month-old baby Carl, Linnaeus settled in Uppsala, where he would be based, apart for some scientific field trips within the borders of Sweden, for the rest of his life. Through a quirk of fate, Rosén, who was more interested in medicine, was in the more botanical chair, while Linnaeus, who was more interested in botany, was in the more medical chair; but, although the two men were to some extent rivals and not on the best of personal terms, common sense prevailed and their duties were re-arranged to their mutual benefit—in effect, they swapped posts.

In his work, Linnaeus was happy and successful. His home life seems to have been less happy. The couple had four daughters, who, along with Carl junior, survived into adulthood, as well as a boy and a girl who died young. But the gloss seems to have gone off the marriage early; Linnaeus's students would later describe Sara in unflattering terms as a rather vulgar, domineering woman, strict with her servants, children, and even with Linnaeus himself.[15] She was a good, thrifty (for which we should perhaps read 'mean') housewife, but little more, according to these accounts. When he was in his mid-sixties, Linnaeus drew up a will which showed very clearly the way things stood between them. It specified that if Sara 'should be so foolish as to remarry, which I have reason to believe she intends', she would receive 'no share in such things as I bought with the money I alone earned by my books, lectures and botanical work'.[16]

But it is that botanical work which is of interest here, along with Linnaeus's other scientific work, rather than his home life. In many ways, his family of students was more important to him than his real family, and we may wonder just how the blame for the lack of domestic bliss should actually be divided. In his personal relation-ships, Linnaeus showed a curious combination of egocentricity and insecurity—he was sure of his own worth (notice the way in his letter to Jussieu he says he has been given back to botany, not botany given back to him) but he wanted people to love him, and was never sure they really appreciated him. He was an excellent teacher who trained many able botanists in seemingly happy circumstances in Uppsala; but most left to make their careers elsewhere, often cutting the ties completely. Johan Falck, who travelled in the Russian Empire between 1768 and 1774 and was one of Linnaeus's favourite apostles, was not untypical. He had been awarded a chair at St Petersburg in 1765, and promptly severed his ties with the teacher he now referred to scornfully in his letters home as 'the Old Guy'. Falck's younger brother, who was then a student at Uppsala, congratulated Johan on his achievements in a letter commenting 'Now you can ask [the Old Guy] to kiss your arse'. Perhaps Linnaeus was too demanding—he could never accept anyone on relatively equal terms. Perhaps the problem was the way he regarded his students as an extension of himself, and took credit for their discoveries. But by the very act of unconsciously driving his star pupils away, he helped to speed and spread the development of a properly scientific botanical classification system.

But this should not obscure the fact that Linnaeus was a *very* good teacher, who wrote brief handbooks that could easily be understood and were small enough to be carried on field trips. He used a format that he took from the Lutheran almanacs, dividing each little book into twelve chapters and 365 aphorisms. These books were, at his insistence, cheap enough to be bought by students, and written in a clear and straightforward Latin. He included instructions on how to prepare a herbarium, how to plan field trips (listing all the equipment needed, from butterfly nets to pocket knives), and even how to lay out and plant a garden.

System, remember, was everything to Linnaeus, and one example highlights both his methods and the ease with which he could be hurt. On Saturdays during the summer, Linnaeus would lead a gathering of students and amateur botanists, sometimes well over a hundred in all, on expeditions to the countryside. The students, at least, had to wear a special light clothing which was referred to as their 'botanical uniform'. This was made up of loose bell-bottomed 'sailor' trousers, a short jacket, a broad-brimmed hat, and an umbrella to act as a sunshade. The expedition always began promptly at 7 am, with a break for lunch at 2 pm and a short rest at 4 pm, while the professor gave demonstrations every half hour. In between, people were not allowed to wander willy-nilly over the countryside, but were divided into platoons, each responsible for a particular area. There was a secretary to keep records, a prefect to keep order, and a marksman to shoot birds for dissection. When the outing was over, the party would march back into town with banners waving, French horns and bugles sounding, Linnaeus at their head like the leader of a victorious army. The students loved it, and there was ample scope for fun in spite of the rules and timetable. But when, eventually, his colleagues complained, asking what it would be like if they all indulged in such activity with scores of students milling about the streets, Linnaeus was deeply wounded by the criticism. He wrote that the criticism 'almost killed him' and that he lay sleepless for two months worrying about it. In a telling letter written in 1764 by Pehr Wargentin, the then Secretary of the Swedish Academy of Sciences, he said of Linnaeus that everybody valued him, but 'hardly anyone loves him, not even here'. Linnaeus, who craved love, must have known this, but never understood why.

We have already dealt with the major contribution that Linnaeus made to botanical classification, the work for which he is remembered, but it's worth mentioning some of his other ideas since they highlight the curious contradictions in his character. At one level, Linnaeus was practical and open-minded. He was concerned about Sweden's poor economic state, and eager to find ways to improve the lot of the people by introducing new plants that could be used for food, for exports, or to reduce expensive imports. The trouble was, he based his efforts on what amounted to no more than a superstitious belief that if plants from warmer places were acclimatized to Sweden, they would begin to thrive there. This was not based on any evolutionary ideas, but on the same principle that a schoolboy who is brought up on a regime of cold baths and early morning runs will be tougher than one who lazes by the fireside all day. Linnaeus made huge and ultimately fruitless efforts to get plants as exotic as tea and bananas to flourish in his botanical garden at Uppsala.

That can be seen as well-intended but mistaken. But Linnaeus could be downright loony and stubborn in his beliefs as well. He was convinced of the truth of the old wives' tale that swallows hibernated during the winter at the bottom of ice-covered lakes, and never seems to have considered the obvious experiment (to an eighteenth-century scientist) of placing a swallow underwater to see if it could survive. He was also one of the last proponents of the old idea that the world is made of four 'elements', earth, fire, air, and water. And ironically, at a time when there were food shortages and Linnaeus was making real efforts to help the agriculture of his homeland, he was firmly convinced that potatoes were poisonous, because they are related to deadly nightshade—even though poor people, including his servants, ate potatoes with no ill effects. He was not alone among the educated classes in dismissing the potato, which actually produces much better yields per acre than grain crops, as a foodstuff. In 1748 Countess Eva Ekeblad became the only woman prior to the twentieth century to be elected to the Swedish Academy of Sciences. Her achievement? Suggesting that the 'useless' potato might be valuable for making wig powder and aquavit.

And yet—and yet. The same Linnaeus who espoused such cranky notions was ahead of his time in espousing new ideas about the age of the Earth and the place of humankind in nature. Like Ray, Linnaeus was a deeply religious man[17] who had been brought up to believe the literal truth of the Bible; like Ray, he came to see that fossil and other evidence implies a much greater age for the Earth than the six thousand years or so generally accepted in his day; unlike Ray, Linnaeus never spelled out these views in print, but he did discuss them and write about them privately. The trigger for this was the realization, which became a hot topic of scientific debate in the 1740s in Scandinavia, that the level of the Baltic Sea seemed to be falling.

We now know that the reason for this is that during the most recent ice age the weight of ice over the land was so great that it forced the solid surface of the Earth to sink deeper into the fluid material beneath the crust; ever since the ice retreated, the land has been slowly rising back to its former level. It isn't that the waters are going down, but that the land is rising up. But none of that was known in Linnaeus's day.

One of the first people to study the phenomenon in detail and make a convincing case that, from the perspective of the land, sea level really is going down was Anders Celsius, Linnaeus's contemporary at Uppsala. He used various pieces of evidence to come up with a fairly accurate estimate that the level of the Baltic was falling by, in modern units, about one metre every hundred years. He suggested that the reason that the seas were in retreat was that water is being turned into solid material by the action of plants—an idea which had also been put forward by, among others, Isaac Newton in the previous century. Linnaeus took up the idea (which is completely wrong) that plants such as seaweed are chiefly composed of water (in fact, they are chiefly composed of carbon dioxide from the air) and that when they die they get turned into sediment (in fact, they decay, releasing carbon dioxide).

Linnaeus also knew about fossils, particularly from the work of the Dane Niels Steensen (1638–86), usually known as 'Steno' from the Latinized version of his name. Steno argued that fossils found today far inland and far above sea level are evidence that the rock strata they are found in were laid down underwater when the sea level was much higher.[18] Naturally, in the eighteenth century, and even later, this was seen by many as evidence for the biblical Flood. Linnaeus appreciated that it required a much longer time scale than anything in the Bible— 'he who attributes all this to the Flood, which suddenly came and as suddenly passed, is verily a stranger to science...himself blind, seeing only through the eyes of others, as far as he sees anything at all'. Linnaeus's own explanation, initially set out in a lecture at Uppsala in 1743 and developed in later years, was that in the beginning the entire Earth had been covered by water, which had since gradually retreated, being continually turned into dry land and leaving fossils behind as the waters fell. The fact that the model is wrong is less important than the fact that Linnaeus, so conservative in some of his beliefs, was open-minded enough to accept that the history of life on Earth extended much farther back in time than six thousand years.

One feature of the debate about the age of the Earth in the eighteenth century was the realization that the conventional Bible-based chronology conflicted with the antiquity of civilization indicated by records from China; in one of his autobiographical memoirs, referring to himself in the third person, Linnaeus says that '[he] would gladly have believed that the earth was [even] older than the Chinese had claimed, had the Holy Scriptures suffered it'. In a book published during his lifetime (*Museum Tessinianum*, 1753) he made his strongest pronouncement on the subject: 'The infinite number of fossils of strange and unknown animals buried in the rock strata beneath the highest mountains, animals that no man of our age has beheld, are the only evidence of the inhabitants of our ancient earth at a period too remote for any historian to trace.'

He was equally open-minded when it came to classifying human beings—'man', as he put it. He was the first person to include man in a system of biological classification, using essentially the classification mentioned earlier. The genus *Homo* and the specific *sapiens* gives us the binomial name *Homo sapiens* (introduced in the 1758 edition of *Systema Naturae*), and today the genus *Homo* has only one member, ourselves. Linnaeus saw things differently, and included other species of man in the genus *Homo*, such as *Homo troglodytes*, based on nothing more than myths and legends; but that is perhaps excusable given the times he lived in. Much more significantly, although in his formal published classification Linnaeus made a clear distinction between man and the apes (including the chimpanzee and gorilla), he did so only because he feared the wrath of the church—remember that Uppsala was still a university primarily devoted to training Lutheran clergy. In the foreword to his *Fauna Svecica*, published in 1746, Linnaeus wrote 'the fact is that as a natural historian I have yet to find any characteristics which enable man to be distinguished on scientific principles from an ape'. The following year, he wrote to the German botanist Johann Gmelin, later Professor of Botany in Tübingen, with a rhetorical question:

I ask you and the whole world for a generic differentia between man and ape which conforms to the principles of natural history. I certainly know of none...If I were to call man ape or vice versa, I should bring down all the theologians on my head. But perhaps I should still do it according to the rules of science.

This from a man who still believed that swallows hibernated under water! But there may be an explanation for the dichotomy, and once again it may stem from the discussions Linnaeus had with Petrus Artedi, when they were both still students.

One of Artedi's manuscripts from the early 1730s draws up a classification of the animal world which in many ways follows the ideas of John Ray, but concludes with a description of 'man' in what seem now very Linnaean terms, culminating with the comment 'dominates by virtue of the power of speech, which the apes lack'. Once again, it's clear that the two men discussed a key component of what became the Linnaean system; and once again it is far from clear that Linnaeus was the leader of these discussions.

The modern view is, of course, that man should indeed be classified as an ape. If we were doing the classifying now, our species would best be included in the same family as the chimpanzees (*Pan paniscus* and *Pan troglodytes*), perhaps as *Pan sapiens*.[19] But it seems unlikely that anyone will change the classification in the foreseeable future.

In spite of all this, the most important thing that Linnaeus did after he became a professor at Uppsala was to train other biologists and send them off to explore and bring back samples of the botanical riches of the world. Linnaeus himself described these young men as his 'apostles'. Altogether, nineteen of his students set out on voyages of discovery between 1745 and 1792; eight of them died on their travels or, as a result of the hardships they endured, shortly after their return. The first of these travellers was also the first to die. Exceptionally, Christopher Tärnström was actually older than Linnaeus (he had been born in 1703), a married clergyman with a family. But he pleaded for an opportunity to travel to China as a missionary and botanist. In 1746 he got free passage in one of the Swedish East India Company's ships, but died of a fever in the Far East before even completing the journey. His widow never forgave Linnaeus. Perhaps as a result of this experience, from then on Linnaeus insisted that the men selected for these expeditions—and there were many clamouring to go—should be young, with no family ties, and preferably poor, so that they would be used to rough living.

At the other extreme of the fate of these apostles, Peter Kalm (1715–79) travelled to North America, arriving in Philadelphia in the autumn of 1748. After more than two years botanizing, he returned with a considerable collection of plants and seeds, a major contribution to the description of more than 700 North American plants in the *Species Plantarum*.

The next victim of the botanical urge, Fredrik Hasselqvist, was such a sickly young man (he had been born in 1722, and probably suffered from consumption) that even Linnaeus tried to persuade him not to travel; but he set out for Palestine and the Middle East anyway in August 1749. He lasted for a surprisingly long time and collected a great deal of material before dying in the Middle East in 1752. By then, he was considerably in debt, and his creditors refused to release his collections and papers until they were paid; the money was eventually contributed by the Queen of Sweden.

Following in the wake of Tärnström, but with rather more success, Pehr Osbeck (1723–1805) obtained a post as ship's chaplain for a voyage to China which lasted from 1750 to 1752. He spent several months in China, and was rewarded for his efforts by having the *Osbeckia* named in his honour by Linnaeus. But each success seems to have been balanced by another failure. In 1750 the Spanish king asked Linnaeus to recommend a student who could do for the flora of Spain what Linnaeus had done for the flora of Sweden, and he chose Pehr Löfling, then 21 years old. Löfling arrived in 1751 and spent a little over two years in Spain, doing an excellent job, before he was sent as the official botanist on a Spanish expedition to South America, where he died of fever in 1756.[20] Even worse, from Linnaeus's point of view, the Spanish authorities simply locked up Löfling's collections for safe keeping, and they were never properly classified in Linnaeus's lifetime.

These are enough examples to give a flavour of how the influence of Linnaeus spread, even though he stayed at home in Sweden, and at what cost. His apostles travelled in the Ottoman Empire, explored the Caucasus and western Siberia, reached Japan, and even circumnavigated the globe. This is not the place to recount all of their stories; but there is one more of them who must be mentioned, because of his importance in carrying the story of the botanists forward. He is Daniel Solander (1736–82), who was in many ways Linnaeus's star pupil. The master hoped that this particular pupil might become his son-in-law, and planned for him to become Linnaeus's successor as Professor of Botany at Uppsala. But in the end Solander turned out to be Linnaeus's biggest disappointment, although he did more than any of the other apostles to promote the botanical exploration of the world.

Like Linnaeus, Solander was the son of a pastor, and the professor seems to have taken a special interest in the young man from his arrival in Uppsala, taking him into his own household in the way that Linnaeus had been befriended by the younger Rudbeck, and treating him like a son. For a time, there was some kind of understanding that Solander might marry the eldest of the Linnaeus girls, Elisabeth (known as Lisa, born in 1743); but in 1760, when Solander was 24, he travelled to England with Linnaeus's blessing. There, he began a successful career and was instrumental in establishing the Linnaean system in England, much sooner than it was accepted in many other countries. Solander seems to have had the same gift as Linnaeus for clear and concise description, and was almost as adept at identifying and defining species. Two years later, Linnaeus arranged for Solander to be offered the chair of botany at St Petersburg, and wrote with what he thought would be the good news, adding that in due course Solander would be able to move from St Petersburg to succeed Linnaeus at Uppsala. It was several months before Solander, to Linnaeus's surprise and annoyance, wrote back to say that he had decided to settle in England, and quite soon the endearments for Lisa faded away from the letters Solander sent to Linnaeus. Linnacus and Solander never met again, and Lisa married a grandson of Rudbeck the younger.

In England, Solander went from strength to strength. In 1763 he was appointed Assistant Librarian at the British Museum, and later became the Keeper of the Museum's Natural History Department—the forerunner of the present-day Natural History Museum in London. Most important of all, as we shall see in the next chapter, he sailed with Joseph Banks on James Cook's first voyage round the world, and later visited Iceland with Banks, becoming his secretary and librarian when they settled down in London in 1771. Any bad feeling between Linnaeus and Solander seems to have been only on Linnaeus's side; when Carl junior visited England in the early 1780s Solander helped him to find his way around, and even nursed him when he fell ill. Solander died in 1782 (of 'apoplexy') when he was only in his midforties, with Carl junior in attendance.

While his apostles travelled the world, Linnaeus stayed at home. He didn't really make any further significant contributions to botany or science other than those we have already mentioned, but two of his more whimsical ideas give more insight into his methodical, orderly mind. The first was a flower clock—not the decorative kind of floral clock you sometimes see in public parks today, but a 'clock' consisting of flower beds in which the time of day was revealed by the opening and closing of different kinds of flowers. It was a nice idea, and great fun for teaching students how different plants open and close their flowers at different times of day, but hardly practical. Such a clock would be very dependant on the climate, and even on the weather, with some of the flowers refusing to play their part if the skies were cloudy.

Linnaeus's other revolutionary idea was slightly more practical, and seems to have had a short-lived influence in France a few decades later. In 1756 Linnaeus came up with a *Calendarium Florae* in which not just the seasons but individual months were defined, and named, not in accordance with an arbitrary chronology, but in accordance with the activities of the natural world. He began the year with the spring equinox, the time of emerging life, and gave Latin names for the months, including *Germinationis* (the month of germination), *Messis* (the month of reaping), and *Brumalis* (the month of fogs). These names are so similar to the names used in the French revolutionary calendar (Germinal, Messidor, Brumaire . . .) that it seems certain that someone in the revolutionary councils had been reading the work of Linnaeus![21]

Linnaeus was always tossing out ideas, and often came up with potentially useful insights—he was possibly the first person to suggest that studying the pattern of rings in wood from long-lived trees could reveal features of past climate. But he was no experimentalist, and never really understood the scientific method, so many of these insights came to nothing at the time.

During his time as a professor in Uppsala, Linnaeus achieved fame and moderate wealth, and was awarded the kind of honours that he always professed to dismiss as mere baubles but which he really loved. But he became increasingly moody and prone to depression, and his last years were marred by illness—he suffered a series of strokes—and the neglect of an ungrateful family. He was already starting to show the strain of years of overwork by the time he was 40, in 1747. That year, the Royal Academy of Sciences, on behalf of the King, asked him to carry out a survey of the Skåne region, and for the first time the thought of an expedition appalled him. He wrote to the Secretary of the Royal Academy listing the reasons against such a trip, including a detailed estimate of the expenses he would incur and concluding:

I shall not make a penny out of it but merely lose 1,800 dalers and wear myself out—when all the time I might have been sitting comfortably in my room...I shall have to publish an account of my travels, which will mean a lot of hard work...I am ready to work and train competent successors—men who can travel until they have travelled as far and worked as hard as I have and who will then have an excuse for being weary.

The only response was that he received permission to delay the trip for a year, until 1748 (in fact, he didn't go until 1749); but his gloom was further deepened by the death of his father the year before the expedition did take place.

Although he had his ups as well as his downs, ten years later, in February 1758, when he was still not quite 51, Linnaeus wrote to his friend Abraham Bäck:

I cannot write more today; my hand is too weary to hold a pen. I am the child of misfortune. Had I a rope and English courage I would long since have hanged myself. I fear that my wife is again pregnant. I am old and grey and worn out, and my house is already full of children; who is to feed them? It was in an unhappy hour that I accepted the professorship; if only I had remained in my lucrative practice, all would now be well. Farewell, and may you be more fortunate.

In fact, Sara was not pregnant; their last child, Sophia, had been born the previous year. Perhaps cheered by this discovery, later in 1758 Linnaeus took the bold step of purchasing two small country estates just outside Uppsala, costing a total of 80,000 dalers, for which he had to raise a loan. It was at one of these estates, Hammarby, about six miles from Uppsala, that he would now spend a lot of his time, secure in the knowledge that as long as he could pay off the loan he would have something to leave his family when he died.

There is just a possibility that at the time Linnaeus already had a cunning plan to pay off the debt, although it did not come to fruition immediately. In the 1740s he had devised a method for farming pearls from mussels, and in 1748 he tried to sell the rights in the technique to the government. Nothing came of the idea at the time; but thirteen years later, in 1761, the rights were indeed purchased by the government, for 3,000 plåtar. This was enough to clear all Linnaeus's debts and assure him of a financially secure old age. Even better, as part of the deal Linnaeus received a promise that he could appoint his own successor to the chair of botany—which meant that he could pass it on to his son. To go with his wealth and country estates, Linnaeus also had titles. In 1753 he had been awarded the Order of the Polar Star, the medal of which he always wore on his coat, and now, in 1761, he was ennobled, using a Swedish version of his name to become Baron von Linné.

The only thing left for his declining years would be to secure the inheritance, both material and academic, for his son. Carl junior studied at Uppsala, and must also have picked up a lot from living in the same household as his father, but he had no inclination towards botany and simply followed in his father's footsteps because it was the easiest option. It certainly was easy—the elder Linnaeus had his son appointed as a Demonstrator in the botanical garden at Uppsala when he was only 18, used his influence to have Carl junior made an honorary Doctor of Medicine at the age of 24, and saw him appointed first as the old man's assistant when he began to need help with his lecturing, then, indeed, as his successor, in 1777, when the younger Linnaeus was 36.

Linnaeus *fils* was obviously not from the same mould as his father, and many contemporary accounts and later histories suggest that he was completely useless. But a closer examination reveals that he carried out his duties with reasonable diligence and was a competent if uninspired teacher and lecturer, simply passing on to the next generation the knowledge gathered by his father. When he visited England in the 1780s, he was received warmly by Solander and Banks as a fellow naturalist, not dismissed as a buffoon. His early death in 1683, when he was only in his early forties, removed any chance he might have had of coming out from under his father's shadow.

By then, the elder Linnaeus had been dead for five years. His final years, particularly after he turned 65 in 1772, had not been enjoyable. One of his students from the 1760s, Johan Fabricius, later wrote:

His family life was not really very happy. His wife was a large, bouncing woman, domineering, selfish, and quite without culture; she often spoiled our parties. Because she could not join in our conversations she did not care for company. So it was inevitable that the children should be poorly educated. Her daughters are all amiable girls, but wholly unsophisticated and without the polish that education might have given them. The son, who succeeded his father in his professorship at Uppsala, certainly lacks his father's vivacity; but the great knowledge he acquired by constantly working at botany, and the many and excellent observations of his father's which he must have found in his manuscripts, combined to make him a very useful teacher.[22]

After his first stroke, in May 1774, Linnaeus never fully recovered his mobility. The 'large, bouncing woman' took only minimal care of him, and contemporary accounts record that on occasions when he tried to get out of his armchair and fell over she would leave him lying on the floor for hours. After another stroke in the winter of 1776–7 Linnaeus was described by one visitor as 'more dead than alive'; but he recovered sufficiently to be taken from Uppsala to spend his final months at Hammarby, where he died on 10 January 1778.

At first, Carl junior looked after Linnaeus's herbarium and books, but he had never married and after his own death (also of a stroke) on 1 November 1783 they became the property of Sara Linnaeus and her daughters. Their only interest was to make money from the collection, which was sold for a thousand English guineas to a wealthy young English naturalist, James Edward Smith, in 1784. Sara Linnaeus had actually offered to sell the collection to Joseph Banks, the obvious person;[23] but he had so much material of his own already that he passed the proposal on to Smith. When the twenty-six chests holding the collection reached England, Smith found that they contained 19,000 sheets of pressed plants, 2,500 books, many other specimens of insects, coral, and shells, and as an unexpected bonus 3,000-odd letters and other manuscript items which Sara had thought worthless and had used as padding in the chests. In 1828, most of this material became the property of the Linnean Society in London, which had been founded in 1788 with Smith as its first President, and chose an Anglicized spelling for its name.

Although the loss of Linnaeus's collection caused much anguish in Sweden, it could not have found a better home. Like the collection itself, the torch of botanical exploration passed, in the late eighteenth century, from Sweden to England, where Joseph Banks picked it up.

IN THE GARDEN

Attempting to cultivate a flower clock is a bold undertaking as so much depends on climate and length of day. Linnaeus had observed the time that flowers capable of growing in Sweden opened and closed each day and he devised a plan which arranged plants opening and closing at different times of day so enabling him to plant a 'floral clock' that could (hopefully) determine the time accurately within half an hour. There is no record of Linnaeus actually managing to cultivate such a clock, and this idea, which he published in *Philosophica Botanica* in 1751, may well have been a theoretical rather than practical garden project. But it may be that he backed off from creating the first flower clock because he did not want to crush the ambitions of his son Carl Linnaeus, who began to write a paper on the project. This thesis (*Horologium Plantarium*) was never completed and Carl seems to have become disenchanted by the idea.

The elder Linnaeus undoubtedly made accurate observations of flowering plants and their opening and closing times and he describes three groups with differing 'opening triggers': *Meteorici* are a category of those which change their opening and closing times with the prevailing weather conditions, *Aequinoctales* are flowers whose opening and closing times are fixed and unaffected by weather, and *Tropici* are flowers whose opening and closing times alter according to the length of the daylight in the course of the day. Obviously *Aequinoctales* are the only flowers suitable for use in growing a flower clock.

The University of Uppsala has a flower clock which has to be constantly maintained because each species has to be replaced after it finishes flowering. Creating a flower clock is time consuming and difficult, but the idea became part of the Victorian vogue for creating more and more exotically creative floral displays. From the mid-nineteenth century onwards the newly affluent middle classes of Britain as well as landowners took great social pride in their gardens. They were prepared to employ skilled gardeners, sometimes teams of gardeners, to carry out their ideas. The idea of creating a flower clock became a cherished dream—one that they were prepared to pay for and maintain.

This 'recipe' for creating a flower clock is taken from a Victorian listing thought suitable for gardening conditions in the milder parts of Britain. Obviously opening times vary according to latitude, season, and the prevailing climatic conditions in the garden:

This flower clock requires a circular flower bed to be laid out like a clock face with a section for each of 12 daylight hours, each section to contain flowers that either open or close during that one hour time slot.

5 a.m. Morning Glory (*Ipomoea*) and wild roses open

6 a.m. Catmint (*Nepeta cataria*) opens

7 a.m. African Marigolds (*Tagetes*) open

8 a.m. African Daisies (*Arctosis*) open

9 a.m. Gentians (*Gentiana*) close

10 a.m. Californian Poppies (*Eschsholzia*) close

11 a.m. Star of Bethlehem (*Ornithogolum*) opens

12 noon Morning Glory Closes

1 p.m. Pinks (*Dianthus*) open

2 p.m. Scarlet Pimpernel closes

3 p.m. Hawkbit (*Leontodon*) closes

4 p.m. Four O'Clock Plant (*Mirabilis jalapa*) opens

5 p.m. White Water Lilies close.

For perfume on a summer's evening plant Evening Primroses (*Oethera*) which open around 6 p.m. and Flowering Tobacco (*Nicotiana*) which opens around 9 p.m.

2

JOSEPH BANKS

(1743–1820)

A USTRALIA BECAME A British colony because of a rare astronomical alignment and the political influence of a botanist. The
botanist, of course, was Joseph Banks, who sailed with Captain
James Cook on his first circumnavigation of the globe; more of him
in a moment. The astronomical alignment was a transit of Venus, when
that planet passes across the disc of the Sun, as viewed from Earth. The
alignments which allow such transits to be seen always occur in pairs,
with two transits observable eight years apart, but the interval between
each such pair of transits is more than a hundred years.[1] Because of the
way the planets line up, the transits are always visible a few days either
side of 7 June and 8 December. Apart from their intrinsic interest, such
events are important because the exact timing of the passage of Venus
across the face of the Sun allows astronomers to use the geometry of the
Solar System to work out the distance from the Earth to the Sun, and
thereby calibrate other astronomical measurements. In the eighteenth
century this was of crucial importance because astronomy was the key
to navigation at sea.

All of this had been appreciated by Edmond Halley, who did much
more than predict the return of the comet that now bears his name.

Among other things, Halley had been in command (with the naval rank of Master and Commander) of a Royal Navy vessel, the *Paramore*, seconded for a scientific expedition at the end of the 1690s; in 1720 he became the second Astronomer Royal. As early as 1691, Halley had published a paper explaining how the geometry of the Solar System could be used, with the aid of a transit of Venus, to measure the distance to the Sun, and he returned to the subject in 1716, when he predicted that the next pair of transits would occur in 1761 and 1769, writing: 'I strongly urge diligent searchers of the heavens (for whom, when I have ended my days, these sights are being kept in store) to bear in mind this injunction of mine and to apply themselves actively and with all their might to making the necessary observations.'

Halley died in 1642, at the age of 84. But his 'injunction' was remembered, and the transit of Venus in 1761 was indeed observed, using the techniques he had spelled out. But the transits are not visible from everywhere on Earth, and to complicate the situation Halley's technique for measuring the distance to the Sun depended on making at least two observations of the transit from widely separated parts of the world. The observations made in 1761, which involved expeditions organized by several countries to far-flung corners of the globe, were far from satisfactory. There was still a need for accurate observations of the transit due in 1769[2]—which is where Joseph Banks and James Cook come into the story.

There was also a political subtext to all of this activity. In spite of Halley's prescience, the two British expeditions of 1761 were hastily planned and poorly funded affairs, put together at the last minute when the Royal Society expressed its dismay (in the summer of 1760) at the news that France had already made plans to carry out such observations. This was in the middle of the Seven Years War, and more than just pride was at stake. One reason why the observations of the 1761 transit turned out to be scientifically disappointing was the war itself: to British delight but to the detriment of science, one team of French observers was unable to carry out their planned measurements from India because the British had captured their intended observing site. But the war ended in 1763, and although this did little to reduce the rivalry between Britain and France it did make planning scientific expeditions more straightforward. Both governments also appreciated that scientific expeditions provided an excellent cover for other kinds of exploration.

Determined that this time the British would lead the way in showing the world how such scientific projects ought to be organized, the Royal Society obtained £4,000 from the King, George III, to fund expeditions. One of them went to the Pacific island of Tahiti,[3] which was ideally located to observe the transit of 1769, due in June that year.

It was a stroke of luck that the Royal Society knew about this possible observing site. The existence and location of Tahiti had, in fact, only just become known in Europe. Although earlier navigators had visited Polynesia and the general existence of the islands was known, the person credited with 'discovering' Tahiti, in the sense of landing there and determining its accurate latitude and longitude, was the English Captain Samuel Wallis, who anchored his ship the *Dolphin* there on 17 June 1767. In April of the following year, only months after the *Dolphin* had left, two French ships under the command of Louis-Antoine de Bougainville (after whom the plant Bougainvillea is named) also visited Tahiti, and took back with them to France a native Tahitian, a living example of Rousseau's 'noble savage'. One curiosity of Bougainville's expedition was that in Tahiti the natives discovered that the botanist's assistant was a woman disguised in man's clothing; in view of the cramped conditions on board ship, it seems astonishing that none of the French sailors had noticed this on their long voyage to the South Seas!

By the time Wallis returned to England, the decision to send an expedition to the Pacific to observe the transit had already been made, but the location for the observations not finalized; it was immediately appreciated that Tahiti would be the perfect spot. The ship for the Tahiti expedition was a converted east coast collier (a kind sometimes referred to as a 'cat'), named the *Endeavour*, commanded by a sailor who had cut his teeth in such vessels, James Cook. The ship, of just 368 tons, was well suited for such an expedition because it had a shallow draft, enabling it to work close inshore in uncharted waters, but a large carrying capacity for all the stores that would be required. Four members of the crew of the *Dolphin*, including her sailing master, sailed in the *Endeavour* with Cook. Cook was chosen for the job because of the skill he had displayed surveying the coast of Newfoundland and in other naval activity during the Canadian operations of the Seven Years War. He had previously served as a Warrant Officer and Master (the person responsible for sailing and navigating a King's ship, under the direction of the Captain) and was commissioned Lieutenant in May 1768, when he was in his fortieth year; because he was in command of the *Endeavour*, like all commanders of the King's ships he had the courtesy title 'Captain', although that was not his substantive rank.

Cook would need all his skills as seaman and navigator—and, as it turned out, cartographer. Very little was known about the southern ocean. New Zealand had been partially mapped by Dutch explorers, and the Dutch had also visited the northern parts of Australia (which they called New Holland) and in addition discovered Tasmania, at its south-eastern extremity. But were these part of one or more larger landmasses? Was there an as yet undiscovered continent in the South Sea east of New Zealand? Cook's secret orders from the Admiralty told him, once the astronomical observations had been completed, to sail south as far as latitude 40° in search of such a continent, then, if nothing were found, to turn west for New Zealand, to find out whether it was an island or the edge of a continent. Any new lands discovered were, of course, to be claimed in the name of the King. Cook was then to proceed home by whatever route he thought best, keeping any discoveries he made secret and sending his sealed logbooks directly to the Admiralty on his arrival back in England.

Without knowing any of this, the Royal Society formally approved the choice of Cook to lead the expedition, and appointed him as one of their 'Observers of the Transit of Venus' with a modest gratuity and an allowance towards his expenses. A second 'Observer of the Transit of Venus' was also appointed—Charles Green, one of the astronomers from the Royal Greenwich Observatory. Green was exactly the right man for the job. At that time, the most accurate way to determine longitude was by measuring the changing position of the Moon against the background stars and comparing this with tables that had been painstakingly compiled over many decades—going back, indeed, to the work of Halley as Astronomer Royal. This was a difficult task, at which Green was an expert—and under Green's tuition Cook soon became one of the few officers in the Royal Navy who understood and had the mathematical skills to use the technique. The value of this skill was about to diminish, thanks to John Harrison's invention of a chronometer which could keep accurate time at sea, enabling longitude to be determined by comparing the time of local noon with the time shown on a chronometer set to Greenwich time. Green had been one of the observers on the voyage to the West Indies and back in 1763–4 when Harrison's chronometer had been tested, but in 1769 it had not yet been adopted by the Navy.[4]

It was the Royal Society that chose Tahiti as the best place for the observations to be carried out; at the same time as making this recommendation the Council of the Society added one further request to the Admiralty:

Joseph Banks Esq., Fellow of this Society, a gentleman of large fortune, who is well versed in Natural History, being desirous of undertaking the same voyage, the Council very earnestly requests their Lordships, that in regard to Mr Banks's great personal merit and for the advancement of useful knowledge, he also, together with his suite, being seven persons more (that is eight persons in all) together with their baggage, be received on board of the ship under the command of Capt. Cook.

Banks, who had been born in 1743 and came into a huge inheritance when he was 21, was used to getting his way, and this occasion proved no exception—not least because the Earl of Sandwich, an influential parliamentary figure who was soon to become First Lord of the Admiralty, was a close personal friend. It also helped that Banks could easily afford to pay for his entourage. We have only sketchy accounts of Banks's childhood and early education, but his family background is well recorded. Banks came from a line of English gentlemen that originated in the parish of Giggleswick in the county of Yorkshire. By the time of this Joseph Banks, a tradition of public service and care for the land had long been established, but the family's wealth had suffered during the Civil War. The fortune which Joseph inherited was largely built upon the work of his great-grandfather, also Joseph, a lawyer who acted as agent for three dukes (Norfolk, Leeds, and Newcastle), acquired estates in Lincolnshire and sat as Member of Parliament for Grimsby. Some sign of his wealth, largely acquired through property speculation, is indicated by the dowry provided for his daughter Mary—£8,000 on her marriage to Sir Francis Whichcote, of Aswarby in Lincolnshire, with the promise of a further £4,000 on the death of her father (though as it happened, she died before he did). The family home that he purchased in 1714 was the estate of Revesby Abbey, dissolved under Henry VIII.

This Joseph's heir, another Joseph Banks, was MP for Peterborough and Sheriff of Lincolnshire, and married an heiress, Anne Hodgkinson, also in 1714. His first son was also given the traditional Christian name, but died young, in his twenties, without having married; so in 1736 the estate was inherited by his younger brother William, who had been born in 1719. Another MP, and an enthusiast for agricultural improvement, he married Sarah Bate in 1741. Their son, Joseph Banks, was born at Argyle Street, in London, on 13 February 1743,[5] and a daughter, Sarah Sophia, on 28 October the following year. Young Joseph had the prospect of a very large inheritance which would enable him to spend his time doing anything he liked, or nothing at all. He chose to do plenty.

There is little record of Banks's childhood, except that he spent four years at Harrow and then, at the age of 13, went to Eton, where he was regarded as an amiable character who enjoyed sport and outdoor activities but had no academic pretensions. Many years later, he told a friend that his interest in botany had been awakened a year after he joined Eton, when he had gone swimming in the river with some friends. Lingering in the evening sunshine and the last to get dressed, he was walking back alone through a lane with high banks on both sides where wild flowers were growing in profusion. Struck by their beauty in the light of the setting Sun, he decided at that moment to learn everything he could about plants. According to his later recollection, the thought stuck in his mind that it would be far more reasonable if his teachers made him learn about the nature of plants rather than trying to stuff his head with Greek and Latin.

By the time Banks went up to Oxford in 1760, he had taught himself what he could about botany from books and was eager to learn more. But the Professor of Botany at the time, Humphrey Sibthorp, was one of the worst examples of the depths to which the university had sunk in those days, and is reputed to have given only one lecture during his thirty-five years in the chair. Banks, used to having his own way, persuaded Sibthorp to provide him with letters of introduction to John Martyn, the Professor of Botany in Cambridge, where teaching was then taken at least a little more seriously. Martyn in his turn introduced Banks to Israel Lyons, the son of a watchmaker, who had no official post but was a self-taught astronomer and botanist of real talent. He had written a handbook of Cambridge plants as a supplement to Ray's famous work, and this had been published in 1763. Banks paid for Lyons to go to Oxford and provide, in the form of a kind of summer school during July 1764, the lectures and tuition that Sibthorp did not. Lyons's lectures were attended by as many as sixty students, and marked something of a revival of botany in Oxford.

In 1761 Banks's father died, when Joseph was only 18. He would come into his inheritance in 1764, at the age of 21, but meanwhile stayed in Oxford, officially leaving the university in December 1763—like many of the 'young gentlemen' of the time, without bothering to take a degree—but actually maintaining contacts in the town and rooms there for several years. He acquired a house in New Burlington Street, in London, but had barely settled there when he began planning his first botanical expedition.

One of Banks's friends from Oxford, Constantine Phipps (later in command of an Arctic expedition, on which Israel Lyons was the official astronomer, and later still Lord Mulgrave) had obtained a commission in the Royal Navy as Lieutenant, and would be sailing in the *Niger*, under the command of Sir Thomas Adams, to Newfoundland and Labrador. It was straightforward for somebody with Banks's wealth and connections to make arrangements, through his friendship with Phipps, to travel on board the *Niger* at his own expense. The voyage lasted from April to November 1766, giving the two friends ample opportunity for botanizing and collecting specimens, which would form the beginning of Banks's own herbarium. Banks kept a detailed journal of the voyage for his own use, but, characteristically, never published it.

While he was on the voyage, Banks had been elected as a Fellow of the Royal Society, at the age of 23. This was unusually young even for those days, and it was not because of any outstanding scientific merit. It was enough that Banks was a rich gentleman interested in science, and with the right connections. The Royal Society was still largely made up of such people, who, by their subscriptions, funded the scientific activities of the society, and by their connections helped to maintain its prestige.

The newly elected Fellow, who was admitted to the Society in person on 12 February 1767, was content to stay in England, attending to his duties as a landowner but finding time for a botanical excursion to the west of England, in 1767. He developed friendships with, among others, Daniel Solander (whom he probably met in the library of the British Museum some time in 1764), and talked of visiting Linnaeus. But in 1768 everything changed when he learned of the proposed expedition to the South Seas. Banks just *had* to go on the expedition, and he began planning for it and pulling the appropriate strings long before the Royal Society formally requested his inclusion.

The request was, of course, granted, and in the end Banks's party was increased to nine by the inclusion of Solander. The others were Sydney Parkinson and Alexander Buchan (both artists); Henry Sporing, a trained doctor and naturalist, but also a skilled draughtsman, who acted as Banks's secretary; two of the servants from Revesby, James Roberts (who was only 16) and Peter Briscoe; and, an essential accoutrement of the time for any English gentleman worth his salt, two Negro servants, Thomas Richmond and George Dorlton. There were also two greyhounds, in case the opportunity arose for any sporting activities. But don't imagine that Banks regarded the voyage as just a kind of Grand Tour around the world. The scientific equipment he provided for the expedition, in addition to the equipment provided by the Royal Society and the Royal Greenwich Observatory for the transit observation, included casks of preserving liquid, hundreds of glass bottles for specimens (and one rubber bottle, a great curiosity in Europe at that time), telescopes and microscopes, and much more. Harold Carter, author of the most comprehensive life of Banks, estimates the total weight of all the baggage and equipment for Banks's party as some 20 tons. To quote a letter sent to Linnaeus by a fellow botanist the week before the *Endeavour* sailed:

No people ever went to sea better fitted out for the purpose of Natural History...They have got a fine library of Natural History; they have all sorts of machines for catching and preserving insects; all kinds of nets, trawls, drags and hooks for coral fishing; they have even a curious contrivance of a telescope, by which, put into the water, you can see the bottom to a great depth, where it is clear...[6]

The letter also quotes Solander as saying that the expedition 'would cost Mr. Banks ten thousand pounds', but this round sum seems to have been meant more as a general indication of the vast expense and Banks's vast wealth than an accurate accounting. Nevertheless, the only comparison you could make today would be with those few multimillionaires who are rich enough and adventurous enough to purchase a visit to the International Space Station.

The final preparation of *Endeavour* for the voyage was made at Plymouth, while Banks and Solander enjoyed their last days in London for several years. Banks, in particular, had some unfinished business there. He had become romantically involved with a Miss Harriet Blosset, an heiress worth ten thousand pounds, and like characters in a Jane Austen novel they had reached an understanding, although they were not formally engaged. Harriet knew of the planned expedition, but Banks seems to have neglected to tell her just how soon he would be leaving. When word came from Cook, on 15 August 1768, for the two botanists to proceed with all speed to Plymouth for embarkation, he carried on with a planned night at the opera with Miss Blosset, failing to pluck up the courage to tell her of his imminent departure. It seems she only learned of Banks's departure the following morning, after he had left for Plymouth, and soon took herself off to the country to live quietly and await his return and their marriage.

Banks was 25, and Solander 32, when the *Endeavour* sailed from Plymouth on Thursday, 25 August 1768. In order to fit everybody in, six tiny cabins, each measuring seven feet by five (roughly two metres by one-and-a-half metres) had been constructed on the quarter deck. There was one each for Cook, Banks, Green, Solander, and two other members of the party. The rest of the officers and crew had less luxurious accommodation. Cook had two lieutenants under him, as well as the ship's Master, a surgeon, and the Captain's clerk, plus the seamen who worked the vessel and a contingent of thirteen marines, including a drummer boy. The total complement of the ship came to ninety-four, in a ship 106' (32 metres) long and 29' 3" (9 metres) across at its widest, crammed with stores that included 7,860 pounds (some 3,500 kilos) of sauerkraut—a ration of 80 pounds (36 kilos) per man—which would be a main reason for the success of the voyage.

The single most important reason for the success of the voyage, however, was Captain Cook himself—and the sauerkraut was part of his method of combating scurvy. We now know that scurvy is a deficiency disease caused by a lack of vitamin C, which can be obtained from fresh fruit and vegetables. In the eighteenth century, scurvy was a scourge which brought sickness and death to sailors on long voyages, and in the 1760s it was just beginning to be appreciated that green vegetables and lime or lemon juice (which the *Endeavour* also carried, mixed with brandy in a small keg) could ward off the symptoms. The Royal Navy officially adopted the practice of issuing lime juice to its crews to stave off scurvy only in 1795, but Cook enthusiastically took up these new ideas on his own initiative. Since sauerkraut was hardly the most appetizing dish in the eyes of the British seamen, he developed a cunning and successful plan to ensure the health of his crew during the long intervals between landfalls. Early in the voyage, he had the dish served only at the officers' table, where it was presented as a treat. Only then did he 'allow' the men a share of what they had come to regard as a delicacy, to such effect that he soon had to ration their allowance:

For such are the tempers and disposition of seamen in general, that whatever you give them out of the common way, although it be ever so much for their good, it will not go down and you will hear nothing but murmurings...but the moment they see their superiors set a value upon it, it becomes the finest stuff in the world.

Apart from Cook's skills as sailor and navigator, which were of the first rank, the avoidance of scurvy made all the difference to the success of the expedition. To put this in perspective, in 1764 an expedition commanded by Commodore John Byron (the grandfather of the poet) took two months to navigate the Straits of Magellan and break out into the Pacific, by which time the crew were in such a state that all they could do was find somewhere to rest and recuperate before heading home, adding very little to the understanding of the geography of the Pacific. By contrast, nobody became seriously ill from scurvy, let alone died of it, on board the *Endeavour*. During their longest passage without a chance to obtain fresh produce, four months, there were a few occurrences of mild symptoms, a loosening of the teeth, which were quickly cured—Banks himself was one of these sufferers and cured the symptoms with lemon juice from the supply he carried with him.

Endeavour's route to Cape Horn was via Madeira and Rio de Janeiro, where the Viceroy of the Portuguese colony refused to believe Cook's tale of an expedition to observe the transit of Venus across the face of the Sun, and suspected some dastardly English trickery. In Cook's words, '[the Viceroy] could form no other idea of the Phenomenon than the North Star passing through the South Pole'. Although the ship was allowed to purchase supplies, for twenty-four frustrating days only Cook was officially allowed to set foot ashore—although Banks, Solander, and the artist Sydney Parkinson did manage to evade the watch on the ship and gather some botanical specimens.

The next stop was in the wilds of Tierra del Fuego, which they reached in January 1769, high summer in the southern hemisphere. Lulled into a false feeling of security by the season, Banks's party suffered their first losses at this point. With the ship safely anchored, friendly relations established with the natives, and fresh water being gathered by the crew, Banks, Solander, and a large party which included all four of his servants, set out into the hills on a day which started out like a bright day in May back home. The going proved harder than they had expected across what turned out to be boggy terrain. The weather changed, and as snow began to fall Buchan, one of the artists, suffered an epileptic seizure. By the time he recovered it was clear that the party would have to spend the night ashore. An advance guard of the fittest seamen was sent ahead to find a good spot and light a fire, while the rest struggled in their wake. Banks had great difficulty assisting Solander through the snow, and the two Negro servants gave up the struggle and laid down to rest; it turned out that they had drunk all of the rum taken ashore by the party. In the morning, they were found dead where they lay, but the others made it safely back to the ship.

With the watering completed and nothing to keep them in this desolate spot, the ship set sail again and rounded Cape Horn before the end of January, having had remarkably good luck with the weather. The traditional route from the Horn was to follow the western coast of South America northwards to the tropics, then head west across the Pacific; but Cook, under orders to search for the hypothetical *Terra Australis*, sailed north-west across uncharted and, as it turned out, empty waters. Navigating with the aid of the lunar technique—it is generally acknowledged that thanks to Green's skill the *Endeavour* was the first ship to sail across the Pacific whose position was accurately known at all times—it was April before the ship passed the first speck of land they had seen since Cape Horn, a tiny coral island that proved the first of many. After three months without sight of any other land, the ship made a perfect landfall at Tahiti, anchoring in Matavia Bay on 13 April. The success of the navigators and the arrival of the crew in perfect health and high spirits could not have been better omens for the transit observations.

By now, as well as his botanical, geological, and other scientific activities Banks had become accepted as Cook's right-hand man in administering the affairs of the expedition. He took a leading part in negotiations with the natives, taking the trouble to learn enough of the local language to get by.[7] In particular he controlled the market between the ship and the shore to regulate the prices paid (in barter items such as iron nails) for the provisions obtained. When the quadrant, a scientific instrument crucial for the observation of the transit, was stolen by some natives, Banks played a key role in recovering it; and he joined Cook on a circumnavigation of the island by boat and on foot to sketch the coast and find any good natural harbours.

Banks also enjoyed the social life on the island, taking full advantage (unlike Cook) of the relaxed attitude of the Tahitians to sexual activity. He also had one of his arms tattooed; Banks's easy manner with the Tahitians was invaluable as he often had to act as an intermediary between Tahitians and members of the ship's crew. The observations of the transit were successfully carried out on 3 June. Well before that date, Green and Cook had accurately determined the longitude of Tahiti by repeated observations using the lunar method—essential if any good use were to be made of the transit observations. And while all of this was going on, everyone, including Banks, was struck by the value of the breadfruit as a local staple—a readily grown, freely available foodstuff which was in no small measure responsible for the easy life of the islanders.

The ship sailed again on 15 July, but only after two of the marines had tried to desert, hoping to remain on the island with the women they had become involved with. They were soon captured by the other marines and brought back to the ship; but for once, as we shall see, an important lesson was not properly learned. When the ship did sail, it carried two extra passengers—a Tahitian called Tupia, who was both a priest and a navigator, and his son Tayeto. Tupia was eager to see more of the world. Banks thought he might keep him in England as a curiosity, 'as well as some of my neighbours do lions and tigers'. Tupia possessed remarkable navigational skills and valuable geographical knowledge of the Pacific. He had already learned a little English and when the *Endeavour* eventually reached New Zealand he turned out to be able to communicate with the Maoris as their language was similar to his own. He was so successful with the Maori people that they honoured him with the gift of a precious dog-skin coat as a mark of respect. But Tupia never did reach England, and the cloak passed to Banks after the Tahitian died of malaria in December 1770 in the notoriously unhealthy port of Batavia.

With the aid of Tupia's local knowledge, Cook spent some time charting the islands near Tahiti, which he called the Society Islands, in honour of the Royal Society. So it wasn't until 9 August 1769 that the *Endeavour* headed south, in accordance with Cook's no longer secret orders, in search of the fabled *Terra Australis*. After struggling some 1,500 miles (about 2700 km) southward in mostly foul weather, *Endeavour* passed latitude 40 °S at the beginning of September, finding nothing but empty sea. It was now more than a year since they had sailed from Plymouth. Cook then turned west, as instructed, and made landfall on New Zealand on 6 October, three months after leaving Tahiti.

There is no space here to describe how Cook circumnavigated both islands of New Zealand, in a figure of eight involving passage through what became called, at Banks's suggestion, the Cook Strait. The bottom line is that the voyage established that New Zealand does indeed consist of two major islands, and is not part of a great southern continent. Among Banks's botanical contributions was the discovery of New Zealand 'spinach', distantly related to our common spinach. This could be cooked and pickled to replace the depleted supplies of sauerkraut in the fight against scurvy. Another was New Zealand 'flax', a fibrous plant which he realized had great potential for making cloth. Since the beginning of the voyage Banks had collected almost 400 plant specimens. New Zealand flax (*phormium tenax*) is now widely grown in gardens as a spectacular architectural plant.

The charting of New Zealand took nearly six months, so it was the end of March before Cook had to decide, in accordance with his instructions, on a suitable route for the voyage home. His own preference was to head east at high latitudes, rounding Cape Horn and establishing once and for all whether there was a southern continent. But, as he noted in his journal on 31 March 1770, 'in order to ascertain this we must have kept in a higher Latitude in the very Depth of Winter but the Condition of the Ship, in every respect, was not thought sufficient for such an Undertaking'. The *Endeavour* was visibly wearing out—her sails and rigging had suffered considerably, and the wooden hull of the ship was being eaten away by marine worms.

Cook was left with two alternatives—either to sail west at reasonably high latitudes (level with the southern part of New Zealand), heading south of the land seen by Abel Tasman on his voyage in the seventeenth century and then round the Cape of Good Hope; or to head slightly further to the north, hoping to strike the unknown eastern coast of the land whose northern fringe had been called New Holland. The second option would involve turning northward up this coastline in the expectation of reaching the Dutch East Indies, where the ship could be overhauled before heading round the Cape of Good Hope. This was the plan which was decided on by Cook, after consultation with his officers and the other gentlemen, not least because 'no Discovery of any moment could be hoped for' on the other route. In making that decision, he actually set the *Endeavour* on the course that would lead to the most important discoveries, geographically speaking, of the entire voyage, and the ones that would have most resonance for Banks in his later life.

Endeavour reached the coast of Australia on 19 April 1770, just to the north of the strait which separates Tasmania and Australia. Although Cook thought it likely that Tasmania (which had been seen in the 1640s by Abel Tasman, who called it Van Dieman's Land) was joined to the mainland, there was no time to test this belief by sailing through what is now known as the Bass Strait, and the ship turned north to make landfall at Botany Bay, missing the discovery of the great natural harbour where Sydney is now located.[8] Cook first named the bay Stingray Bay and recorded it on the admiralty chart under that name on 6 May 1770. He wrote in the ship's log on that date 'the great quantity of these sort of fish found in this place occasioned my giving it the name of stingrays harbour'. Later, Cook changed the name to Botany Bay after 'the great quantity of plants Mr Banks and Dr Solander found in this place'. Banks and Solander built up a large collection of new species in Botany Bay. These included the now popular garden trees and flowers eucalyptus, mimosa, grevilleas, acacias, and, perhaps most famous of all the genera named in his honour, *Banksia*. There are around eighty species of *Banksia*, all with the characteristic flower spike and fruiting 'cones'. Their growing form varies from low growing shrubs to 30-metre-high trees. Because *Banksias* produce so much nectar, they are a vital part of the food chain in that part of the world; today they are a staple of Australia's cut flower industry, lasting for many weeks after cutting. Another of Banks and Solander's finds in Botany Bay was the Illawarra flame tree. This spectacular tree, growing up to 40 metres high and covered in vibrantly colourful bright red bell-shaped flowers, was a particularly spectacular find.

Following the coast northward, the *Endeavour* was soon, unknown to its crew, inside the Great Barrier Reef, among the shoals and lesser reefs off the coast of modern Queensland. On 11 June, around 11 o'clock in the evening, the ship struck a reef and stuck fast on the falling tide while water poured in through a hole in the hull. It was literally a case of all hands, and all gentlemen including Banks and Solander, to the pumps, in a desperate attempt to stop the water level inside the hull rising. Even after dumping the six cannon carried by the ship overboard, it proved impossible to refloat the ship on the next high tide. After dumping more equipment and continuing to pump in relays for more than twenty-four hours, *Endeavour* was refloated the following night, and the hole in her hull was temporarily patched with a fother—a sail into which masses of wool, oakum, and anything else that might serve was sewn. The sail was manoeuvred over the hole and pressed into it by the pressure of water outside, slowing the inrush sufficiently for the vessel, still pumping, to make the shore. There, Cook found a river (now named after his ship) where *Endeavour* could be unloaded and careened (hauled over on her side) so that the damage could be repaired.

Cook described what he discovered:

The Rocks had made their way through 4 planks quite to, and even into, the timbers and wounded 3 more. The manner these planks were damaged or cut out, as I may say, is hardly credible. Scarce a splinter was to be seen, but the whole was cut away as if it had been done by the Hands of Man with a blunt edged tool. A large piece of Coral rock was sticking in one Hole and several pieces of Fothering, small stones &c. had made their way in and lodged between the timbers, which had stopped the water forcing its way in in great quantities.

Without that lump of coral wedged into the hole, *Endeavour* would surely have been lost. But it would also have been lost if it had not had a fit, healthy crew with high morale—the sauerkraut and Cook's leadership also played a part.

Banks wrote:

During the whole time of this distress I must say for the credit of our people that I beleive every man exerted his utmost for the preservation of the ship, contrary to what I have universally heard to be the behaviour of sea men who have commonly as soon as a ship is in a desperate situation began to plunder and refuse all commands. This was no doubt owing intirely to the cool and steady conduct of the officers, who during the whole time never gave an order which did not shew them to be perfectly composed and unmoved by the circumstances howsoever dreadfull they might appear.

The near-disaster provided ample opportunity for plant hunting, studying the local fauna, and making limited contact with the natives while the repairs were being carried out at the mouth of what became known as the Endeavour River. Specimens joining their swiftly growing plant collection included tulip wood, yellow wood, and cedar wood, together with the Moreton Bay Pine, a valuable, light, even-textured wood. These timbers later contributed greatly to the trade in fine woods used in the manufacture of fine furniture and marquetry. They also came across Kangaroo Grass (*Themeda triandra*), a grass whose ripe seeds could be ground and baked into cakes. One of their most stunning finds was the Coastal Cottonwood (*Hibiscus tiliaceus*), a shrub so profuse that it can carpet a whole hill, covered in large bright yellow scarlet-centred flowers. Each flower deepens from yellow to orange over the course of a day, finally turning red and falling to the ground.

By the time the ship sailed again on 10 August, all but two months after the near-shipwreck, the thought uppermost in everyone's mind was going home. After a difficult journey northward through reefs in a worn-out ship, leaving the tip of Australia behind[9] and heading for the Dutch settlement of Batavia (now Jakarta) at last, Banks described the feelings of the company: 'The sick became well and the melancholy looked gay. The greatest of them were now pretty far gone with the longing for home which the Physicians have gone so far as to esteem a disease under the name of Nostalgia;[10] indeed I can find hardly any body in the ship clear of its effects.'

But fate had one last cruel trick to play on the nostalgic crew. Batavia was a notoriously unhealthy port, which sailors knew to avoid if at all possible. Unfortunately, with the *Endeavour* worn out and in need of an overhaul it was not possible. Although Cook never lost a man to scurvy, and arrived in Batavia with the healthiest crew yet to reach the Dutch East Indies via Cape Horn, during three months spent in Batavia seven of the party died of malaria, including the Tahitian Tupia and his son, the surgeon, three seamen, and Green's servant; many others, including Banks and Solander, were ill. On the voyage home, before reaching Cape Town twenty-three more died, mostly of dysentery, including the astronomer Green, the ship's Master, one of its lieutenants, and the cook. Banks himself was again ill, possibly with typhoid, and Solander was laid up for two weeks with a combination of the diseases sweeping the ship. Out of Banks's original party of nine, as well as the two Negro servants who died in the snow of Tierra del Fuego, the artist Buchan had died in Tahiti after suffering an epileptic seizure, and both Parkinson and Sporing were among those who died between Batavia and the Cape of Good Hope, where replacements for the dead seamen were recruited. Of his own party, only Banks, Solander, and his two servants from Revesby returned to

England in the middle of July 1771, nearly three years after their departure.

When he heard the news, Linnaeus wrote to a colleague: 'I cannot sufficiently admire Mr Banks who has exposed himself to so many dangers and has bestowed more money in the service of Natural Science than any other man. Surely none but an Englishman would have the spirit to do what he has done.'[11]

Banks had collected more than 1,300 new species and discovered 110 new genera. Specimens were brought back as dried herbaria, not as seeds or living plants. It was only much later that transporting the varieties of plants Banks had found halfway round the world became viable as a trade. But many, including hebes and the vastly popular everlasting flower (*Helichrysum bracteatum*), eventually became firm garden favourites.

Because of his position in society, if anything Banks's immediate fame overshadowed that of Cook in the months after the voyagers returned. As early as 2 August Banks was presented to the king, George III, at the Court of St James, and on 10 August both Banks and Solander were presented to the king at Kew, by the President of the Royal Society, Sir John Pringle. Banks and the king, who was keenly interested in agriculture and popularly known as 'Farmer George', immediately hit it off and became friends. Just over a week later, on Sunday 18 August, Banks and Solander dined with Pringle and a distinguished visitor from the American colonies, Benjamin Franklin, who was also a Fellow of the Royal Society. Rather less agreeably, Banks had to face up to Harriet Blosset, breaking the news that he no longer felt himself suited for marriage. He settled a large sum (rumoured to be £5,000) on her in compensation, and in due course she married a clergyman. Banks always enjoyed female company, and had at least one illegitimate daughter, but did not marry until 1779.

The connection with George III and Kew would become one of the most important features of Banks's life, and *the* most important as far as our present story is concerned. During Banks's time, some seven thousand new plants from overseas were introduced into Britain, mostly through his efforts on behalf of the Royal gardens.

Kew Gardens came into the Royal family through George's father, Frederick Prince of Wales. Frederick was the heir apparent to George II, and in 1730 he obtained the lease of Kew House and its surrounding land from the Capel family, descended from Sir Henry Capel, who had built up a collection of exotic plants during the reign of Charles II. Frederick married Augusta of Saxe-Coburg-Gotha, and their son George was born in 1738. But just thirteen years later Frederick died after being hit on the head by a cricket ball, and the teenager became heir to the throne. The dowager Princess Augusta, herself a keen gardener, made her home at Kew, where her close friend (the rumours said more than just a friend) John Stuart, the third Earl of Bute, bought a house, Richmond Lodge, in 1754. Bute's property joined on to her grounds, and Bute played a major part in developing the gardens, as well as in the upbringing of Prince George. The two gardens were combined, and under Bute's direction an expert botanist, the Scot William Aiton, was appointed to lay out and maintain a 'physic garden' in the style of the one at Chelsea, where Aiton had trained. George became king in 1760; he would reign until 1820, longer than any other king of England but not as long as Queen Victoria, and Bute rose to become Prime Minister at the time of the Seven Years War, resigning once peace was achieved and retiring from public life.

George III is famous for having 'lost the American colonies' and for being mad. In fact, he was not responsible for the policies which alienated the Americans (although he was responsible for the failure of attempts at Catholic emancipation in the early 1800s, with disastrous repercussions in Ireland); and the 'madness', which did not kick in until late in his life, was probably linked to a hereditary illness called porphyria. For most of his reign George was popular, astute, and the first king (discounting the dilettante Charles II) to have any serious interest in science. There could scarcely have been a better mesh between his interests and those of Joseph Banks.

Just after Banks came on the scene, Princess Augusta died in 1772 and Bute's remaining connection with the gardens at Kew came to an end. George bought the property outright, and made Kew House his home for much of his reign; although Banks was never given any official post, he became the king's botanical adviser, with essentially a free hand in running the gardens. He was still only 29, and the King just 34; they would remain firm friends for the next thirty years. One of the first, and most important, suggestions Banks made was to send one of the younger gardeners, Francis Masson (born in 1741), on a botanical expedition to South Africa at the King's expense; we tell his story in the next chapter. But Banks had one last adventure of his own to experience before he settled down into the role he was ideally suited for, as a scientific administrator and adviser to the king and, before long, the government.

The voyage of the *Endeavour* was so successful that almost as soon as he had returned to England Cook, promoted to Commander, was asked to lead another expedition to the South Seas, this time with two ships. Banks was naturally offered the chance to go with him, and leaped at the opportunity; but his new-found fame seems to have slightly over-inflated his own opinion of his importance, and in the end this prevented his participation. The problems were partly caused by Banks's determination, based on experience, to have an even larger party with him; but they were exacerbated by his intransigence and refusal to compromise. He proposed a party of sixteen people (half of them servants), including Solander, the chemist Joseph Priestley, and James Lind, a Fellow of the Royal Society and physician to the royal household. Priestley accepted the invitation but was rejected by the authorities because of his nonconformist religious beliefs (he was a Unitarian minister), leading him famously to write to Banks:

What I am and what [my views] are, with respect to religion, might easily have been known before the thing was proposed to me at all. Besides, I thought that this had been a matter of *philosophy* and not of *divinity*... I am truly sorry that a person of your disposition should be subject to a choice restricted by such narrow considerations.

There were, though, other natural philosophers eager to voyage with the famous Joseph Banks in Priestley's place. A bigger problem was that in order to accommodate this retinue and their supplies and equipment, Banks demanded major modifications to the ship chosen to lead the expedition, another converted collier called the *Resolution*.[12] It is a sign of his influence that the changes, involving considerable additions to the upper deck, were actually carried out; but even though the *Resolution* was bigger than the *Endeavour*, after the modifications the ship proved top-heavy and unseaworthy. All the additions to the upperworks had to be removed, and Banks, in something of a huff, withdrew from the expedition. This caused some temporary ill-feeling between himself and his friend Lord Sandwich[13] at the Admiralty, and left Banks and his party, with all their expensive equipment (once again described as costing '£10,000', though as before this should not be taken literally) at something of a loose end. So he chartered a brig, the *Sir Lawrence*, and sailed from Gravesend, on the Thames, for Iceland, visiting the Western Isles of Scotland on the way, on 12 July 1772—the day before Cook's second expedition, carrying Francis Masson as a passenger to the Cape, set sail from Plymouth. The expedition to the Western Isles was not of any great botanical significance, but it perhaps gave Banks a chance to reflect on his rather arrogant behaviour in the spring, and restore his equanimity. After stopping off in Scotland on the way home, Banks left Edinburgh for London via Revesby on 19 November, his voyaging days behind him, although he did visit the Netherlands early in 1773.

It was during 1773 that Banks, still living in his house in New Burlington Street when in London, became established in his role, unofficial but no less real, as botanical adviser to the king and *de facto* head of the botanical work at Kew. At the end of the year he was elected to the Council of the Royal Society, where he was involved in the discussions that led, in February 1774, to the proposal that when Cook returned from the South Seas again he should be sent back to the Pacific to investigate the possibility of finding a passage around the north of North America back into the Atlantic—the fabled 'Northwest Passage'. But the highlight of 1774 was the return, a year earlier than anticipated, of the *Adventure*, which had got separated from the *Resolution* and came back to England carrying, among other things, a real live Polynesian, Omai. He was a sensation in England, and naturally became part of Banks's entourage, meeting the king, learning English, and enjoying the theatre and the opera.

Cook himself returned to England in the *Resolution* at the end of July 1775, having circled Antarctica at high latitudes, finally disproving the existence of *Terra Australis*. He made many discoveries, and kept his crew so healthy that he lost only one man on a voyage covering more than 20,000 miles (well over 30,000 kilometres) and lasting just over three years. Banks was away from London at the time the *Resolution* returned. The first shots in what was to become the American War of Independence had been fired on 19 April 1775, and as it was clear that the Royal Navy would soon be in action the First Sea Lord, Sandwich, had gone on a tour of inspection of naval shipyards, taking Banks with him as a guest. Following this journey, in the Admiralty yacht *Augusta*, Banks had travelled north to visit friends in Yorkshire. It was more than a month after the *Resolution* returned before Banks was back in London and met up with Cook, who had meanwhile been promoted to Captain ('made post'). They had plenty to talk about. As well as hearing firsthand news of the voyage, Banks was involved in planning Cook's third expedition, again in the *Resolution* (this time accompanied by the *Discovery*), although this time he does not seem to have seriously considered sailing with Cook. The *Resolution* set off again in July 1776, after less than a year at home, but not before Cook had been elected a Fellow of the Royal Society; this was Cook's last voyage—he was killed in Hawaii in 1779. Omai returned with the expedition, and Cook's sailing master on the *Resolution* was a certain William Bligh.

Bligh will soon feature in the story of Banks's continuing botanical work. But in the summer of 1776 Banks's personal circumstances were about to change dramatically, and it makes sense to skim over the rest of his life story before focusing on the role he played in sending botanical explorers out around the world.

In 1777 Banks moved from New Burlington Street to a house in Soho Square. This was not the most fashionable part of town, but convenient for the British Museum and the premises the Royal Society then occupied in Crane Court; the house, which has since been demolished, was large, with ample accommodation at the back for Banks's library, his collections (including an ever-growing herbarium), and the various people he employed to work on his behalf. These included Solander, when not busy with his duties at the British Museum, and another former pupil of Linnaeus, Jonas Dryander (1748–1810), who arrived in London in the summer of 1777 and was a fixture at 32 Soho Square almost from the beginning of Banks's residence. After Solander died of a stroke in May 1782 Dryander took over his duties, including looking after the herbarium and library, as Banks's right-hand man. He carried out that role for the next twenty-eight years, until his own death. Banks's mother, who lived into her mid-eighties and died only in 1804, also lived in Soho Square with him—and there was room for another addition to the household that he cannot have been expecting when he bought the house in March 1777.

In October 1778, Banks was introduced to Dorothea Hugessen, a 20-year-old heiress with a fortune of about £14,000. Dorothea and her sister Mary, aged 17, were orphans being looked after by relatives. Just six months later, Joseph Banks and Dorothea Hugessen were married at St Andrews's Church, in Holborn, and both sisters moved into the house in Soho Square, where Mary stayed until her own marriage, in July 1780. After Mary left, Banks's sister Sarah Sophia (Sophy) became part of the family at 32 Soho Square, and travelled almost inseparably with her brother and sister-in-law. A fascinating woman in her own right, in another age she might well have become a distinguished scientist. She never married, and was an avid collector who helped her brother in his work; her greatest service to posterity was to copy out enormous quantities of his journals and other writings, often almost illegible to other people, in her beautifully clear handwriting.

The lack of a garden at Soho Square was compensated for by the acquisition of the lease on a country house called Spring Grove, in the parish of Heston, near Hounslow. This was only a couple of miles farther west than Kew, on the other side of the Thames, in what was then, indeed, still the countryside. Joseph and Dorothea seem to have been happy together, although the marriage was childless. Their house in Soho Square became not only a home but a kind of private research institution and museum, open to anyone interested in the natural world, where visitors were particularly welcome at breakfast. This, taken in the library overlooking Dean Street with both ladies (initially Dorothea and Mary, later Dorothea and Sarah Sophia) in attendance, was the best time of day to catch Banks for a conversation.

Marriage also turned Banks's mind to his duties at Revesby, where the house, somewhat neglected since his father's death, was refurbished to suit Dorothea's taste and they began a routine of visiting the estate for a couple of months every autumn. But London remained the centre of Banks's life from now on, not least because he had been elected as President of the Royal Society in November 1778 (early in his courtship of Dorothea), and took his duties very seriously.

Banks was only 35 when he was chosen for this honour, but he was exactly the right man for the job both because of his skill as an administrator and, particularly important at that time, because he was on good terms with the king. The Society needed to restore friendly relations with George III because of a bizarre wrangle about lightning conductors, which became entangled in the politics of the American rebellion. In 1772 the government had asked the Royal Society to advise them on the best form of lightning protection, and a report was duly prepared by their (and the world's) leading expert on electricity, Benjamin Franklin, who was then living in London.

The report correctly recommended pointed lightning conductors as the best means of drawing the electricity generated inside storm clouds safely to Earth. But there was a minority view that lightning conductors with ball-shaped ends would be more effective. The chief proponent of this idea, one Benjamin Wilson, was provided with ammunition when powder magazines at Purfleet were struck by lightning (though happily not destroyed) even though they were protected by Franklin-style conductors. The king, who naturally had no sympathy for American revolutionaries, was persuaded that Franklin was just as bad a scientist as he was a subject, and supported the Wilson camp, eliciting the crisp response from Sir John Pringle, the President of the Royal Society, that 'I cannot reverse the laws and operations of nature'.

By 1778, with the American war at its height, the argument was blown up out of all proportion (echoing the argument in *Gulliver's Travels* over which end to break into a boiled egg), and in the eyes of many people it became unpatriotic to believe in the utility of pointed lightning conductors. As much in response to the bad feeling between himself and the king caused by this hassle as anything else, Pringle, who was 71, resigned the post he had held for only six years. A candidate who was a rich gentleman with a sound scientific record, essentially apolitical (Banks remained on good terms with Franklin without offending anybody, including George) and a close friend of the king, was just what was needed to soothe the situation, and Banks got the job. He was arguably the most effective President of the Royal Society since Isaac Newton, attending 417 Council meetings out of the 450 held during the forty-one years he was in the post; but such diligence left little scope for any adventurous voyaging.

Banks was so effective in this post that he became, in all but name, the first scientific adviser to the British Government, becoming a Privy Councillor in 1797, when the congratulations included one from his friends Sir William Hamilton and his wife Lady Emma. But he several times turned down the offer of a safe seat in Parliament. As he explained to a correspondent: 'My independence of action & opinion I value beyond any thing that can be given to me and as I am not or ever have been in Parliament I have not even a Vote which I can give to a Minister.'

As an independent, his influence covered the entire difficult period of the wars with revolutionary and Napoleonic France, and enabled him to maintain scientific contacts with France throughout this time. He was made a baronet in 1781, and a Knight of the Bath (a much more prestigious title) in 1795.

As a botanist Joseph Banks, through collecting and through his work at Kew, introduced more than 7,000 new species into Britain. A whole book could be written about Banks's non-botanical activities, including the way he engineered not only the introduction of Spanish merino sheep into England (at one time using the returning transports that had carried Wellington's troops out to the Iberian peninsula), but also the introduction of tea cultivation from China into India; his influence in persuading George III to provide financial support for, among others, the astronomer William Herschel and his sister; his own financial support for the pioneering geologist William Smith; and his decisive role in establishing the British colony of New South Wales. Banks was also a key figure (at the beginning of the 1800s) in founding the Royal Institution, where Humphrey Davy and Michael Faraday would become the great science popularizers of the early nineteenth century. In later life he became very fat and suffered severely from gout (an ailment which often provokes mirth in non-sufferers, but was in reality extremely painful and debilitating), so that he ended up being transported in a chair; but he remained mentally active and fully in command of his various projects almost up to the time of his death, in 1820 at the age of 77. We only have space here, though, to look at the legacy he bequeathed to botany by developing Kew into the leading botanical centre in the world, encouraging the activities of plant hunters, and promoting the use of plants from different parts of the globe in new locations where they could bring economic benefits. Like Linnaeus's disciples, these pioneers suffered a high attrition rate.

After Francis Masson, the next young man to be sent by Banks on a botanical voyage of exploration on behalf of Kew was David Nelson, who sailed in the *Discovery* on Cook's third expedition to the Pacific. He brought back many new species in 1780, and in 1787 sailed again on behalf of Banks on the ill-fated voyage of the *Bounty*. He was one of the loyal followers set adrift in a 23-foot-long boat with William Bligh by the mutineers, and died of a fever after they reached the East Indies.

The purpose of the *Bounty* expedition, of course, had been to obtain living breadfruit trees from Tahiti and take them to the West Indies, where it was hoped they would provide a cheap and plentiful supply of food. The whole project, including the choice of Lieutenant Bligh to lead it, was very much Banks's idea; the story of how the mutineers under Fletcher Christian, seduced by the soft life in Tahiti, took over the ship and abandoned Bligh and fifteen other men to their fate in the overloaded open boat is too familiar to need elaboration here. But it is worth mentioning that Bligh, although perhaps an unfortunate choice of leader, was handicapped by the astonishing failure (doubly so in the light of Banks's experience of Tahiti) of the Admiralty to provide him with any junior officers or marines. Whatever his faults, Bligh's skill as a seaman and navigator were shown by the epic voyage of his open boat across the Pacific to the East Indies, across nearly 6,000 kilometres of sea, without any loss of life. When he led a second attempt to transplant breadfruit to the West Indies in 1791, with two ships (*Porpoise* and *Assistant*), competent junior officers, and a complement of marines, the project was completely successful.

Between Bligh's two voyages to Tahiti, in 1789 two gardeners from Kew, George Austin and James Smith (the brother of John Smith, who was Banks's gardener at Spring Grove), sailed for Australia in a convict ship, the *Guardian*, carrying plants that Banks thought might be useful in the infant colony. But the ship was wrecked, and both the

gardeners and their plants were lost. Even one of Banks's most successful collectors, the Scot Archibald Menzies (1754–1842), had his
share of difficulties, which highlight another of the hazards, apart
from shipwreck, disease, and natural disaster, confronting the traveller
in the eighteenth century—the absolute authority, especially in Royal
Navy ships, of the captain.

Menzies was an example of what became a common breed of Royal
Navy surgeons with a passion for botany and zoology, the real-life
counterparts of Patrick O'Brian's fictional Stephen Maturin (O'Brian's
character Joseph Blaine is said to be based on Banks). He trained as a
doctor in Edinburgh, then worked as a naval surgeon, botanizing
whenever he got the chance and sending seeds back to Banks from
the United States and the West Indies in the mid-1780s, after the
American war had ended. They eventually met in 1786, when Menzies
was in London, after his ship had paid off. Banks found him a post as
surgeon for a commercial trading expedition to the Far East involving
two ships, the *Prince of Wales* and the *Princess Royal*. The ships
travelled round Cape Horn and up the west coast of America before
crossing the Pacific to Japan and China; the expedition was a success
on all fronts—commercially, botanically, and even medically, with
only one man dying of sickness out of both crews in the three years
it lasted. It is said that when Menzies attended an official dinner with
the Viceroy of Chile, he noticed that the dessert included a kind of nut
that he had never seen, and managed to secrete some of them in his
clothing. When they were planted, they sprouted into seedlings that
he brought back for Banks. The plant introduced into England in this
way was *Araucaria imbricata*, the monkey puzzle tree; one of the
saplings was planted at Spring Grove, where it thrived.

Thanks to Banks's influence, in 1791 Menzies travelled as naturalist
on board the Royal Navy ship *Discovery* (not the same ship as the
Discovery that accompanied Cook on his third voyage), sent to survey
the north-west coast of America. The snag was that the captain of this
small ship (similar in size to the *Endeavour*) was George Vancouver.

Vancouver, who had been a junior officer on both Cook's second and third voyages, was a fine seaman and navigator (witnessed by the number of geographical features that bear his name), but lacked what would now be described as interpersonal skills. After a disagreement about the priority which should be given to looking after Menzies's collection of seedlings, Vancouver confined the botanist to his cabin (which must have been about the same size as the tiny cabins in the *Endeavour*) and the neglected plants died.

You might think this was just one of those things; but Vancouver was known as a disciplinarian with violent rages, and on this voyage he picked out one midshipman for special attention, having him beaten repeatedly[14] and eventually throwing him off the ship at Hawaii to make his own way home. This was clearly a rather extreme punishment, although within the captain's rights; what has led people to question Vancouver's sanity is that the midshipman in question was the teenage Thomas Pitt, who became Lord Camelford when his father died before Thomas got back to England. He was a cousin of the Prime Minister; another cousin was First Lord of the Admiralty, and his brother-in-law was Foreign Secretary. Vancouver had clearly not made a wise career move—but soon after returning to England in failing health he died, on 12 May 1798 at the age of 40, before any action could be taken against him.

Stories like this put the happy relationship between Banks and Cook in perspective, and show the wisdom of Cook's appointment. But Vancouver's irrational behaviour failed to deter Menzies, who served once again as a surgeon in the Royal Navy on the West Indies station before settling in London as a medical practitioner.

Many of the botanists influenced by Banks, or directly under his orders, didn't just travel, but also settled overseas. Bligh's second, successful, breadfruit expedition, which was generally better equipped than his first, carried two botanists, Christopher Smith and James Wiles. Smith later went to Calcutta, where he had a long career, while Wiles stayed in the West Indies. Both spent the rest of their lives where they had settled, developing botanical gardens and sending back samples to Kew at regular intervals. Banks was also involved in organizing early expeditions into Africa, including those of Mungo Park (1771–1806), another Edinburgh-trained surgeon, who carried out a highly successful journey inland from the mouth of the Gambia river between 1794 and 1797, but died, probably in 1806, on a second expedition into the African interior.

Australia always featured in Banks's thoughts, and he was able to send George Caley (1770–1829) out to New South Wales on behalf of Kew in 1800; he stayed there for ten years, sending back a wealth of material and becoming a prominent member of the settler community, but returned to England in 1810, then spent several years in the West Indies before finally returning home to retire. But while New South Wales was a corner of Australia that was beginning to become a more or less civilized part of the British Empire, most of the coast, let alone the interior, remained unexplored. The first full circumnavigation of Australia, a project dear to Banks's heart, was carried out by Matthew Flinders, in command of the 334-ton sloop *Investigator*. When he set off on his epic voyage in 1801, during the uneasy peace between Britain and France that preceded the Napoleonic Wars, he carried with him the naturalist Robert Brown (1773–1858), who would feature large in Banks's declining years.[15] Brown was yet another Scottish surgeon-naturalist, but this time one who had served in the Army, not the Navy. He met Banks in 1798.

Flinders, just a year younger than Brown, formed a relationship with his botanist almost as successful as that between Cook and Banks; he completed his task of surveying the entire coastline of Australia,[16] but wore his ship out in the process. On the way home in another vessel he suffered shipwreck and was then, war having broken out again in the meantime, imprisoned on the French island of Mauritius, in the Indian Ocean. His captivity lasted until 1810, when the island was captured by the British. Brown, however, had stayed behind in Australia to complete his botanical work, and arrived safely back in

England in 1805—he arrived in London the day after the news of Nelson's victory at Trafalgar.

It took Brown five years, working in rooms at 32 Soho Square provided by Banks, to prepare all the material he had gathered for publication. The first volume of what had been planned as a larger work sold so poorly when it was published in 1810 that he abandoned the project; but the same year he became Banks's librarian, following the death of Dryander. His name is immortalized in science by the term 'Brownian motion', used for the curious jiggling dance of pollen grains and other tiny particles suspended in air, which Brown described in the 1820s; in 1905 Albert Einstein proved that this motion is caused by the battering the particles receive from the molecules the air is made of.

The last of Banks's botanical protégés that we want to mention didn't achieve as much in the way of exploring as the likes of Brown, Park, or Masson; but he lived to a ripe old age, and saw Kew passed on as a thriving concern to later generations. He was William Hooker (1785–1865), who was (eventually) the first official Director of the Royal Botanic Garden at Kew.

William Jackson Hooker was born in Norwich in 1785, and trained as an estate manager, although he had no need of a profession, having inherited enough to live on (in the language of the day a 'competency') from his cousin and godfather, William Jackson, at the age of 4. He was a botanical enthusiast, and in 1804, when he was only 19, discovered a kind of moss which he could not identify. His search for a botanist who could identify the moss—it turned out to be a species never before recorded in Britain, *Buxbaumia aphylla*—led him to get in touch with the banker and botanist Dawson Turner, ten years his senior, and through him to make contact with Banks. Hooker eventually (in 1815) married Turner's daughter, Maria, and bought into the family brewing business, but spent most of his time working in botany. Hooker became a Fellow of the Linnean Society in 1806, and in 1809 Banks arranged for him to travel to Iceland as botanist on what

turned out to be a rather bizarre adventure. The leader of this expedition was a Danish adventurer called Jorgen Jorgensen, who professed
to be aiming to restore trade with the Icelanders, who had been badly
affected by the Napoleonic Wars,[17] but who was really, unknown to the
botanists, intending a coup which would see him installed as dictator
over the Icelanders. Suffice it to say that the coup failed, and Hooker
remained a rather bemused spectator to the political shenanigans
while botanizing as best he could. As if that weren't enough, on the
way home all Hooker's specimens were destroyed by fire, and he was
lucky to escape with his life.

In the wake of this disaster, there was some talk of Hooker making
up for his disappointment by travelling to Ceylon (as Sri Lanka was
then known) and the Far East. Banks offered to use his influence to
obtain funding for such an expedition, but before anything could be
set in motion Hooker had a change of heart. After pressure from his
family, who had heard all the stories about the terrible losses from
sickness on the *Endeavour* voyage, he pulled out. Banks tried for
some time to persuade the young man to proceed with what would
have been the old man's last adventure by proxy, but in June 1813
(when Banks was 70) he wrote a last letter to Hooker on the subject,
rather grumpily conceding defeat. Referring to a planned visit to Java,
he wrote:

Tho I cannot think it Possible that your Relations and friends in Norfolk can
consider an Island half as large as England to be of a deadly & unwholesome
nature because one Town upon it [Batavia] is notoriously so, I see their
objections are urged with so much determination & eagerness that I am far
indeed from advising you to despise them. . . .

Let me hear from you how you feel inclined to prefer Ease & indulgence to
Hardship and activity I was about 23 when I began my Peregrinations you are
somewhat older but you may be assured that if I had Listend to a multitude
of voices that were Raised up to dissuade me from my Enterprise I should
have been now a Quiet countery Gentleman ignorant of a multitude of

matters I am now acquainted with & probably have attained to no higher Rank in Life than that of a countrey Justice of the Peace.

In fact, Banks's parting shot missed its mark. Although Banks would never know it, Hooker, who remained on friendly terms with Banks and often visited him after 1813, ended up as much more than a quiet country gentleman. He became Regis Professor of Botany at Glasgow University, partly thanks to Banks's influence, in 1820 (the year both Banks and George III died); was knighted in 1836; and in 1841, the year he was 56, became the Director of Kew Gardens. In Banks's time as unofficial Director of Kew, the day-to-day running of the gardens had been in the hands of two 'supervisors', first William Aiton senior (1731–93) and then his son, also called William Aiton (1766–1849). Both were good men who did their work well, but there had been no powerful figure to look after the interests of the Royal Botanic Garden since Banks—nor, indeed, during Banks's final years, when he was often ill. Hooker's appointment, as a result of the Government taking over the gardens from the Crown, came just in time. The gardens were in a run-down state when he was appointed, with just eleven acres of botanical garden and a few decrepit buildings. By the time he died, in 1865, the area covered by the botanical garden had been extended to 250 acres and the famous Palm House and Temperate House, along with other buildings, had been erected.

On 16 March 1820, not long after his 77th birthday, Banks presided over a meeting of the Royal Society for the last time. A few weeks later, he offered his resignation on the grounds of ill-health, but the Society, to his gratification, rejected it at the end of May. Everyone knew that it was only a matter of a short time before a new President would be needed anyway, and Banks died on 19 June, a Monday, at about 3 a.m.

Banks left his library and his herbarium to Robert Brown, with the stipulation that as and when Brown wished they could be passed on to the British Museum. The transfer duly took place in 1827, forming the core of the botany department at the Museum (now at the Natural

History Museum in South Kensington). Brown himself stayed on at Soho Square, where he inherited the lease after Lady Banks died in 1828 (Sophy had died in 1818). The Banks connection finally came to an end with Brown's death, in 1858. By then, the torch of botanical exploration had been passed on to William Hooker's son, Joseph, who was arguably the greatest botanical explorer of the nineteenth century, and whose story forms the climax of our book. But first we want to tell you about the adventures of Banks's other spiritual heirs, including his greatest protégé, Francis Masson.

IN THE GARDEN

B anks's plant and flower introductions enrich gardens in many parts of the world. Perhaps the most readily associated with Banks are the many varieties of *Banksii* (Australian Honeysuckle). *Banksia integrifolia* has spectacular cone-shaped spikes with yellow flowers, *Banksia speciosa* has flowers which are greenish yellow, and the swamp *Banksia* (*Banksia occidentalis*) is a riot of flaming orange flowers. *Eucalyptus banksii* (the Blue Gum Tree), *Grevillia banksii* (Red Spider Flower), and the Bottle Brush Tree (*Callistemon citrinus*), whose strange red bottle-brush-shaped flowers have become something of a symbol for Australian botany, are all associated with Banks. Joseph Banks was the key figure in the botanical investigation of Australia, particularly during the first thirty years of settlement.

New Zealand gave Banks the architecturally magnificent *Phormium tenax* (the New Zealand Flax, so called because the indigenous Maoris used its fibres to make a type of cloth). *Phormiums* are now popular garden plants and the sword-shaped spikes of *Phormium tenax* can grow almost four metres high. Another New Zealand favourite is the yellow-flowered *Sophora tetraptera*. Banks found many varieties of flowering evergreen *Leptospermum*, with their broom-like flowers ranging from pale pink to dark purplish brown, throughout Australasia.

Tahiti produced beautiful Jasmines, Lobelias, and Gardenias and Tierra del Fuego the autumn red-berried *Gaultheria mucronata* (Checker Berry). Australia's coastline was home to Eucalyptus, Mimosas, Grevillias, Baureas, Acacias, *Banksia arctinotus* (the Flannel Flower), Angophora (the Gum Myrtle), and Telopeas (Waratahs). Telopeas are so called from the Greek *telepos*, which means 'seen from afar', because their vivid crimson flowers make them visible from a great distance away. Joseph Banks also introduced the more everyday garden favourites Helychrysum (Everlasting Flowers), Geraniums (Cranesbill), Senecios (Lambs Ears), and Pelargoniums and Hebes. Plants named in honour of Banks include the Hydrangea Joseph Banks and *Rosa banksiae* (Lady Banks's Rose), which was named in honour of his wife Lady Dorothea Banks.

Joseph Banks has an interesting link with Pierre Joseph Redoute (1759–1840), a flower painter of extraordinary ability and arguably the finest of all botanical illustrators. At one time Redoute was library assistant to Banks and during his time in London he learned the techniques of stipple engraving for colour printing, which was to do so much to make his botanical prints famous.

3

FRANCIS MASSON

(1741–1805)

and

CARL PETER THUNBERG

(1742–1828)

F RANCIS MASSON WAS the first plant collector officially sent out
from the Royal Botanic Gardens at Kew to obtain foreign plants to
enrich Kew Gardens themselves and then the gardens of England. His
finds included *Amaryllis*, *Streptocarpus*, *Lobelia*, *Gladioli*, *Cinerarias*,
Agapanthus, the beautiful white Arum Lily (*Zantedeschia aethiopica*),
the dramatic Bird of Paradise flower (*Strelitzia reginae*), spectacular
Proteas, Red Hot Pokers (*Kniphofia*) and almost fifty different varieties
of *Pelargonium*, which became valued plants in Victorian hothouses
and gardens. He was responsible for bringing one potted Cycad
(*Encephalartos altensteinii*) back to Kew in 1775, where it still lives
today—the oldest pot plant in the world.

Strictly speaking, Masson was not a botanist—at least, he did not
have a formal botanical education. He rose through the ranks, starting
out as a garden boy in Aberdeen, where he had been born (in 1741) and

brought up, with only the most basic education. When he was in his early twenties, Masson moved south to London, where he obtained a job as under-gardener to his fellow Scot William Aiton in what was then still Princess Augusta's Royal Garden. A forerunner of the hard-working 'self-improvers' that are often thought of as typical of the Victorian era, alongside his gardening duties Masson taught himself botany and became a skilled botanical artist while working at Kew, where he was well established, and highly regarded by Aiton, before Joseph Banks, two years younger than Masson but the hero of Cook's circumnavigation of the globe, came on the scene.

When Banks's plans to sail with Cook on his second great voyage of exploration fell through, as a consolation he was able to obtain permission from the Admiralty and sponsorship from the Royal Society for a plant collector to travel as far as South Africa with the *Resolution*, briefed to collect living specimens of native South African plants and ship them back to England. Masson was the ideal man for the job. Banks always approved of the hardy nature and appetite for work of the Scots he employed, and Masson was also recommended by Aiton. But it is fortunate that he was such a good candidate, since Banks and Aiton seem to have had little choice in who they picked. Writing in 1796, Masson commented of his first South African exped-ition that 'his Majesty was graciously pleased to adopt the plan, though at that time so little approved by the public, that no one but myself chose to undertake the execution of it'.

On his second circumnavigation, Cook sailed the other way around the world from the *Endeavour* voyage, so that after stops at Madeira and the Cape Verde Islands he reached the Cape of Good Hope on 30 October 1772, stopping only to take on provisions, and to drop off the 31-year-old Masson, before heading east. The official naturalists on Cook's expedition were the Germans Johann Reinhold Forster and his son Johann Georg Adam Forster, two rather arrogant individuals who looked down on Masson as their social inferior and regarded him as a mere gardener. When Masson's account of his travels was later published, the elder Forster noted that since it had not been translated into German it must be a 'poor product' and 'we need not waste words over it'. The truth is he was a jealous individual who could never bear to acknowledge the success of his colleagues, and was mortified to have been outdone by a 'mere gardener'.

Most of what Masson achieved was a result of his own hard work and ability. But he had the great good fortune to meet up with two men in South Africa who would prove to be ideal companions on his expeditions. The first, Franz Pehr Oldenburg, was a tough Scandinavian who had been employed as a mercenary by the Dutch East India Company, and knew his way around the harsh, uncompromising, and sparsely settled land. Oldenburg had an interest in botany, having met Banks during his visit to the Cape and been on collecting expeditions with the Swede Carl Peter Thunberg, of whom more shortly. He also spoke not only Dutch, but several of the native dialects; he introduced Masson to the techniques needed to survive and travel outside the main colonies on a couple of short expeditions, trial runs for the work to come.

Settlements in South Africa had been established by the Dutch as early as the 1650s, although the first European sailors to reach the Cape of Good Hope were the Portuguese, at the end of the fifteenth century. Britain did not begin to take a formal interest in the region until the 1790s, with, as we shall see, repercussions for Masson at a later stage of his career. The best analogy for the situation there in the 1770s would be the familiar image of the North American wild West, with scattered settlements, homesteaders, and sometimes hostile natives. The main difference from this picture is that in South Africa at that time many of the native people worked for the Dutch homesteaders, under conditions which shocked Masson; he noted that they were paid for their long hours of labour, but only with beads or tobacco mixed with marijuana—a convenient way to keep them stupefied and unlikely to cause trouble.

The value of a guide like Oldenburg was brought home to Masson during his first weeks at the Cape, when he was getting acclimatized and learning to know his way around. Although he only made short journeys out to the country to collect plants, on one of his earliest trips he lost track of time and was far from the settlement when dusk fell. He had been warned that a gang of escaped convicts was in the area, and was alarmed when the sounds of voices and clanking chains reached his ears. Afraid that the men might take him hostage as a bargaining counter, and certain that the tough Dutch settlers would let him die rather than meet any of the escapees' demands, he spent the night cowering in an abandoned shepherds' hut, clutching his only means of defence, a clasp knife. Fortunately, when dawn broke there was no sign of the convicts and he was able to make his way back to what passed for civilization.

Masson's first real trip into the interior began on 10 December 1772, under the guidance of Oldenburg. He travelled in a covered wagon pulled by eight oxen, accompanied by the native driver of the wagon and the Scandinavian mercenary. It's a sign of just how vast the region open to exploration was that this round trip of 400 miles was regarded by all concerned as minor excursion, mainly a chance for Masson to experience the difficulties of travelling by ox-cart, crossing rivers and negotiating rough tacks. But even this short expedition opened up a wonderland of plants unknown in England; it was on this trip, Masson wrote, that 'I collected seed of so many beautiful species of Erica which have succeeded so well in the Royal Garden at Kew', and which we now regard as domestic British garden plants.

Having cut his teeth on this minor expedition, after returning to Cape Town on 20 January 1773 Masson spent the late summer organizing his collections, making further short trips out of the city, and drawing some of the plants. In May, as winter was approaching, he made a brief excursion into the nearby mountains with a Colonel Robert Gordon and the Swedish naturalist Carl Peter Thunberg, who would soon become his companion on much longer trips into the interior, and whose story merits recounting at length in its own right.[1]

Thunberg was just a year younger than Masson, having been born on 11 November 1743 at Jönköping, in Sweden. But unlike Masson he had followed the traditional route of a formal education in botany— indeed, the best possible education of its kind, since he studied under Linnaeus at Uppsala and obtained his MD in 1770. Thunberg's father, Johan, had been a successful trader, but died relatively young; his mother, Margaretha, was the daughter of the Alderman of the Guild of Pistol Makers in Jönköping, and married a second time, to a merchant, Gabriel Forsberg. Carl Peter and his only brother were comfortably provided for, and expected to go into trade; but he was such a promising student that he was allowed to continue his education into his teens and beyond. One of his tutors later became the Dean of Växjö Cathedral. Thunberg entered Uppsala University in 1761, and after taking his degree in 1767 obtained his doctorate in 1770 with a thesis on sciatica. Following the traditional route of Linnaeus and others, he then spent eight months travelling and studying—in his case, from Sweden via Denmark and Holland to Paris, where he attended lectures by, among others, Bernard de Jussieu. In Holland, he visited the botanical gardens at both Amsterdam and Leiden. While in Paris, he purchased a set of the most modern medical instruments, which caused great interest when he later visited Japan.

The idea of a trip to Japan seems to have been planted by the botanist Nicolaus Burmann, who Thunberg met in Amsterdam when he was en route to Paris. The mysterious eastern country was of great interest both in medical and botanical terms, but in the second half of the eighteenth century it was barely open to Westerners. Specifically, it was only open at all to a limited number of Dutch traders, and in order to visit Japan Thunberg would have to be able to pass himself off as a Dutch doctor.

Although early European explorers had been able to enter Japan, and attempts had been made to introduce Christianity, since 1603

power had been in the hands of a succession of military rulers, the
Shogun, with a policy of maintaining only the minimum contact with
the outside world. A Chinese trading settlement was permitted in
Nagasaki, and the Dutch East India Company was allowed to maintain a trading station (known as a 'factory'[2]) on an artificial island
called Deshima (sometimes spelled Dejima), in the bay of Nagasaki.
By the 1770s, some of the original restrictions on contact with Westerners had been relaxed, since there seemed no prospect of Christianity gaining a foothold in Japan, and apart from using the Dutch as a
conduit for the export of valuable trade goods such as copper and
camphor, there was particular interest in Western medicine and in the
use of medicinal plants. Which is why a Dutch doctor with a knowledge of botany would be ideally placed to obtain permission to travel
in Japan and learn about Japanese medicine and plants in exchange
for information about Western medicine and plants.

Thunberg met all the requirements except one—he wasn't Dutch.
But this seemed a mere detail to be overcome. After leaving Paris,
Thunberg returned to Holland in the autumn of 1771, and arranged
with the Dutch East India Company to travel to the Cape of Good
Hope, where he could live for several years among the Dutch settlers,
learning their language and their ways well enough to be able to
appear Dutch to the Japanese.

He sailed as ship's surgeon on the *Schoonzigt*, at the end of December 1771. Almost immediately, an incident occurred which showed
Thunberg's resilience and his keen analytical mind. By some mis-
chance, lead white had got mixed in with some flour that was used
to cook pancakes, and the officers who ate the poisonous pancakes,
including Thunberg, suffered a violent, life-threatening illness. For
three weeks, in spite of his physical condition, Thunberg managed to
keep a detailed scientific record of his symptoms. Happily, he survived
the ordeal, and arrived in Cape Town on 16 April 1772, just six months
before Francis Masson. He would remain at the Cape for a month
under three years, not only learning to become a surrogate Dutchman

but going on several long botanical expeditions into the interior, which we shall describe when we pick up the threads of Masson's story.

Having satisfied himself and his Dutch colleagues that he could pass for a Hollander, Thunberg sailed for Batavia in the *Loo* on 2 March 1775. He arrived there on 18 May, and was officially appointed as ship's surgeon on the *Stavenisse*, which was sailing for Japan, and contracted to stay on for a year as doctor to the traders at the Dutch Factory on Deshima. Part of his duties would be to accompany the head of the factory on his annual journey to Edo (the city which was renamed Tokyo in 1868) to pay his respects to the Shogun. Thunberg's preparations for the trip included the purchase of some fine new suits, 'some silk, some cloth with froggings and other finery, in order to be able with dignity to show myself among the curious Japanese'. He also found time while in Batavia to put together a little Malay phrasebook, based on the master–servant relationship of Europeans with the natives and including such gems as 'whose fault is it that I have not yet had any coffee?'

The *Stavenisse* arrived in Nagasaki Bay on 13 August 1775. As far as the Japanese were concerned everybody on board the ship was officially Dutch, although in fact the crew included Danes, Germans, Portuguese, Spaniards, and Swedes. A diplomatic blind eye was turned to this, since there was no chance of ordinary sailors being allowed off the tiny island of Deshima, just 120 metres by 75 metres, where the 'village' consisted of just two streets. Indeed, the conditions were so strict that all the Europeans had to carry passes which listed not only their personal details but every item they carried on them. Nobody, not even the Captain himself or the head of the factory, was exempt from a careful search and a check against these passes every time they moved from ship to shore or vice versa. Thunberg even had to get explicit permission every time he was called ashore in his capacity as ship's doctor to attend to a sick sailor or one who had been injured while handling the cargo. Thunberg described the conditions on the island in heartfelt terms: 'A European, who has to remain here, is as though dead and buried in a corner of the globe... One's will is completely infirm and inert, since for the European there is no other will here but that of the Japanese, which must be strictly observed in every detail.'

But even under these restrictions Thunberg found ways to botanize. The Dutch kept livestock on the little island, and the animals had to be fed with fodder brought over from the mainland. Before the animals got a look in, Thunberg went through the fodder carefully, looking for rare plants and seeds which he could send back to Europe. He also wrote down a detailed description of the buildings on the island, and the way the trade was organized—including his own successful trade of 'unicorn horn' (actually rhinoceros horn), which was in great demand in Japan for its supposed medicinal value, and which he had judiciously obtained before setting sail. The profit he made was enough to cover the expenses of all his scientific work in Japan. But there would be further delays before he could get on with some serious botanizing.

While the *Stavenisse* stayed in the bay, preparing for the return voyage, Thunberg was chiefly occupied with his medical duties, because of an outbreak of diarrhoea and other minor ailments which afflicted the crew. Although he was able to visit some of the other small islands in the bay, where he was the object of great curiosity to the Japanese villagers, and managed to take temperature and other meteorological readings every day, it wasn't until November, when the ship sailed, that he really had much time to himself. Like the other thirteen Europeans who remained on Deshima, Thunberg had too much time on his hands. With their day-to-day living requirements supplied, and money in their pockets from their salaries, the officers alleviated the boredom by entertaining each other at dinner parties or spending their cash on what Thunberg disapprovingly referred to as 'the Sex'. Prostitutes could be hired by the day or for any time up to a year, and for more casual liaisons both the Chinese traders and the Dutch were allowed to visit brothels in Nagasaki. Thunberg seems not to have indulged, writing that 'Christians...should never degrade themselves to licentious commerce with the more pitiable than unfortunate daughters of the Country', even though 'the Japanese themselves, as Heathens, do not consider Lewdness a Vice'. He was almost equally censorious about the habit of smoking tobacco, and must have been something of an outsider (quite apart from the fact that he wasn't even Dutch) in the small community.

But Thunberg was remembered by his contemporaries as a cheerful character, who made friends easily in spite of his abstemious way of life. His open, friendly nature helped him to establish good relations with the Japanese interpreters, many of whom were doctors and eager to exchange information about the different medical approaches, science, and cultures of East and West. Some of the friendships Thunberg established became so firm that his Japanese counterparts smuggled maps and coins onto the island for him, at considerable risk to themselves, as such a breach of the regulations risked severe punishment.

Eventually, Thunberg's cultivation of these contacts bore fruit when he was granted permission by the Governor of Nagasaki to collect plants in the nearby countryside. Part of the reason for this permission was that a precedent had been established several years earlier when another Dutch doctor had been allowed to seek out medicinal plants in the vicinity—but there was a further delay when it was realized that technically Thunberg outranked the previous physician, so that in the eyes of the legalistic Japanese letting *him* go ashore would create a new precedent. Once the legal niceties were sorted out, Thunberg was able to begin real botanizing on Japanese soil on 7 February 1776—even though he was forced to take with him a retinue of guards, interpreters, and servants, who not only got in the way but had to be entertained to tea, at Thunberg's expense, at roadside teashops.

On 19 February 1776 Thunberg was able to attend and describe the festivities of the Japanese New Year; by then the preparations for the journey to Edo were already well in hand. The three Dutch representatives (the head of the Factory, his secretary, and Thunberg) were just a tiny part of a procession of some two hundred Japanese travelling on this formal visit. As honoured guests, they each rode in a palanquin of the kind used by senior samurai, reclining on velvet cushions with space for books, writing material, beer, wine, and food for the journey. It was an ideal conveyance from which Thunberg could observe the countryside as he passed at walking pace, and he took every advantage of the opportunity to take notes not just about the plant life but the people and places they passed through and their nightly stops.

The city of Osaka made a particular impression on the Europeans, and Thunberg called it 'the Paris of Japan' (hard to believe for anyone who knows modern Osaka!). The party spent four days in Miyako (now Kyoto), then still the imperial capital of Japan even though the emperor was a figurehead, with real power residing in the person of the Shogun. Thunberg described the emperor rather neatly as 'now-adays a Pope who only possesses power in Matters of the Church'. If Osaka and Miyako were high spots, the big disappointment of the journey was that Japanese farmers were so efficient at tilling their fields and getting rid of weeds that there were hardly any interesting plants to be discovered by the roadside, except when the travellers crossed the Hakone mountains, where on the difficult paths Thunberg had to get out of his palanquin and walk, taking the opportunity to sprint ahead of his companions and gather up what plants he could in his handkerchief.

It took the procession until 27 April to reach Edo, where Thunberg, a rare example of a Western scientist in the midst of Japan, received visits from many physicians and astronomers. The Japanese had an impressive collection of Western texts, and were eager to learn more; their discussions on physics, botany, medicine, and other matters continued well into the night, for day after day. Although Thunberg was exhausted at the end of three weeks in Edo, he wrote 'I cannot deny that I have spent many enjoyable and edifying hours in their company'. One of the more practical contributions he made was to introduce to Japan the use of mercury in the treatment of venereal disease, and he kept up a correspondence with many of his new friends long after he returned to Europe.

The audience with the Shogun took place on 18 May, and with the formalities completed the party returned to Nagasaki, with Thunberg enjoying the more relaxed atmosphere that set in once the business of the expedition had been accomplished. In Osaka, in particular, the party rested for two days, and the Europeans were allowed considerable freedom. Thunberg was delighted to find a small botanical garden where he bought several plants that were eventually shipped back to Amsterdam alive in tubs of earth. It wasn't until 29 June that Thunberg got back to Deshima, where he spent the summer enjoying further visits into the countryside around Nagasaki and putting his notes and collections in order. Although the Dutch were eager for him to stay for a further year, Thunberg 'was lucky enough to be able to tear myself loose and return to the places where I could have more freedom and space to collect and scrutinise the admirable treasures of Nature without constraint', leaving Deshima to rejoin the *Stavenisse* on 23 November and travelling via Batavia to Ceylon. There, he spent several more months botanizing, finally leaving on 6 February 1778 and arriving back in Holland on 1 October, almost seven years after he had set out for the Cape to learn how to be Dutch. On the way home, the ship he was travelling in, the *Loo*, called in at Cape Town, where Thunberg learned of the death of Linnaeus.

Thunberg stayed in Holland for ten weeks before starting his journey home to Sweden. On the way, he visited London, where he arrived in mid-December, and met Daniel Solander and Joseph Banks. After sharing botanical knowledge with them, at the end of January 1779 he set off for Sweden, where he arrived on 14 March. Although he was offered prestigious posts in other countries during the remainder of his career, he never left Sweden again.

At the time Thunberg returned to Uppsala, Linnaeus the younger occupied the chair once held by his father, and the great Linnaean herbarium and other material had been sold to John Smith in London. Botany in Uppsala wasn't exactly in the doldrums, but it had certainly declined since the heyday of the first Linnaeus. Thunberg was appointed as a Demonstrator in botany, and in 1781 he became Professor of Medicine, although clearly he was more suited to the chair once held by his mentor. It must have chafed at least a little to see that post occupied by the younger Linnaeus, but his willingness to accept the reality of the situation paid off when Linnaeus junior died in 1784, and Thunberg was appointed as his successor. The same year, he married Brita Charlotta Ruda, who at 32 was eleven years his junior. Thunberg did as much as was possible to rebuild the damage that had been suffered to the collections at Uppsala and the botanical gardens; he spent more than forty years, as the historian Catharina Blomberg has put it, devoted 'to the consolidation, improvement, and augmentation of the scientific heritage left by Linnaeus'. This included publishing a string of books and scholarly papers and supervising the dissertations of no fewer than 293 students.

Like Linnaeus, Thunberg mixed with royalty and received high honours for his work. In 1785 he became a Knight of the Order of the Vasa, and in 1815 he was promoted to Commander in the same order—the first academic, let alone the first scientist, to achieve this status. At a ceremony to mark the centenary of the birth of Linnaeus, in 1807, Thunberg gave an address in which he summed up his own outlook on life:

Although it is so seldom felt, and seldom fulfilled, it is nevertheless one of our foremost duties—to know Nature, to realize the value of Nature's great and wonderful Chain,—to regard its splendour devoutly and with admiration,—to use its products wisely and with consideration.

Those words are as apposite now, two centuries later, as they were in 1807. They stand as a fitting epitaph for Thunberg, who died on 8

August 1828, at the age of 84—the last, and arguably the greatest, of the Linnaeans.

Thunberg had outlived Francis Masson, his one-time companion on botanical expeditions, by twenty-three years. But unlike Thunberg, Masson kept on botanizing around the world right up until his death. Indeed, this urge to explore may well have contributed to his demise.

Masson and Thunberg had clearly hit it off on their short journey into the nearby mountains with Colonel Gordon in the late autumn of 1773, in spite of (or perhaps because of) the fact that they had very different personalities and came from very different backgrounds. They decided to pool their resources for further botanizing exped-itions, the first of which began on 11 September 1773, at the start of the southern spring. They were accompanied by a third European, a servant whose name has not come down to us, and three or four natives known to Masson as Hottentots, members of the Khoi people whose descendants now live mainly in Namibia and the Kalahari Desert of Botswana. They were hired both to act as servants and to drive the wagons (Masson and Thunberg were on horseback). In Thunberg's words, the little group 'were to penetrate into the country together, put up with whatever [they] should find, whether good or bad, and frequently seclude [themselves] from almost all the rest of the world, and of the human race'. Heading north from Cape Town, initially following the line of the coast, they passed through country which, Masson reported, afforded 'a fine field for botany, being enamelled with the greatest number of flowers I ever saw, of exquisite beauty and fragrance'. They also encountered large packs of wild dogs, which 'destroy the antelopes wherever they go, by hunting them down in the same manner as our hounds do a stag'.

At St Helena Bay, the botanists were forced to turn south-east for a while to follow the course of the Berg River, which they crossed on 7 October, heading into country where there were 'oranges and lemons in great plenty'. This gave way to mountainous terrain, where the passage was 'one of the most difficult in this part of Africa', and the horses of Masson and Thunberg had to be led for three hours in incessant rain along a slippery, rock-strewn track. On the other side of the pass they found a 'miserable cottage' belonging to a Dutchman, and were glad to take refuge in a corner of the single room.

After crossing the Oliphants River, some 130 miles north of Cape Town, they visited a hot spring, where Masson, the first European to describe these springs, saw an orange tree growing 'in a seam of the rock where the water boiled out, which to my surprize flourished amazingly'. The party spent a few days in mid-October travelling slowly along the bank of the Oliphants River, giving the oxen a chance to enjoy the good grazing there, before they attempted to cross a high ridge of mountains to the north; but this proved impossible, and they decided to send the wagons eastward by an easier route while the two botanists headed on horseback through the wild country. On 17 October:

We directed our course Eastward through Elans Kloof, a narrow, winding passage through a high chain of mountains, which lies to the N.E. of Olyfant's River. This road is rugged beyond description, consisting of broken and shattered rocks and rugged precipices, encompassed on each side with horrid impassable mountains; the sides of which are covered with fragments of rocks that have tumbled down from the summits.

Although Masson and Thunberg found few plants on the 'melancholy' high Veld, where the season seemed to be two months behind Cape Town, even though the plateau was about a hundred miles closer to the equator, when they descended to the lower Veld they were 'delighted to see the luxuriance of the meadows, the grass reaching to our horses bellies, enriched with great variety of *ixiae, gladioli,* and *irides*'. The way on to the rendezvous with the wagons took them through an even wilder pass than Elans Kloof, involving narrow paths with precipitous drops to one side and four fordings of the wild river which had cut the pass through the mountains. But 'we thought our labour and difficulties largely repaid by the number of rare plants we found here . . . the precipices are ornamented with *ericae* and many other mountain plants never described before'. Late on 22 October, after night had fallen, the exhausted pair arrived at the rendezvous where their wagons and servants were waiting; they spent the next day resting and putting their collections in order.

Compared with this adventure the next phase of the journey provided easy travelling, although on 26 October Thunberg and Masson left the wagons again to take a detour to the top of the mountain known as the Winter Hoek. They found some curious plants growing alongside the streams which ran down the mountainside, but many more 'remarkably fine flowers' as they travelled through the lush country along the Broad River. On 10 November, the day before Thunberg's thirtieth birthday, a relatively minor incident occurred which, thanks to the different accounts of it provided by the two botanists, provides some insight into their different characters. They had come to Davenhoek's River, where Thunberg took the lead in finding a crossing. According to Masson,

The Doctor imprudently took the ford without the least inquiry; when on a sudden, he and his horse plunged over head and ears into a pit, that had been made by the *hippopotamus amphibius*, which formerly inhabited this river. The pit was very deep, and steep on all sides, which made my companion's fate uncertain for a few minutes; but, after several strong exertions, the horse gained the opposite side with his rider.

In Masson's cautious eyes, Thunberg survives the incident, caused by his own rash behaviour, only thanks to the strength of the horse. According to Thunberg, however:

I, who was the most courageous of any of the company, and, in the whole course of the journey, was constantly obliged to go on before and head them, now also, without a moment's consideration, rode plump into the river, till, in a moment, I sank with my horse into a large and deep sea-cow hole, up to my ears. This would undoubtedly have proved my grave, if my horse had not by good luck been able to swim; and I, who have always had the good fortune to possess myself in the greatest dangers, had not, with the greatest calmness and composure, guided the animal (which floundered about violently in the water) and kept myself fast in the saddle, though continually lifted up by the stream. After having passed over this hole, I was likewise successful in my attempts to get safe out of it, though the edges of these holes are in general very steep, in so much that they seldom afford one a sure footing. All this time my fellow travellers stood frightened on the opposite bank and astonished, without daring to trust themselves to an element that appeared to them so full of danger.

Dare we suggest that there does seem to be just a hint of the Baron Munchausen about Thunberg's version?

Although the eastern extent of their travels was limited by the presence of hostile 'Hottentots' beyond the Zondags River, Masson and Thunberg experienced few further alarms on their journey, and were sometimes able to find comfortable lodgings with settlers such as Jacob Kock, a German who 'had built a handsome house, made gardens and vineyards, possessed numerous herds of cattle, and had upwards of a hundred Hottentots in his service'. While staying on Kock's farm in December 1773, Masson and Thunberg discovered two 'new' Cycads, and Masson sent a specimen of one of these, *Encephalartos altensteinii*, back to Kew, where it arrived in 1775. This very specimen still survives—the oldest pot plant in the world.

On the return journey to Cape Town, the party had several encounters with dangerous wildlife, taking detours to avoid contact with lions and buffalo, and once being attacked by a pack of hyenas which injured one of the oxen. Masson and his companions arrived back in Cape Town on 29 January 1774, four months and fourteen days after setting out, having covered roughly a thousand miles. Once again, Masson spent much of the winter months classifying and sorting his collection, and arranging for specimens (including *F. longifolius*) to be sent back to England. But once again, there were short collecting trips to be made, often with Thunberg and sometimes in the company of an Englishwoman, Lady Anne Monson.

Lady Anne was an interesting woman in her own right. Born Lady Anne Vane, she was a great-granddaughter on her mother's side of Charles II, through one of his illegitimate offspring, Charles, the first Duke of Southampton, who took the family name FitzRoy. Then in her late forties, she was an independent spirit who had divorced her first husband and was now the second wife of Colonel The Honourable George Monson, a career soldier in the service of the East India Company, who by 1774 was in India as one of the 'Council of Four' set up to curb the power of Warren Hastings, the Governor-General. Since Hastings chaired the Council and had the casting vote in case of ties, the ability of the Council to limit his activities depended on Monson and the other two members acting together. Lady Anne was on the way to join her husband in India, but she was a keen naturalist and took advantage of the stopover in South Africa to study the local flora; she was sufficiently well regarded in botanical circles to have a native South African genus, the *Monsonia*, named after her by Linnaeus. But there would be no time for more botanical honours to come her way. She died in India in 1776, at the age of 50; Warren Hastings was among the men who carried her coffin to the cemetery gates in Calcutta, where it was handed over to six ladies 'of gentle birth' to be conveyed to the grave.

The accounts Masson and Thunberg have left us of their second expedition together give slightly different versions of how it started. According to Thunberg, they set out together on 29 September 1774; but Masson tells us that he set out on the 26th accompanied only by his servants, and was joined by (or joined) Thunberg on 2 October, just before they climbed the Paarle Mountain together, where 'we added greatly to our collection'. This time heading north across the Berg River, initially through country 'every where decorated with flowers of the greatest beauty', they soon moved into more arid regions, which among other hazards were infested by snakes.[3] The journey took them past a mountain called the Piquet Berg, which lies due north of Cape Town and was of particular interest to Masson since it had been one of the observation sites used by Abbé Nicolas Louis de la Caille (as he was later to become) to measure one degree of latitude along the meridian passing through Cape Town, in 1750. Usually referred to today as Lacaille, the future Abbé spent the years 1750–4 studying the stars of the southern hemisphere of the Cape, and named many of the southern constellations. At the time, it was of keen interest to astronomers to establish whether the Earth was actually spherical, or whether its 'roundness' was different in different places, like, for example, the shape of a pear. This was assessed by determining the length on the surface of the Earth of arcs covering precisely measured angles (in this case, one degree) determined from astronomical observations; so Lacaille's work was at the cutting edge of research. On the top of the mountain he observed from, 'which is very high but easy of ascent', Masson and Thunberg found verdant plains populated by zebra, before descending to the coast at the mouth of the Verloore River. Then 'we left the shore on our left hand, and directed our course Northward', reaching the Oliphants River on 25 October, where they were able to stay at a Dutch homestead for several days.

Masson was surprised to see large flocks of sheep subsisting in the arid landscape by eating only 'succulent plants, and all sorts of shrubs; many of which were aromatic, and gave their flesh an excellent flavour'. Many of the succulents were new to European eyes, and were eagerly collected by the botanists. Continuing north and then east, the travellers experienced similar conditions to those of their first joint venture, but including a crossing of the Tanqua Karoo, a near-desert where they had to travel in the evening and early morning, resting up by day to avoid the worst of the heat, and where only small amounts of brackish water were available. In order to preserve the lives of their oxen, they had to press on along their direct route without detouring to botanize, but even 'only collecting what we found growing along the road side, [this] amounted to above 100 plants'.

In mid-November, following the course of the Renoster River, they arrived at the Roggeveld Mountains and ascended by an 'extremely rugged' road to the Veld, at an altitude of about 1,200 metres. Buffeted by fierce storms, with the temperature dropping so far that ice formed on the pools even in early December (equivalent to northern hemisphere June) and the local farmers, described as 'peasants' by Masson, feared for their crops, they decided to descend back to the plain. But this was only possible down a path so steep that the rear wheels of the wagons had to be made fast with chains to stop them turning, while teams of natives had to hold the wagons back with long thongs of leather attached to the upper parts of the wagons, to stop them overturning. After all that, 'we arrived at the foot of the mountain, where we found the heat more troublesome than the cold had been at the top'.

It was, clearly, time to call it a day. With their collections increased even more greatly, they arrived back in Cape Town at the end of December, where Masson stayed on until March 1775 putting everything in order before he returned to England. At Thunberg's suggestion, shortly before he died Linnaeus gave the name *Massonia* to a genus of succulent plant that Masson had collected at the Cape. In passing on Thunberg's suggestion with the specimen, Masson wrote to Linnaeus that:

The enclosed specimen I think is a new genus, to which my worthy friend, Dr Thunberg, had the great desire of giving the name Massonia, honouring me with this mark of his friendship. But...I have declined receiving this honour from any other authority than the great Linnaeus, whom I look upon as the father of botany and natural history, in hopes that you will give it your sanction.

The botanical material Masson provided for Kew from the Cape gave Banks just the ammunition he needed to convince the king and the Royal Society of the value of the Royal Botanic Garden itself and of the need to send plant hunters out to explore the world. Masson himself arrived back in England at the end of 1775, to a warm reception and acknowledgement that his status was now much more than that of a mere gardener. One enthusiastic visitor to Kew, the Revd M. Tyson, wrote in May 1776 that 'Mr Masson showed me the New World in his amazing Cape hothouse, Erica 140 species, many proteas, geraniums and cliffortias more than 50'. Apart from tending his plants and establishing the hothouse, Masson was busy writing up an account of his travels in the Cape for the *Philosophical Transactions of the Royal Society*, where it appeared in 1776—in this article he was the first person to use in print the name 'Royal Botanical Gardens at Kew'. But in spite of the recognition he received, Masson found it hard to settle to a routine working life at the gardens, and pestered Banks to send him on another expedition. Banks obliged, and on 9 May 1778 Masson departed on what should have been a peaceful journey around the islands of the Atlantic, botanizing from Madeira via Tenerife, in the Canary Islands, and the Azores to the West Indies, following the established trade route determined by prevailing winds and currents. He even hoped to visit mainland South America—the 'Spanish Main'.

Things didn't turn out as peacefully as Banks and Masson had hoped, however, and for reasons which will become clear no detailed journal recording that voyage survives. It started well enough, with Masson sending back to Banks many specimens from Madeira and the Canary Islands. His account of his visit to the island of São Miguel, in the Azores, was sent back to William Aiton, and published in the *Philosophical Transactions*. But by the time he reached the West Indies, trouble had flared up between the British and the French. There was often trouble between the British and the French in the eighteenth century, and the French, of course, supported the American rebellion against British rule. At the beginning of July 1779, Masson was on Grenada, the most southerly of the Windward Islands, when it was attacked by a French force. Along with other able-bodied men, he was conscripted into the militia and took part in the defence of the main port, St George's, where he was captured and imprisoned by the

French. All his plant collections were lost, and he was released only after Banks intervened with the French authorities to confirm that he was merely a botanist who had been in the wrong place at the wrong time.

Having put all that behind him, Masson moved on to St Lucia and started to rebuild his collection, only to have the specimens, all his equipment, and his journal lost in a hurricane which devastated the island in October 1780. It was almost the last straw, and although Masson did visit some of the other islands, before long he sailed for England, arriving in November, most probably in 1781 but possibly not until 1782.

It didn't take long for Masson to recover his spirits, and with his wanderlust restored in 1783 he departed on a much less alarming journey through Portugal (where he spent some time in Lisbon), Spain, and Algeria, with a detour back to Madeira before returning to Kew two years later. This was a relatively unremarkable expedition, compared with what came before and after. Late in 1785, after only a short time back in London, Masson departed once again, this time going back to South Africa, where he had enjoyed his greatest success. He arrived at Cape Town, on board the East Indiaman *Earl of Talbot*, on 10 January 1786, only to find that the political situation had changed dramatically in the decade since his previous visit. Britain and the Netherlands were now at war, and although Masson's status as a civilian botanist was not in question, British citizens in particular were suspected of being potential spies. Masson was given orders not to 'approach the coast nearer than the distance of 3 hours on foot', since the planners of any British seaborne invasion would naturally desire intelligence about suitable landing sites. There is at least a hint that Masson may have been under instructions from England to gather such information and that he ignored it. Banks pressed Masson to explore certain regions of the coast, and in a letter dated 3 June 1787 wrote: 'I hope that before this time you have taken up your headquarters as I directed at False

Bay; the most rare plants to be met with in Europe are from that place, & you know that one rare described plant is worth two nondescripts.'

Given that an invasion force under Admiral Elphinstone did land at False Bay in 1795 (the beginning of the British takeover of the Cape), it is hard not to read this as a veiled request for military intelligence—not least since False Bay is not of particular botanical interest. But Masson ignored it (in any case, he didn't get the letter until 1790), and all his activities were consistent with a statement he made in a letter to Thunberg written in March 1793, that 'the sole intention of my second visit to the Cape [is] to furnish the Royal Garden at Kew with living plants'.

Although initially intending to spend only a year or so at the Cape, Masson ended up staying there until 1795, leaving in March that year, not long before the British invasion force arrived. For a long time, communication with England was intermittent and slow. Masson sent seeds and other material back via Holland and on a Danish ship, but got little back in response. One letter from Banks, written in April 1787, reached Masson in November the same year, having been carried on the first convict ship taking settlers to New South Wales. But this was the exception rather than the rule. Communications improved somewhat later, and many specimens were sent back to Kew, but Masson has left no record of what must have been his extensive travels in the Cape between 1786 and 1795. We do, however, have a copy of a letter he wrote to Banks on 30 April 1790, in which a couple of familiar names appear. It begins: 'I received your letter dated June 3rd 69 which came by the L. Juliana. I have wrot several times this year viz by Mr. Bligh, Mr. Tarquharson of the Guardian, Mr. MacDonald from Madras, Mr Hayward of the Bounty, all of them took charge of small collections of seeds . . .'.

When he returned to England, Masson was in his fifty-fourth year, and might have been expected to settle down at last. But after two years devoted mostly to writing a book about what seem to have been his favourite plants, the succulents known as *Stapelia*, the restless Masson started on his travels yet again. Heading this time for Canada, he set sail in September 1797 on a ship which had the misfortune to be attacked twice by French pirates. On the second occasion the ship was commandeered, and the passengers were crammed into a vessel from Bremen bound for Baltimore. This ship already had its own quota of passengers and crew, so everyone was forced to survive on half a pound of nearly indigestible bread a day, with strict rationing of the foul water supply. As if that weren't bad enough, the weather also turned against them. But the ship made it to North America, where Masson recovered his strength in New York before crossing the border into Canada, visiting Queenstown, Fort Erie, and Niagara. Although he did send many samples of seeds back to Kew, Masson found the climate of Montreal, where he was based, far less agreeable for his ageing body than the climate of South Africa. Banks urged him to return to England in 1801, but Masson chose to stay on in Montreal in virtual retirement. His health deteriorated, and he died during a particularly severe winter on 23 December 1805, at the age of 64. Through all his adventures, his salary from Kew had never amounted to more than £100 a year. The last image we have of him comes from a Colonel George Landmann, serving with the Royal Engineers in Canada, who met Masson on one of his last field trips and wrote:

Mr Masson was at that time about sixty years of age or perhaps more, very kind in his manners, very plain and unassuming, and I thought him very scientific. He accepted of a shelter and what trifling nourishment I could provide, with unaffected diffidence, and submitted to the thousand inconveniences of the want of every comfort, without an expression of regret, except his frequent mention of the fear he entertained of incommoding me.

IN THE GARDEN

Gardeners and florists have much to remember Masson by. His introductions brighten gardens, houses, and parks today.

Almost fifty types of Pelargonium brighten summer borders together with Gladioli, Lobelias and the beautiful White Arum (Calla) Lily (*Zantedeschia aethiopica*). From South Africa came the Bird of Paradise flower (*Strelizia reginae*) and *Protea cynaroides*. The very name *Protea* hints at the variety and diversity of this genus—it is named after Proteus, the Greek god of the sea who had the power to change his form at will. The vibrant Amaryllis is named after Amaryllis, a beautiful shepherdess lauded in both classical and English pastoral poetry. Masson brought back *Amaryllis disticha* and *Amaryllis belladonna*. In the mountains behind Cape Town he found the Heather *Erica tomentosa* and near the Great Thorny River he found *Geranium spinosum* and the cactus-like plants *Stapelia euphorboides* and *Stapelia incarnata* (Carrion flowers).

The dramatic African Lily (*Agapanthus*) is as beautiful as its name, which comes from the Greek *agape* (love) and *anthos* (flower). Gladioli are so named for their leaves, which are reminiscent of a small sword (*gladiolus*).

Many of the plants that Francis Masson found growing in spectacular plenty won't survive in frost-prone gardens but bring great joy as pot plants. We also have Masson to thank for Cinerarias, whose vivid clusters of flowers contrast so dramatically with their grey downy leaves, and *Streptocarpus* (Cape Primrose).

4

DAVID DOUGLAS

(1799–1834)

D AVID DOUGLAS WAS the greatest of the Scottish botanist-explorers. His collecting adventures took him 12,000 miles on foot, horseback, and canoe, often through unexplored territory. There are more than 200 plants named after Douglas, probably more than for any other person in the history of scientific nomenclature. The plants that he introduced into Britain, in particular the trees, had a huge impact on the Victorian landscape. Both the already landed gentry and the rising merchant middle-class landowners were eager to pay to have the latest imports as growing status symbols on their land. His impact on the forestry industry in Britain and North America was enormous, as he discovered many of the pines normally grown for timber, including the Sugar Pine, Sitka Spruce, Douglas-fir, and Monterey Pine. In Britain, as well as being 'trophy trees' for landowners, they could be planted to form shelter belts to prevent wind damage to exposed newly created gardens surrounding the new country houses being built by the newly rich. As well as fashionable (and useful) trees Douglas was largely responsible for the introduction of the Flowering Currant (*Ribes sanguineum*) that flowers in so many gardens every spring, and the cottage garden favourite, Lupins.

Douglas is not normally remembered for the flowers that he introduced into our gardens, which is unfortunate, because they are wonderfully ornamental and would be sadly missed. He brought us California Poppies (*Eschscholzia*), *Penstemons* (Beard Tongue), the fragrant Evening Primrose (*Oenothera*), and the only peony native to the Americas. The Kew gardens flagpole, which is the tallest in the UK, is made from a section of just one Douglas-fir tree.

The hardships Douglas endured and the distances he covered in the north-west of North America, at great cost to his health and ultimately costing his life, would alone have been enough to make his name as an explorer, even if he had not been encumbered by his scientific equipment and specimens, which he carried through uncharted forest, on expeditions lasting weeks, in preference to such luxuries as a change of clothes or something to eat. Such single-minded devotion to his task would have surprised his early schoolteachers—although with hindsight many of the characteristics that made him such a successful plant hunter, including a stubborn insistence on doing things his own way and a fascination with the natural world, can be seen in the child.

Douglas was born on 25 June 1799, in Scone, the former seat of Scottish kings. The importance of Scone had long since declined, but at the end of the eighteenth century there was a revival in its fortunes brought about by the Earl of Mansfield, who had a new residence, Scone Palace, built. The old village was wiped off the map and replaced by new dwellings located out of sight of the house, so as not to spoil the view. All of this provided work, and one of the workers on the Scone estate was John Douglas, a strict Presbyterian, who styled himself a stonemason but could turn his hand to most building work. The region also experienced a mini-boom around this time as mills and other industrial activity sprang up. David Douglas was the second of six children fathered by John Douglas, stonemason, and brought up fairly comfortably thanks to John's steady income of one shilling and eight pence a day.

In the eyes of David's parents, like so many Scots, the most important thing that the stable income provided was an opportunity for the children to be educated. His elder brother later recorded that at the age of 3 David was first sent to a 'school' kept by an old lady in the village, but that even at that age he proved so headstrong and unmanageable that he was soon moved to the Parish School at Kinnoull, where the master, a Mr Wilson, was barely able to keep him under control and frequently handed out punishment—using the inevitable leather strap, or tawse—when David played truant, or got behind with his work because he spent so much time birdwatching or fishing. The walk of six miles each way, in all weathers, between home and the school gave ample opportunity for the boy to disappear, as well as toughening him up at an early age. When he did show up at school, in between his punishments he got a reputation for asking awkward questions and refusing to bow mindlessly to authority, whatever the consequences; his fellow pupils remembered being deeply impressed by the way he shrugged off his encounters with the tawse.

Douglas would have seen great changes in the countryside while he was playing truant from school since this was the time of land enclosures, when hedges were planted in profusion to mark the boundaries of fields. The introduction of the new farming practices enriched the landowners (and paid for extravagances like Scone Palace) while depriving the smallholders of what little they had, with little or no common land left for grazing. One of the fashionable new features of a great house like Scone Palace was the landscape garden; so when Douglas left school for good in 1810, at the age of 11, he was able to get a job as an apprentice gardener at the big house. Like many intelligent, independent-minded children who rebel against a rigid educational system, Douglas now decided that education was a good thing. As well as working hard at his job, which he enjoyed, he studied in the evenings, even improving the Latin that he had unwillingly learned at school. After serving his seven-year apprenticeship, the now well-regarded (and well-read) young man took up a position as one of the under-gardeners to Alexander Stewart at Valleyfield, the home of Sir Robert Preston, about twenty-five miles (some 40 km) south of Scone.

This was a key moment in Douglas's life, since Sir Robert was not only an enthusiastic amateur botanist with wide scientific interests, but lacked the haughty arrogance of many members of his class. Finding that Douglas shared his enthusiasm for the natural world, Sir Robert allowed the under-gardener free access to his extensive botanical library, and encouraged him to study. After a year, Douglas was promoted to Foreman under Stewart, and after two years he obtained a position at the Botanic Garden in Glasgow—arriving there in April 1820, at almost exactly the same time that William Hooker arrived there as Professor of Botany. Douglas was not only able to attend Hooker's lectures, but struck up a firm friendship with the older man, accompanying him on field trips botanizing in the Highlands and Islands of Scotland. Hooker saw first hand the independence of character and physical ability to withstand harsh conditions, as well as the enthusiasm, that would make Douglas one of the best botanical explorers of his time; Douglas learned not only botany but also basic herbal medicine from Hooker's lectures, and saw the door opening to the wider world. Before long, Hooker would recommend Douglas as a botanical collector to the Horticultural Society in London.

The Horticultural Society had been in existence since 1804. Its founders (at a meeting held in Hatchard's bookshop in Piccadilly on Wednesday, 7 March) included Joseph Banks, William Forsyth (the gardener to George III whose name is immortalized in the Forsythia) and John Wedgwood, a member of the famous pottery family and uncle of Charles Darwin. Since 1815, the affairs of the Society had been handled by its Secretary, the lawyer Joseph Sabine, and in 1818 it had taken over a garden extending to one and a half acres (0.6 hectares) in Kensington. Now the Royal Horticultural Society, it is famous worldwide today for hosting the annual Chelsea Flower Show.

One of the early aims of the Society was to send collectors out around the world to obtain not just a few specimens of exotic plants for scientific study, but large numbers of living specimens and seeds that could be propagated and sold to the burgeoning numbers of affluent people in Britain with an interest in gardening—the Society had 1,500 members in 1823, and landowners like the Earl of Mansfield and Sir Robert Preston would pay handsomely for plants for their gardens. In 1821, the first gardener sent out by the Society on such an expedition, John Potts, travelled to India and sent back a huge consignment of material. But he became seriously ill, and although he did make it back to Britain, bringing with him the seeds from which many modern Primulas are descended, he died in 1822. The second collector sent out by the Society was even less fortunate. John Forbes sent home Orchids and other plants from the coastal region of east Africa, but eventually succumbed to fever while on the Zambezi River in 1823. It was third time lucky for John Damper Parks, who made a successful visit to China, brought back twenty varieties of Chrysanthemum, and lived to tell the tale. Encouraged by this success, Sabine began looking for another young man to make a second trip to China, and discussed the possibilities with Hooker.

David Douglas, now 23, had just been promoted to Head Gardener at the Glasgow Botanic Garden, and had little prospect of anything more exciting. When Hooker recommended him to Sabine, he jumped at the chance, and travelled south to London in the spring of 1823. The Chinese expedition had to be postponed because of political unrest in the region, but the Horticultural Society decided to send Douglas instead to the eastern part of North America, travelling as far west as Lake Erie to seek out interesting plants—not just exotics, but species of Oak unknown in Europe and the American apples, which had a reputation for size and flavour that had already crossed the Atlantic.

The political map of the North American continent where Douglas arrived on 2 August 1823, after a tedious two-month crossing, was very different from that of today. It was only twenty years since the Louisiana Purchase, when France sold a huge area of North America (not just modern Louisiana) to the United States for $15,000,000; the US President at the time was Thomas Jefferson, only the third incumbent of the post, who was instrumental in establishing the principle of westward expansion for the Union. Jefferson had been collecting books on the exploration and geography of the western territories of North America since the 1780s, almost as soon as the United States became independent. He had a vision of the West as a paradise where white settlers and 'Indians' would live peacefully together, and although this idealistic dream never came to anything, his fascination with the West was a driving force in turning the eyes of the young nation towards the Pacific. Even in 1823, though, this was still little more than a vision. The Florida peninsula had been bought from Spain in 1819; but what are now the states of California, Nevada, Utah, Arizona, New Mexico, Texas, and most of Colorado were part of the empire of Mexico. What would become the states of Washington, Oregon, and part of Idaho were mostly under British influence, although nobody had established sovereignty over this Pacific Northwest region, and Alaska belonged unequivocally to Russia.

Douglas stayed in New York until 19 August, checking out the local market produce, orchards, and the remains of what had been the fine Botanic Garden, 'now, I am sorry to say, in ruins'. He then travelled by boat to New Brunswick, on overland to Burlington, New Jersey, then by steamboat again to see the landscape gardens of the rich gentlemen who lived around Philadelphia. This was the gentlest introduction to his new role as a botanical collector, but even in the most civilized parts of the United States there were new varieties (including the famous apples) to obtain and send back to London. As he gained experience, Douglas spread his wings and undertook longer journeys—hardly expeditions—which provided a sketch for what was to come. In September 1823 he travelled by steamboat up the Hudson

River into upper New York State, then overland to Buffalo and by boat across Lake Erie to Amherstburg. It was here that he had his first taste of what was to come, crossing the Detroit River to the Canadian side[1] in a birch-bark canoe accompanied by a Native American guide. As he wrote in his journal on 16 September:

This is what I might term my first day in America. The trees in the woods were of astonishing magnitude. The soil, in general, over which we were passing was a very rich black earth…I gathered seeds of some species of *Liatris*, which along with *Helianthus* [Sunflower], *Solidago* [Golden Rod], *Aster, Eupatorium* [Boneset] and *Veronica* form the majority of which I had an opportunity of seeing in perfection.

Although this was still largely a natural forest, there were settlers who gave Douglas advice and help on his travels, and he had a fairly easy time of it except for one occasion, which he recorded ruefully, when he took off his jacket to climb a tree in order to gather seeds and other specimens, only for the man he had hired as a guide to gather up the coat and run off with it before Douglas could descend: 'He escaped in the woods. I had in my [coat] pockets my notes and some receipt of money, nineteen dollars in paper, a copy of Persoons *Synopsis Plantarium* with my small vasculum. I was thus left five miles from where I had left the car, in a miserable condition…'. A few years later, Douglas would hardly have noted such a trivial incident, nor regarded his resulting situation as 'miserable'.

Making his way back to New York, Douglas detoured to view Niagara Falls, but gave much more space in his journal to describing the plants nearby than to the Falls themselves. The worst of his difficulties were painful attacks of rheumatism, but these didn't stop him heading off to Philadelphia once again early in November before finally returning to England. The great majority of his plants and seeds reached the Horticultural Society safely, and their official response was that:

The mission was executed by Mr Douglas with a success beyond expectation: he obtained many plants which were much wanted, and greatly increased our collection of fruit trees by the acquiring of several sorts only known to us by name. It would be unjust here to omit mentioning the uniform kindness and attention with which he was received in every part of the United States that he visited. It is most gratifying to have to add, that the presents of cultivated plants to the Society embraced nearly everything which it was desirous to obtain; and that the liberality with which they were given was only equalled by the hospitality with which the collector was received.

The seeds and plants that Douglas transported to England included twenty-one varieties of Peach, nineteen varieties of Oak, Orchids, varieties of Evening Primrose, and (a special coup) the Oregon Grape (*Mahonia acquifolium*), which had only recently been brought to the east coast of North America from the west coast by the explorers Lewis and Clark. It would be Douglas's destiny to follow them to the Pacific Northwest of North America—but by sea, not overland.

Meriwether Lewis (1774–1809) and William Clark (1770–1838) were the leaders of the first successful overland expedition which crossed from the Atlantic coast of North America to the Pacific coast and back, in the years 1804–6. Lewis, born near Charlottesville, Virginia, had been a boyhood neighbour of the future president Thomas Jefferson. In 1801, when Jefferson became president, Lewis was a captain in the army, with experience fighting the British in the north-west of the nascent United States. Jefferson gave him a post as his aide, already having the idea of what would become the Lewis–Clark expedition in mind. As we have mentioned, Jefferson had the vision of opening up the continent for settlement, and the expedition was the first step towards creating the continental United States that we know today. Funds for the expedition were approved in 1803, with Lewis appointed as its leader; but he soon decided that he would need a colleague to help with such a big project, and chose William Clark, a friend who was also an army captain.

The two men were a classic example of opposites attracting and complementing one another. Lewis was an introvert, a planner, and a thinker but subject to gloomy moods; Clark was a gregarious extrovert, a pragmatic man of action, just the man to keep the spirits of the expedition up. They began their epic journey in May 1804, just five months after President Jefferson's historic decision to purchase Louisiana from France. It took them by boat, with forty-five men and a dog, mostly along the Missouri and Columbia rivers through land that eventually became eleven separate States of the Union, reaching the Pacific on the coast of what is now Oregon in November 1805. On their return to St Louis in September 1806, having covered some 8,000 miles (12,800 km), Lewis was originally selected to edit their journals for publication; but he died (probably murdered) in Tennessee in 1809. Clark did not feel up to the task, and eventually enlisted help from a Philadelphia lawyer, Nicholas Biddle, and a journalist from the same city, Paul Allen, who finished the job and saw the resulting book into print in February 1814.

British interest in the Pacific Northwest came in the form of the Hudson's Bay Company, which had penetrated from Canada in the east and by sea from the Pacific to exploit the fur trade—in particular, beaver. As we have seen, official government interest in the region had led to the surveying expedition under Captain George Vancouver in the *Discovery* (accompanied by the *Chatham*) in the 1790s, when the unfortunate naturalist Archibald Menzies had to suffer the indignity of being confined to his cabin while his carefully gathered plants were neglected nearby. The relationship between Menzies and Vancouver deteriorated so much that even while he was on board the *Discovery*, off California on 18 November 1793, on the way home, Menzies was reduced to writing to the Captain rather than speaking to him:

It is really become so unpleasant to me to represent to you verbally any thing relative to the Plant-frame on the Quarterdeck that I have now adopted this method, to mention to you all the alterations or rather additions which I wish to be made to its original plan...the Fowls have been in it again last night, and have done irreparable damages...

The detailed proposals that Menzies put forward in that letter came to nothing, of course, and his specimens were destroyed. But in spite of the difficulty of working under Vancouver, Menzies was the first botanist to see (in 1792) the conifer forests of what is now British Columbia and Washington State, and to describe (though not collect) what has become known as the Douglas-fir. He was responsible for introducing into Britain the California Poppy, the tree Lupin and the Sitka Spruce. But he seems to have been most proud of the fact that when the surgeon on the *Discovery* became ill and had to be sent home, Menzies, who, remember, had studied botany and medicine in Edinburgh and served as a ship's surgeon on the Halifax Station of Nova Scotia, took over his duties to such good effect that nobody on the ship died of sickness on the entire voyage. After his voyage with Vancouver, Menzies served as a ship's doctor in the West Indies on board the *Sans Pareil* during the Napoleonic Wars; after he retired from the navy he settled in London and practised medicine.

So although Lewis and Clark had blazed the land trail across the North American continent, it was not in their footsteps but in Archibald Menzies's wake that Douglas followed when he sailed from Gravesend on behalf of the Horticultural Society, on one of the Hudson's Bay Company's supply ships, the *William and Ann*, on 26 July 1824.

We have plenty of information about this trip, because, as with his first journey undertaken on behalf of the Horticultural Society, Douglas kept a detailed journal. The driving motive for the expedition was commercial—the Society intended to market the plants that he would send back to them. It wouldn't be difficult to show a profit, since the budget for the entire three-year expedition, including Douglas's salary and expenses, was £400; he was expected to live off the land for most of the time. But there was also a scientific side, which cost hardly anything once Douglas was in place, since naturally the Society and its members wanted to know all they could about the botany, zoology, and other features of this largely unexplored terrain; although Douglas did not know it, his reports would also be eagerly studied by the politicians back home (not least Banks), since he would be travelling through a region where the political boundaries were uncertain and undefined, and there was at least the prospect of international tension in years to come.

Douglas's voyage to the north-west of North America was by what had already become, less than sixty years after Cook's pioneering voyage, an established trading route round Cape Horn. The first port of call was Madeira, where Douglas had the opportunity to visit local fruit and vegetable markets, as well as vineyards, and climbed to the highest point on the island, Pico Ruivo de Santana. Although a modest 1861 metres above sea level and representing no more than 'a laborious day's work', the climb was the first of many to be described in the journal, as Douglas developed a passion for getting to the tops of mountains just because they were there. From Madeira the *William and Ann* sailed to Rio de Janeiro, where as well as taking a keen interest in the local flora and fauna Douglas, brought up in a strict Presbyterian household, attended a Roman Catholic Midnight Mass. This may scarcely seem worth mentioning today, but his tolerant and broad-minded attitude towards other people's religious beliefs was unusual for the time, and would stand him in good stead on his travels.

Douglas sent back two boxes of plants to the Horticultural Society from Rio, including fine orchids such as *Brassavola nodosa* and *Oncidium pubes*. The success of these plants in the hothouses of England meant that he was already repaying the modest investment made by the Society before he had even reached the Horn. His description of the conditions when the *William and Ann* did round the Horn highlights that although such voyages were by then routine, they were far from comfortable: 'The weather was stormy with generally a fine clear sky. The motion of the vessel was great, the waves frequently breaking over it, and no sleep until completely worn out with fatigue. When the wind blows from the south or south-west the cold is insupportable...'.

The rounding of the Horn was completed on 16 November 1824, and conditions gradually improved as they sailed north, the days becoming so dull that Douglas simply wrote 'nothing worthy to be noticed' in his diary. The tedium was broken, however, when they came to the Juan Fernandez Islands, some 400 miles (640 km) off the coast of Chile. These were the islands where the Scot Alexander Selkirk had been put ashore in 1704 (at his own request, after an argument with his captain) and lived alone for just over four years; his story was the inspiration for Daniel Defoe's *Robinson Crusoe*, published in 1720. After Douglas and his companions had convinced themselves that they had identified the very cave where Selkirk had lived, the botanist explored gardens that had been planted by Spanish settlers before they abandoned the islands:

In the old gardens were abundances of three or four different peaches in a half ripe state, very luxuriant; one apple, a quince, and two pears; a quantity of the last three we took for puddings...I sowed a small portion of vine, pear, and some other fruit seeds which I had...and some culinary vegetables.

The next feature on the voyage was a call at the Galapagos Islands, in January 1825—just over ten years before Charles Darwin visited the islands with Robert FitzRoy's *Beagle* expedition. In January 1825 Darwin, aged 15, was still at school. The variety of bird life that would before long become one of the key factors that inspired Darwin to develop the idea that evolution operates by a process of natural selection also impressed Douglas, but in different way:

The birds are very numerous, and some of them pretty, so little acquainted with man's devices that they were readily killed with a stick; a gun was not necessary except to bring them from the rocks or from the tops of the trees.

Many of the smaller ones perched on my hat, and when I carried my gun on my shoulder would sit on the muzzle. During my stay I killed forty-five, of nineteen genera, all of which I skinned carefully, and had the mortification to lose them all except one species of Sula by the almost constant rain of twelve days after leaving the Island. I could not expose them on deck and no room for them below.

Nearly four weeks after leaving the Galapagos, on 12 February the *William and Ann* reached her destination at the mouth of the mighty Columbia River, which today marks the boundary between the states of Oregon and Washington, but was then in the British sphere of influence. To the frustration of all on board, this still wasn't quite the end of the voyage. The weather was so severe—described by Douglas as 'a thousand times worse than Cape Horn'—that it was six weeks before the ship could actually approach the coast close enough for a landing to be made, on 7 April 1825. 'Thus', wrote Douglas, 'my long and tedious voyage of 8 months 14 days from England terminated.'

Among the first trees that Douglas saw when he got ashore was the species that now bears his name, the Douglas-fir.[2] As we have mentioned, the tree had been described by Archibald Menzies, in 1792, a fact reflected in its Latin name, *Pseudotsuga menziesii*.[3] But it was Douglas who sent the first cones and seeds from the tree back to Britain, where the first examples of the species in Europe were grown from those seeds. The name originally given to the species, before it was renamed in Menzies's honour, was *Pinus taxifolia*. In his notebook Douglas reported his first sight of the tree that would bear his own name without any special mention: 'The ground on the south side of the river is low, covered thickly with wood, chiefly *Pinus canadensis*, *P. balsamea*, and a species which may prove to be *P. taxifolia*...'.

Before long, the ship was visited by friendly natives, Douglas's first encounter with the people he sometimes referred to as 'Indians'. On 11 April, a Monday, the ship was moved up river about seven miles, to a base (factory) called Fort George (the site of present-day Astoria,

Oregon) established by the Hudson's Bay Company. The representatives of the Company were in the process of abandoning this base and moving to one some seventy miles up river; Douglas left the ship on the following Saturday (although he had been ashore every day during the week) and began his adventure proper, receiving every assistance from the Company, under the direction of its Chief Factor, John McLoughlin.

Like the East India Company, the Hudson's Bay Company was more than just a trading organization, and worked closely with the British Government. Although its commercial purpose was to supply furs to the European market, and it had been established for that purpose as long ago as 1670, by the early nineteenth century its political role was to establish and maintain British influence over the parts of the North American continent still claimed by the British. In fact, the Pacific side of the continent had been largely opened up by the rival North West Company, but in 1821 the two companies had merged, with the Hudson's Bay Company very much the senior partner and the North West name being consigned to history. The new base that was being established when Douglas arrived was called Fort Vancouver, and was located close to the present-day city of Portland, Oregon, with the spectacular mountain scenery including a view of Mount St Helens to the north.

From the outset, Douglas mostly slept in a tent or under the stars, since accommodation at the incomplete Fort Vancouver was at a premium. Far from regarding this as a hardship, a few weeks later he wrote: 'The luxury of a night's sleep on a bed of pine branches can only be appreciated by those who have experienced a route over a barren plain scorched by the sun, or [become] fatigued by groping their way through a thick forest, crossing gullies, dead wood, lakes, stones, &c.'

After a few weeks botanizing in the immediate vicinity of the fort, in June Douglas began to venture farther afield along the Columbia and Multnomah (now the Willamette) Rivers, culminating in a much longer expedition on which he set out on 20 June, up the Columbia River, following part of the route blazed by Lewis and Clark two decades earlier. This was a serious expedition, on which he was accompanied by two natives and one of the Canadian 'voyageurs'— the tough descendants of French explorers and native women, who transported furs and other goods for the Company along the water ways of Canada in birch-bark canoes.

The natives themselves were mostly friendly—there were no serious conflicts with settlers until European immigration into the region began in earnest in the 1840s. But the country itself was a serious challenge. After passing through the Cascade Mountains, although still following the course of the river the travellers passed through the arid plains mentioned above, where Douglas detoured on foot to botanize:

Nothing but extensive plains and barren hills, with the greater part of the herbage scorched and dead [in] the intense heat. I had to cross a plain nineteen miles without a drop of water, of pure white sand, thermometer in the shade 97 degrees. Suffered much from the heat and reflection of the sun's rays; and scarcely can I describe the state of my feet in the evening from the heat in the dry sand; all the upper part of them were in one blister.

Douglas continued with his collecting expeditions through the summer, and in September made a journey on his own into the mountains near what Lewis and Clark had called the Grand Rapids:

This took three days, and was one of the most laborious undertakings I ever experienced, the way was so much over dead wood, detached rocks, rivulets, &c., that very little personal effects could be carried. Indeed I was obliged to leave my blanket at my first encampment.

My provision was 3 oz. tea, 1 lb. sugar, and four small biscuits. The next day I caught no fish, and at such a great altitude the only birds to be seen were hawks, eagles, vultures, &c. I was fortunate enough to kill one young white-headed eagle, which . . . I found very good eating. I roasted it, having only a small pan for making tea. On the summit of the hill I slept one night. I made a small fire of grass and twigs and dried my clothes which were wet with perspiration and then laid myself down on the grass with my feet to the fire. I found it very cold and had to rise four times and walk to keep myself warm, fortunately it was dry and a keen north wind prevented dew.

The second half of September was devoted to packing up twenty-four large bundles of plant specimens, a large chest of seeds, another of 'birds and quadrupeds', and one containing samples of dress and other native work. Douglas did everything he could in duplicate, sending one set of specimens and seeds by sea back to England and the other overland across the North American continent the following spring. He was unable to supervise the loading of his specimens onto the *William and Ann*, however, since he fell on a rusty nail, injuring his knee so badly that he was laid up for three weeks. Having recovered, he renewed his exploration of the country, this time bot-anizing in the coastal region near the mouth of the Columbia River. He stayed on the coast until 15 November in spite of foul weather, his journal full of comments such as 'the rain fell in torrents all day', and 'the wind about midnight increased to a hurricane with sleet and hail'. Hardly surprisingly, all this took a toll on his health, aggravating the rheumatism from which he had suffered in New England, while his eyesight began to deteriorate, partly a result of snow blindness. And the knee injured by the rusty nail never really fully recovered. By New Year's Day 1826 Douglas was in a gloomy mood, and wrote:

Commencing a year in such a far removed corner of the earth, where I am nearly destitute of civilised society, there is some scope for reflection. In 1824 I was on the Atlantic on my way to England; 1825, between the island of Juan Fernandez and the Galapagos in the Pacific; I am now here, and God only knows where I may be the next [New Year]. In all probability, if a change does not take place, I will shortly be consigned to the tomb. I can die satisfied with myself. I have never given cause for remonstrance or pain to an individual on earth. I am in my twenty-seventh year.

But Douglas' self-penned obituary was a little premature. Even in the north-west of North America, winter ends eventually, and in the spring he was sufficiently restored mentally and physically to make a crucial decision—ignoring his instructions from the Horticultural Society in order to stay on in the north-west for a further year. According to those instructions, he should have returned to England in 1826, either by ship from the Columbia River or by joining the annual west-to-east trek, known as the Hudson's Bay Express, to York Factory, on Hudson's Bay itself. This left Fort Vancouver in early spring, and took four months to cover the two thousand miles across the continent. Douglas would eventually follow this route—becoming the first 'civilian', or non-Hudson's Bay Company employee, to cross Canada—but not for another year.

To get him on his way for another season in the wilds, Douglas set out with the Express in March, getting well up river before setting off on his own. He didn't exactly travel light, carrying scientific equipment for his botanizing which included thirty quires of paper, weighing 102 pounds, for preserving specimens; but in order to accommodate all this he had no scope for luxuries, and carried for his own use only two shirts, two handkerchiefs, a blanket, and a cloak, and 'one pair of shoes but no stockings'. 'On the afternoon of Monday, the 20th, at four o'clock, I left Fort Vancouver in company with John Mcleod, Esq., a gentleman going across to Hudson's Bay, and Mr Francis Ermatinger,[4] for the interior, with two boats and fourteen men.'

Because the winter had been unusually severe, McLeod's expedition experienced considerable hardship on the journey, struggling in places through snow up to thirty feet deep, and McLeod himself had to cut up a pair of leather trousers to make shoes when the ones he set out with wore out. Douglas didn't suffer anything quite as severe—or at least, when he did so, it was from choice. Apart from the usual hardships of botanizing in the wild, carrying heavy loads of specimens and equipment on a trip which would last until the end of August, while crossing the Blue Mountains Douglas didn't just stick to the easiest passes but climbed the highest peak he could find, about 2,000 metres above sea level:

In the lower parts I found it exceedingly fatiguing walking on the soft snow, having no snowshoes, but on reaching within a few hundred feet of the top, where there was a hard crust of frost, I without the least difficulty placed my foot on the highest peak... (Thermometer at 5 P.M., 26 Fahr.)

Getting back down to camp was another matter, as Douglas was caught in a storm on the way down—and not just any storm:

I never beheld anything that could equal the lightning. Sometimes it would appear in massive sheets, as if the heavens were in a blaze; at other, in vivid zig-zag flashes at short intervals with the thunder resounding through the valleys below, and before the echo of the former peal died away the succeeding was begun, so that it was impressed on my mind as if only one.

He reached the camp at 8 p.m., with the storm still raging and making lighting a fire impossible:

As all my clothes were wet, and having nothing to change, I stripped and rolled myself in my blanket and went soundly to sleep shortly afterwards. Precisely at twelve [midnight] I was so benumbed with cold that on endeavouring to get up I found my knees refused to do their office. I scoured them well with a rough towel, and as the storm was over made a cheering fire.

I could not resist the temptation of making a little tea, which I found restored me greatly (thermometer 26 degrees F). If I have any zeal, for once and the first time it began to cool.

Hung my clothes up to dry and lay down and slept until three o'clock.

We have gone into some detail about this little side trip by Douglas because it is so typical of the man—except for the momentary cooling of his zeal. Often living off the land,[5] but taking advantage of any opportunities to trade and send samples back to Fort Vancouver from other Hudson's Bay Company outposts and usually accompanied only by native guides, Douglas acquired the 'Indian' name 'Walking Man

Who Gathers Grass', earning the respect even of the natives, not least since he took the trouble to learn their languages.

Sometimes, even Douglas's enviable fortitude wavered, as on the day when he:

Travelled thirty-three miles, drenched and bleached with rain and sleet, chilled with a piercing north wind; and then to finish the day experienced the cooling, comfortless consolation of lying down wet without supper or fire. On such occasions I am very liable to become fretful.

Hardly surprisingly, by the time he returned to Fort Vancouver itself, he looked like the ragged survivor of some disaster to a boat on the river:

I had the satisfaction of arriving safe at Fort Vancouver at midday [29 August], after traversing nearly eight hundred miles of the Columbia Valley in twelve days and unattended by a single person, my Indian guides excepted. My old friends here gave every attention a wayworn wanderer is entitled to. On their discovering me plodding up the low plain from the river to the house alone, unpleasant thoughts struck them...but as soon as I dispelled the cloud of melancholy that sat on every brow I had that unaffected welcome so characteristic among people so far from home. I had a shirt, a pair of leather trousers, an old straw hat, neither shoe nor stocking nor handkerchief of any description, and perhaps from my careworn visage had some appearance of escaping from the gates of death.

Douglas was just in time to send samples of 120 species of seeds back to England on the Company ship *Dryad*, which sailed at the beginning of September. They received an ecstatic welcome when they arrived in London—and the package included the first seeds of the Douglas-fir to reach Europe.

Time, you might think, for Douglas to put his feet up for a good long spell. But not a bit of it. On 20 September he set off to explore the mountainous region south of Fort Vancouver. A month later, already suffering severely from chilblains and rheumatism (or arthritis) in the damp weather, he was a mile from his camp when, hunting deer, he fell into a deep gully where he lay unconscious for more than five hours, waking up flat on his face in the mud with a severe pain in his chest. He was found by six 'Indians of the Calapooie tribe', who helped him back to camp and undoubtedly saved his life. Yet he still stayed out in the wilds until 19 November, giving up his botanizing only when overcome by 'fatigue and constant exposure to the rain and cold'. Typically, by 9 December he was so bored that he set off on one last quick trip down to the mouth of the Columbia River and back to Fort Vancouver before Christmas—he actually got back at noon on Christmas Day. By then even Douglas had to admit that the weather was too severe for any more field trips, and there was nothing to do but regain his strength and wait for spring and the departure of the Hudson's Bay Express.

The small party set out by boat on 20 March 1827. Douglas would be accompanied all the way to Hudson's Bay by Edward Ermatinger, a representative of the Company; four others (McLoughlin, the Chief Factor, McLeod, Annance, and Pambrun) would take their leave at Fort Colville, on the western side of the Rocky Mountains, and head off on an expedition into the interior of the country. The parting of the ways came on 16 April, leaving Douglas, Ermatinger, and their voyageurs to proceed up the headwaters of the Columbia River and across the Rockies:

Having now just bid farewell to my Columbian friends, I cannot in justice to my own feelings refrain from acknowledging the kindness shown to me during my stay among them, a grateful remembrance of which I shall ever cherish. My society now is confined to Mr Edward Ermatinger, a most agreeable young man who goes to Hudson's Bay with us, and seven men— four Canadians and three Iroquois Indians. Our next stage is Jasper House, in the Rocky Mountains, distant about 370 miles. Laid down to sleep at 2 A.M.

By 27 April they had gone as far as they could by boat. The precious vessel was hauled ashore and secured to await the arrival of the westbound Express in the autumn, while Douglas and his companions now had to cross the Rockies on foot. This seemed to Douglas a good time to summarize his travels in the north-west. Adding up all his journeys over the past couple of years he calculated that in 1825 he had travelled a little over 2,100 miles, and in 1826 just under 4,000 miles; the route of the Express from the lower Columbia River to the Rockies added in another thousand miles or so. The total came to more than 7,000 miles, and although some historians have suggested this may be a slight overestimate, it was certainly an impressive achievement. By this time, Douglas's personal wardrobe consisted of four shirts, three handkerchiefs, two pairs of stockings, two jackets, two vests (waist-coats), and two pairs of trousers, one blanket, seven pairs of mocca-sins, shaving materials, a towel, and 'half a cake of Windsor soap'. His other baggage—seeds, specimens, and scientific equipment—weighed around 20 kilos.

Thus encumbered, Douglas trekked through the pass in the Rock-ies, experiencing piercing cold and plunging through snow up to seven feet deep. On 29 April they managed fifteen miles in the day; on the 30th, 'the ravines or gullies unmeasurable, and towards noon becoming sinking, ascending two steps and sometimes sliding back three'. Progress that day, nine miles; 'find no fault with the food, glad of anything'.

The next day, being at about the highest point of the pass, Douglas decided on a little diversion, and set out on his own to climb the highest peak in the vicinity. The ascent took five hours. 'I remained twenty minutes, my thermometer standing at 18° [Fahrenheit] night closing fast in on me, and no means of fire, I was reluctantly forced to descend. The sensation I felt is beyond what I can give utterance to.' The price Douglas paid for that sensation was to exacerbate the eye problems caused by snow blindness, and further weaken his health. Meanwhile, he took the opportunity to name two of the highest peaks he could see—one Mount Brown, in honour of the botanist remembered today for observing 'Brownian motion', and the other Mount Hooker, after his old friend and patron in Glasgow.

As April gave way to May, with advancing spring the party was also descending the eastern side of the Rockies and beginning to enjoy warmer weather. The symbolic end of their journey through the mountains came when they reached the Company post known as Jasper House, a little to the north of modern Jasper, and enjoyed a day of rest in temperatures touching 61 °F. It was now possible to travel again by river (the Athabasca), in birchbark canoes, nearly two hundred miles to Fort Assiniboine. From there, an exhausting overland trek of a hundred miles took them to Fort Edmonton, where the North Saskatchewan River provided the highway to the east and York Factory. Douglas arrived there at the end of August. In the past two and a half years, he had covered almost 10,000 miles.

But he still had one more adventure to endure before joining the ship for the voyage home. A few days before the ship was due to sail, Douglas and three other gentlemen set out in a boat rowed by eight oarsmen to visit the vessel, which was anchored a little way out in the bay. On their way back, a storm blew up (Douglas, with understandable hyperbole, describes it as a 'hurricane') and the boat was swept far out into the bay in heavy rain accompanied by thunder and lightning. There was no hope of doing anything other than desperately bailing out the boat with their hats to keep it afloat; by the time the storm abated, about thirty-six hours later, they had been swept some seventy miles (115 km) out into Hudson's Bay. All twelve survived, but it was a long row back to York Factory. Hardly surprisingly, with this coming on top of his earlier exertions, Douglas was quite worn out and spent the entire four-week voyage back to England, in the *Prince of Wales*, resting in his cabin, unable to rise or even to write up his journal, with an uncertain future ahead of him.

The return of their collector to London on 11 October 1827 was almost as much a surprise to the Horticultural Society as a delight. A few months earlier, their President, Thomas Knight, had written:

Our collector proposes, when he has sent all he can home by a ship, to march across the continent of America to the country of the United States on this side, and to collect what plants and seeds he can in his journey: but it is probable that he will perish in the attempt. Mr Sabine says, that if he escapes, he will soon perish in some other hardy enterprise... It is really lamentable that so fine a fellow should be sacrificed.

Sabine's gloomy prophecy would indeed come true, but not just yet. Douglas would have been greeted as a returning hero in London, but at first he was too ill to enjoy the adulation, and even had to leave it to Sabine to read a paper he had written to the Linnean Society on his behalf. Once Douglas had recovered enough to enjoy his success, he became the toast of the town, entertaining fashionable society with his tales of life in the wilderness. He was made a Fellow of the Geological, Linnean, and Zoological Societies, with the usual membership fees waived in each case.

Although he had sent back more material than any collector before him, the total cost of the expedition was less than £400, and Douglas's personal expenses, including food, came to £66 for three years. Sales of the Flowering Currant, *Ribes sanguineum*, alone covered the entire outlay of the Horticultural Society on the expedition. But Douglas began to become disenchanted when he discovered that his salary was less than the pay of the hall porter at the Society's office, and he became increasingly grumpy and bad-tempered. As William Hooker later spelled out in a biographical memoir of Douglas,[6] although he was ideally qualified as a traveller and surveyor of 'the wonders of nature in its grandest scale', he was now ill at ease in his native land, and especially among London society. The highlights of Douglas's time in Britain, the honours notwithstanding, were a visit to Glasgow in the autumn of 1828 to renew his acquaintance with Hooker (and to teach the young Joseph Hooker, who had been born in 1817, how the native Americans caught fish), and a meeting with his fellow traveller Archibald Menzies in London a little later. He was also pleased to be asked to advise the Colonial Office on the appropriate placing of the boundary between Canada and the United States in the north-west. From a British perspective, it is a pity his advice was not followed:

There is not any natural boundary which would give a plea to the American Government to claim this fine country up to the 49th degree. Neither have they priority of discovery either on the Coast or in the Interior. The boundary line ought to extend (from my observations on the spot) from the 'Lake of the Woods' keeping the same parallel to the Rocky Mountains, from thence south on the Eastern Base, to the pass of Lewis and Clark 46 degrees North Latitude and then cross over the dividing side of the continent to the sources of the Solomon [Salmon] River which stream those travellers descended until they came on the Columbia in 46 degrees 37 North latitude 119 degrees West long and from that point to the sea on the Columbia leaving the river open to both powers.[7]

It is intriguing to speculate on the implications if what is now Washington State and some of the territory farther east had become part of Canada; but with the Colonial Office occupied with expansion in South Africa, Australia, and India it is hardly surprising that in the end the boundary settled upon (in 1846, essentially following the 49th parallel) was much more favourable to the United States than the one suggested by Douglas.

The obvious solution for Douglas's disenchantment with London was to send him on another botanizing expedition. At first, the Society prevaricated, reluctant to commit itself to further expense in spite of the commercial success of the previous expedition. But in the end it was agreed, not least thanks to Hooker's efforts, that Douglas should return to the west coast of America, but this time doing most of his collecting in California, in search of different species from those he had found farther north. Douglas had greater ambitions, and wrote to Hooker on 6 August 1829 to tell him that although 'my principal objects are to make known the vegetable treasures of the Interior of California', he intended if possible to 'cross to the opposite shore' and complete his journey by travelling overland through Russia and back to England from east to west.

At that time, Alaska was Russian territory,[8] and the Russians also maintained a base in California to supply their Alaskan settlements, so the plan made a certain political sense, even if it was ambitious even by the standards of Douglas's previous exploits. Douglas was, though, no longer as capable of such exploits as he had been. One ominous portent was the effort he went to to obtain a Bible with 'good bold legible type' that he would be able to read with his weakened eyesight; a happier acquisition, obtained on a trip to Scone to say farewell to his family, was a Scots terrier, called Billy, who would travel with him when he sailed once again for the Columbia River, this time on board the Hudson's Bay Company ship *Eagle*, on 31 October 1829.

Because so little was known about California, on this trip, in addition to his botanizing, Douglas was asked by the Colonial Office to do some surveying of the region he would visit. He was supplied with good instruments for the task, and the Colonial Office agreed to cover his expenses for the trip, while the Horticultural Society only contributed his specific botanical expenses and his still meagre salary. He even had to ask for an advance of £40 against that salary to purchase his personal equipment. Douglas was taught how to use the surveying instruments by the astronomer Edward Sabine, the brother of Joseph Sabine, at the Royal Greenwich Observatory; he would study the mathematical techniques involved, and practise with the instruments on the voyage out, turning himself into a competent surveyor. An impressive achievement for a man who had been virtually unteachable as a schoolchild! Perhaps the best thing about Douglas's new status as a surveyor for the government was that he carried letters from the Colonial Office requiring all Royal Navy ships in the region to provide him with 'such facilities as they may have in their power to grant him'.

Although many of Douglas's own letters home from what proved to be his last expedition survive and give us an outline of his travels from

1829 until his death five years later, his journals and diary covering most of this period were lost. The most complete account of his adventures during this period can be found in *Douglas of the Fir*, where A. G. Harvey reconstructs the story from those letters and accounts by people who met Douglas on his travels. We shall only sketch in the bare outline here.

En route to the Columbia River, the *Eagle* called at Honolulu, where Douglas took the opportunity to botanize, climb Mauna Parii, and do some surveying. He became intrigued by the botany of the Hawaiian islands, and determined to return there for a longer visit if he could. The ship arrived at its North American destination on 3 June 1830, and although Douglas received a warm welcome from his old friends at Fort Vancouver, one of the newer residents described him as a 'florid partially bald-headed Scotsman of medium stature and gentlemanly address about forty-eight years of age'. In fact, Douglas was just 31; this is one of the clearest indications we have of how much he had suffered for his work.

It would be five months before Douglas could obtain a passage south to California, and he spent the time botanizing in the northwest, sending back several chests full of seeds to Hooker and to his colleagues in London. These included *Pinus nobilis*, the Noble Fir, which was later renamed *Abies procera*, one of the Silver Firs. It became very popular as a Christmas tree, especially in Germany and Holland;[9] in the 1830s single plants of the variety were sold to Fellows of the Horticultural Society for as much as 20 guineas, which again puts Douglas's salary of less than £100 a year in an interesting perspective.

Later in the summer, the entire region was swept by a killing fever, probably influenza, which wiped out entire villages of the native population and took the lives of twenty-four of the Company men at Fort Vancouver:

The houses are empty, and flocks of famished dogs are howling about, while the dead bodies lie strewed in every direction on the sands of the river. I am one of the very few persons among the Hudson's Bay Company people who have stood it, and sometimes I think, even I have got a great shake, and can hardly consider myself out of danger.

But he did survive, and in November was able to head south as a passenger in the Company brig *Dryad*, arriving at Monterey, in California, on 22 December. This far south, it was possible to explore and botanize even in winter; but to Douglas's frustration the Mexican Governor of the region was suspicious of his motives, just as the Dutch authorities had been suspicious of Masson's motives in South Africa in the 1780s, and refused to grant him a passport to travel into the interior until 20 April 1831.[10] He spent the time improving his Spanish and botanizing locally, discovering among other things the 'Baby Blue Eyes', *Nemophila menziesii*, which is now a popular garden flower.

In May, Douglas set off south to Santa Barbara, staying at Catholic missions on the way. He found the priests friendly and hospitable, and saw that they did good work among the natives, in spite of what he regarded as the errors of their faith:

Their errors are the errors of their profession, and I thus make bold to say so, having had reason to know the individuals in question are honourable exceptions to priests in general. I am no friend to Catholicism, still I should desire to maintain my own opinion without hurting the feelings of others.

Would that there were more people who felt that way about their religious beliefs!

After his trip south, Douglas headed north from Monterey to San Francisco and the Mount Diablo area, then on to the Russian settlement, Fort Ross, in the region still known as the Russian River. There, he met the farmers who grew crops to supply the settlers in Alaska, and found them 'a set of people whose whole aim is to make you happy'. Although 200 miles north of Monterey, this still left him some

300 miles away from the farthest south he had travelled from Fort Vancouver on his previous expedition.

Writing home from Monterey in August, Douglas commented on the heat and lack of rainfall of the climate, but mentioned that this was alleviated by the heavy night-time dews which made it possible for life to survive. 'It is the land of the vine, the olive, the fig, the banana', he enthused. 'The wine is excellent, indeed, that word is too small for it; for it is very excellent.' But the glare of the Sun did his eyesight no good. More ominously, to Hooker he apologized for any errors in his handwritten letters for: 'I can never read what I write, so do pardon my blunders and if you can fathom what I wish to say I am for once happy... tell Joseph I caught two fine trout yesterday, twenty seven pounds each.'

Douglas was now ready to head back to Fort Vancouver, but had to wait for a ship on which he could hitch a ride. In the winter, he was busy cataloguing his material and packing it to be sent back to England, but in January he was conscripted into a 'Company of Foreigners' raised to help keep the peace at a time when there were uprisings against the Mexican rulers of California. It's hard to see what use the half-blind Douglas would have been in the militia, but he seems to have managed to avoid any serious military duties by heading off to the Santa Lucia Mountains, where he found the Monterey Pine, *Pinus radiata*, which became a staple of the timber trade around the world. Altogether, his botanizing in California was as successful as his botanizing in the north-west, and the Horticultural Society had trouble coping with the vast quantities of material he sent back.

Douglas also found gold, some seventeen or eighteen years before the California Gold Rush of 1849. When he got back to Fort Vancouver, he mentioned that in one location he had found flakes of gold in the dirt clinging to the roots of plants he had gathered, and had put together enough of this to melt down and have made into a little seal[11] to hang on his watch chain. But he left no written record of the discovery—perhaps it was in the lost journals—and it is intriguing to speculate how history might have been changed if he had kicked up more of a fuss about it.

Douglas eventually managed to obtain passage on a ship sailing to Honolulu, where he arrived on 7 September 1832. While he was there, he learned that Sabine had been forced to resign his post as Secretary of the Horticultural Society, having overspent their budget to the tune of £3,000 (somehow, you have to admire such an achievement!) Out of personal loyalty to Sabine, who had given him his big break back in 1823, Douglas promptly sent off a letter resigning his own post with the Society, and, now regarding himself as a free agent, sent all of his later specimens to Hooker alone. He soon found passage in an American ship bound for the Columbia River, and arrived at Fort Vancouver on 14 October. This was less than two months after leaving Monterey, having crossed half the Pacific, and a little less than sixty years since the success of Cook's voyage opened up the Pacific to routine travel by Europeans. As Douglas put it, 'what would have been thought [of such an achievement] forty years ago?'

After another winter at the rapidly growing settlement of Fort Vancouver, where he kept himself occupied making astronomical ob-servations, which he sent back to Edward Sabine, and some surveying when the weather eased, Douglas started to put in to action his plan to travel home via Alaska and Siberia. Before he left London, he had obtained enthusiastic approval for the idea from the Russian Governor of Alaska,[12] and he set off for the coastal community of Sitka, in what is now British Columbia, on 20 March 1833. From there, he could take a boat to Otosk, in Siberia. But the omens were not good. Another bout of fever struck the settlement just before he left, and although once again Douglas survived, his health was failing. Apart from frequent bouts of rheumatism, he was now literally more than half blind, having lost the sight of his right eye entirely while the left gave him blurred vision at best. He was supposed to wear purple-tinted glasses to help what remained of his vision, but did so only reluctantly, 'as every object, plant and all, is thus rendered of the same colour'.

Once again, the first stage of Douglas's journey was with the eastbound Hudson's Bay Express, which he left at Fort Okanogan to head north with a group of traders styled the New Caledonia Brigade. It took two and a half months of hard travelling, mostly following the courses of the Fraser, Quesnel, Nechaco, and Stuart Rivers, before trekking overland for the last stage of the journey, to reach Fort St James, more than 1,100 miles from Fort Vancouver. It was already 6 June, and a further 800 miles of largely uncharted country lay between Fort St James and Sitka.

Even Douglas realized that he had bitten off more than he could chew, and would have to turn back. It was on the return journey, travelling down the Fraser River in a birchbark canoe with his servant, a man called Johnson, and the terrier, Billy, that disaster struck. The canoe was overturned in rapids, and Douglas was trapped in the water, swirled around in whirlpools and swept downstream, for an hour and forty minutes before scrambling ashore. Johnson and Billy also survived, and Douglas was able to recover from the river scientific instruments and his astronomical notes. But he lost all his food, spare clothing, and blankets, together with more than four hundred plant specimens and, worst of all from our perspective, his journal. Having replaced the canoe and provisions at the nearby post of Fort George,[13] which they had left not long before the disaster, Douglas, Johnson, and Billy had a relatively easy time on the remainder of their journey south to Fort Vancouver, where they arrived in August. Describing the fruitless journey north in a letter to Hooker, Douglas wrote:

I cannot detail to you the labour and anxiety this occasioned me, both in body and mind, to say nothing of the hardships and sufferings I endured. Still I reflect, with pleasure, that no lives were sacrificed. This disastrous occurrence has much broken my strength and spirits. Such are the not infrequent disasters attending such undertakings. On the whole I have been fortunate, for considering the nature and extent of the Country

I have passed over (now 8 years here) and the circumstances under which I travelled my accidents have been few.

But Douglas soon regained his enthusiasm, not least since two young doctors, protégés of Hooker, had arrived in Fort Vancouver to tackle the recurring fever problem. William Tolmie and Meredith Gairdner were both keen botanists, as you might expect of Hooker's students, and also enjoyed mountaineering. In their company, Douglas made the most of his remaining time around the Columbia River, before setting out for warmer climes on what would be his last adventure.

Ever since his visit to Honolulu on the way out from England, Douglas had hankered after a longer excursion among what were then still known as the Sandwich Islands. In order to get there, he had to leave on 18 October on the *Dryad* for San Francisco, where they arrived on 4 November. Storms prevented the little ship leaving California until 28 November, but after a rough crossing of the Pacific she finally arrived in Honolulu on 23 December. There, they stayed for a few days over Christmas before moving on to Hawaii, where Douglas landed on 2 January 1834, eager to botanize and climb mountains.

For this trip, we once again have a detailed journal, plus several letters to Hooker, describing his experiences. Douglas's first target was the highest mountain in the Hawaiian chain, Mauna Kea, which rises 4,205 metres above sea level, and is today the home of one of the great astronomical observatories, with a variety of telescopes near its summit. Douglas stayed with an American missionary, Joseph Goodrich, who was also a keen geologist and had climbed the mountain several times. With his help, Douglas hired the necessary guides and porters, but as usual insisted on carrying his scientific instruments (weighing about 60 pounds, or 27 kilos) himself on the twenty-seven mile (43 km) trek. The ascent took four days, and at the summit he was nearly overcome by the volcanic gases:

The great dryness of the air is evident to the senses, Walking with my trousers rolled up to my knees, and without shoes, I did not know there were holes in my stockings till I was apprised of them by the scorching heat and pain in my feet, which continued throughout the day; the skin also peeling off my face. While on the summit I experienced violent head ache, and my eyes became blood shot, accompanied with stiffness in the lids.

Pretty much just another day at the office by Douglas's standards.

His next target was Mauna Kilauea, at 4,000 meters, an active volcano where at the summit crater: 'The nearly full moon rose in a cloudless sky and shed her silvery brightness on the fiery lake roaring and boiling in fearful majesty, the spectacle became so commanding that I lost a fine night for making astronomical observations, but gazing at the volcano.' In spite of his experiences on Mauna Kea, Douglas decided to take a closer look at the crater, descending into it and (this time wearing shoes!) walking over a crust of solidified lava at the edge of the molten lake:

The thermometer, held in the hand five feet from the ground indicated a temperature of 89F...on the lava if in Sun 115F...I remained on the rim of the crater for upwards of two hours and suffered from an intense headache, my tongue parched...the intense heat corroded my shoes so much they barely protected my feet from the hot lava.

All that was left now in the way of mountaineering was to climb Mauna Loa, a 4,169-metre-high peak which Douglas reached on 29 January, having climbed all three mountains in a single calendar month.[14] As usual, he had pushed himself to exhaustion in the process, and caused further damage to his one functioning eye. This was virtually the end of Douglas's adventuring, and in April he went back to Honolulu, planning a quiet stay while waiting for a ship that could take him back to England.

Over the next few weeks Douglas became friendly with a local chaplain, John Diell, who worked at the seamen's mission. With his strength restored by the rest in Honolulu, Douglas, restless as ever, offered to take Diell over to Hawaii to climb Mauna Kilauea, but on the boat trip Diell stopped off to visit the island of Molokai. Douglas, his dog Billy, and Diell's servant landed at the northern tip of Hawaii, planning to walk the ninety-odd miles (145 km) to the town of Hilo (then known as Byron's Bay), the jumping-off point for the planned ascent, where they would meet up again with Diell. Ninety miles was a stroll in the park for Douglas and Billy, but the servant soon gave up and left them to carry on without him. On the morning of 12 July, within a month of his thirty-fifth birthday, Douglas and Billy met up with a tough character called Ned Gurney, who subsisted by trapping feral cattle in pits that he dug, selling the meat and other products to visiting ships.

Gurney was in Hawaii partly as a result of the Cook voyage and Joseph Banks's subsequent influence on government policy. He was a convicted thief who had been transported to Australia at the age of 19 in 1818, but had turned up in the Sandwich Islands in 1822, having either escaped or (less likely) been pardoned. He later reported to the authorities that he had given Douglas breakfast and directions for the next stage of his journey, taking care to warn him of the pits he had dug just off the track a little farther along the way towards Byron's Bay. He last saw Douglas at about 10 a.m.; around noon, two natives found Douglas's mangled body in one of the pits, together with an angry but still very much living bull. Billy was sitting next to Douglas's pack by the side of the track, not far away.

The most likely reason for the tragedy is that Douglas, ever curious but almost blind, had heard the bellowing of the trapped bull, gone to the edge of the pit to investigate, missed his footing and fallen in to meet his fate. There were inevitably, given the lack of witnesses and human love of a mystery, suggestions that he had been murdered, based on the fact that Gurney was a convicted criminal and a rumour that Douglas had been carrying a large sum of money. But both his chronometers were still on his body, together with a small amount of cash, and this dramatic interpretation of the tragedy seems rather far-fetched.

Douglas was buried on Hawaii; Billy was sent home to an honourable retirement, together with the more valuable scientific instruments, astronomical and other observations, and the last collections of botanical specimens made by David Douglas. He was arguably the greatest botanical explorer/collector of them all, although in many ways he was also a transitional figure. Before Douglas, explorers such as Banks and Masson had operated largely as official representatives of the Government (or the king), usually with the Royal Society, which was specifically not interested in commercial profit, also involved. Douglas represented a learned society of a different kind, one that was also very interested in the commercial possibilities; he would never have been sent out if there had been no prospect of making money from his finds. But after Douglas there would come the great age of commercial exploitation of the flora of the world. To be sure, as we shall see, there would still be botanists whose primary motive in seeking new species was scientific; but there would also be those whose paymasters held no scientific brief and were straightforwardly commercial in their aims. Two brothers from Cornwall, a county whose wealthy coastal estates feature many Monterey Pines, and their employers became the archetypal examples of this breed.

IN THE GARDEN

The legacy of David Douglas has changed the shape of forests, country estates, and to a lesser extent private gardens. His introductions became expensive status symbols for the upper and rising middle-class landowners of Victorian Britain from garden features to the pinetum. *Pinus radiata*, *Pinus ponderosa*, and *Pinus lambetiana* are all conifers introduced by Douglas. *Abies grandis*, the world's tallest Fir tree which grows profusely in North America, has leaves which smell of tangerines when they are crushed. The Douglas-fir, one of the fastest growing trees in the world, the Sitka Spruce, and the Monterey Pine formed the foundation of the North American forestry industry. *Umbellaria californica* (California Laurel), *Arbutus menziessii* (Strawberry Tree), *Garrya elliptica* (Silk Tassel or Fever Bush), and *Mahonia aquifolium* add beauty to woodland estates, parks, and suburban gardens.

David Douglas also brought us many beautiful flowering plants including *Clarkia*, *Penstemons*, Lupins, *Liatris*, and Lilies.

In many gardens in Britain the prettily pink but strangely smelling Flowering Currant (*Ribes sanguineum*) is a real sign of spring.

5

WILLIAM LOBB

(1809–1864)

and

THOMAS LOBB

(1817–1894)

A LTHOUGH THE BROTHERS who did the collecting described in this chapter came from Cornwall, the botanical connection with Scotland was maintained through their employers, the Veitch family, who ran the greatest commercial horticultural nursery of the nineteenth century. Part of their commercial success was due to their expansionist policy of employing their own plant hunters, whose global explorations were designed to discover and introduce into Britain plants that could be sold as a valuable commodity, not just for the interest of botanical science. These nurserymen (and eventually, one nurserywoman) were descended from John Veitch, who headed south by sea from Edinburgh to London at the age of 16, in 1768—the year Cook and Banks set sail in the *Endeavour*. John was the son of a gardener, Thomas Veitch, who worked for Sir William Scott, at Ancrum House in the county of Roxburgh. John already had the basics of a sound Scottish education behind him, and a two-year apprenticeship in a tree nursery. But like David Douglas, he could have expected to rise no higher than head gardener on a country estate, if he hadn't struck lucky with his eventual employer.

Veitch took up a further apprenticeship with the Vineyard Nursery, which occupied three acres of land in Hammersmith, then still a village outside London, on the main road west to Bath and beyond. He worked under James Lee, a fellow Scot from the border region, who after two years recommended the young man to Sir Thomas Acland, who was building a new house in Devon and needed a gardener to lay out his grounds and plan the necessary tree planting to create a country park. Sir Thomas had the good sense to send his new gardener to visit other west country estates before starting work, including one then being laid out by Lancelot Brown (1716–83), who earned the nickname 'Capability Brown' not just from his skill at meeting the requirements of rich landowners like Sir Thomas, but because his usual first response on seeing a property was that it had 'capability for improvement'. It was Brown, more than anyone, who established the English tradition of a naturalistic style of landscaping in preference to more formal (and more expensive to maintain) gardens.

His head full of new ideas, Veitch set to work on the landscaping. Sir Thomas originally intended, when the landscaping was complete, to have a grand new house built for him in the grounds at Killerton, leaving his other properties (he had estates in Somerset and North Devon, as well as the Killerton estate in South Devon) to his son, John. All those plans were thrown into confusion by the rebellion of the American colonies in 1776. John Acland, fighting as a Major with the British forces in Canada, was wounded and captured by the rebels. Until he could be brought back home, Sir Thomas was too preoccupied to think about the new house; after John returned to England and his wife gave birth to a son there was no time to carry through the original grand design, and a less extravagant 'temporary' house was thrown up between July 1778 and July 1779. It still stands, and both the house and the gardens are now owned by the National Trust.

Sadly, though, Sir Thomas had to change his plans again. In November 1778, John Acland had died of a chill, at the age of 34, and Sir Thomas would have to keep a close eye on all his properties until his grandson came of age. He would need help with the task, and appointed John Veitch, who had proved his abilities over the previous nine years, to be Head Steward on all the Acland estates. In a gesture of gratitude for everything Veitch had done and would be doing, Sir Thomas also gave him the tenure for life of enough land on the Killerton estate (at the tiny village of Budlake) to develop his own tree nursery, and the money to get the project started.

With his future secured, John paid his first visit to Scotland in twelve years. The extended visit included work—ordering trees for the Killerton estate—but also gave time to visit his family, and to marry. He returned to Budlake with his bride, Anna, who over the next decade produced six children—Mary, Margaret, John, Thomas, Anna, and James. Sir Thomas died in 1785, and just a few weeks later his grandson and heir also died. The estates were inherited (along with the baronetcy which gave Sir Thomas his title) by a second son, another Thomas, a wastrel who had been estranged from his father and had huge debts which could only be paid by selling off some of his inheritance. Fortunately, this sale did not include Killerton.

The new Sir Thomas had no interest in Killerton, and lived on the estate in Somerset. When he too died, in 1794, everything passed to his son, another Thomas, who was only 7 and took no part in running the properties until he came of age in 1808. For all that time, although John Veitch carried out his duties as steward diligently, he was left with enough time free to develop his own tree nursery and build up both a good trade and an excellent reputation.

Veitch suffered a personal tragedy when his own eldest son, John, was killed serving with the Royal Navy at the Battle of Trafalgar in

1805; but by the time the latest Sir Thomas came into his inheritance Veitch was 56 and the tree nursery was so successful that it was being run full time by his younger sons Thomas (now 21) and James (15). This was just as well, as the new Sir Thomas Acland would take up a lot more of John's time. Sir Thomas was 21 in March 1808, got married a month later to Lydia Hoare, a member of the famous banking family, and moved into the house at Killerton which had been empty for so long, full of plans for improving the estate.

There were other changes over the next few years. John's wife, Anna, died of tuberculosis in 1809, and three years later the daughter named after her, who had married a doctor from Hull, died from complications following the birth of her second child. The two infants, both boys, were left with their father, William Betty, in Hull; but only after James Veitch had promised his dying sister that he would look after their interests. James himself married a local girl, Mary Tosswill, who produced six surviving children—James Junior, John, Thomas, William, Robert, and Anna—in quick succession. At least one other baby, Theresa (the twin of William) died at birth. The siblings were among the beneficiaries of one of the first improvements that the new baronet introduced to the village, a new school built in 1809.

While Thomas Veitch followed in his father's footsteps raising trees for landscaping estates or to provide fruit, James became more interested in flowering plants, especially the exotic varieties being raised in the hothouses (then often referred to as 'stove houses') of the gentry. These stove houses were the pride of many great houses; the exotic plants, flowers, and fruits grown in them were the centre of all great dinners held in the house, where they were proudly displayed as signs of the owner's fashionability and wealth. It was James who took over the day-to-day running of the nursery, now known as John Veitch & Sons, and in 1825 he became a Fellow of the Horticultural Society. As we have seen, this was at that time the leading organization in the world for collecting exotic plants from far-flung places and distributing them to the gardeners of Britain and Europe. David Douglas was already on his first trip to the Pacific Northwest when James Veitch became a Fellow of the Society.

In 1827, James's wife Mary died (like his mother, of tuberculosis). His eldest son, James Junior, was only 12, and Mary's sister, Rebecca, came to live with the family as housekeeper to look after the six children. Two years later, she married James, and almost immediately their household was increased, not by her own children but by the addition of James's nephews. The two sons of his sister Anna seem to have been the victims of a stepmother so cruel she could have stepped out of the pages of a melodrama. She had beaten the boys, starved them, and treated them so badly that she was eventually sent to prison; their father, the doctor William Betty, had then died penniless, leaving the boys without a home. So the brothers, William and Thomas Betty, were taken in by their uncle and his second wife. The home they joined was one based on the same principles of hard work and evangelical Christianity that James Veitch applied to the nursery (which *never* opened on a Sunday), with education a high priority for all the boys; girls were not then thought to need much education. But although James was old-fashioned in those regards, when it came to plants he was always looking to the future.

The Veitch business had the tenure of the nursery at Budlake only for the lifetime of old John Veitch, but by 1830 the business was so successful that the family were able to purchase twenty-five acres of land in Exeter, seven miles away, for £50,000—some indication of how far John Veitch had progressed since his days as an apprentice on 8 shillings a week. The astute purchase gave them a site at Mount Radford near the middle of the rapidly expanding city, where no landlord would be able to eject them to make way for new housing. And they would be smack in the middle of their new customers, not the old landed gentry but the new wealthy middle class that was building avenues of houses with large gardens in which they could try to put one over on the neighbours with bigger and better displays of flowerbeds and hothouses filled with exotica. James set up the new nursery at Mount Radford, where he had a new house built for his large family, while his brother Thomas and father John kept the tree nursery at Budlake. Looking to the future, James sent his eldest son James Junior, now 15, to train in London, initially at a nursery in Vauxhall and then with William Rollison of Tooting, a nurseryman specializing in orchids. For more immediate help with developing the nursery in Exeter, which would be ready to open in 1832, he took on new staff, including a 13-year-old apprentice, Thomas Lobb, from Cornwall. Eventually, Lobb and his brother, William, would become the collectors that took the success of the Veitch nurseries to new heights.

Thomas was, in fact, the younger of the two brothers, who also had several other siblings. Their father, John Lobb, probably worked on the Pencarrow estate owned by Sir Arscott Molesworth, who died in 1823, and then by his son, Sir William Molesworth. John married a Jane Rowe at Bodmin in 1803, and the parish records reveal that he was educated enough to be able to sign his name in the register, although his wife could only make her mark. The marriage produced eight children (one of whom died in infancy) including William, born on 12 March 1809, and Thomas, born on 5 November 1817. They were all baptized in the parish church at Egloshayle, and the fact that the family was living in a cottage in the hamlet of Lane End (just a farm and seven cottages) on the Pencarrow estate is a clear sign that John Lobb was working on the estate. The records give his occupation as carpenter.

Very little is known about the early life of the Lobb brothers, but it is most likely that they attended the local parish school (that is, the boys' school; girls were taught separately) where one teacher was responsible for all ages in a single classroom. Some rather fanciful accounts suggest that the two boys received a good basic education at a school in the town of Wadebridge up to the age of 12; but there is no evidence to support this. Just one letter from each of the Lobb brothers survives today, in the archives at Kew. Both were written to

Sir William Hooker, as the Director of the Royal Botanical Gardens, in the 1850s, and both show a straightforward ease with writing that indicates a decent basic education somewhere along the line, but exactly where remains a mystery.

By 1841, when a census was carried out, the family had moved to Perran Wharf, in the parish of Parranarworthal, between Truro and Falmouth. Although there is no record of when the move took place, this gave the boys an opportunity to work in the stove houses at the estate of Carclew, owned by Sir Charles Lemon, who inherited the property in 1824. Sir Charles was a keen plant collector with widespread contacts; from 1830 (just too late to benefit Thomas Lobb) to 1853 he employed as head gardener William Booth, well known to his peers as an expert on camellias and frequent contributor to horticultural journals. The likelihood is that Thomas Lobb, at least, was recommended to James Veitch by Sir Charles Lemon, and worked for him for many years. There is more confusion about what William Lobb was up to between 1830 and 1840. One plausible suggestion is that William worked at the Veitch nurseries (we don't know which one) briefly, before returning to Cornwall in 1837 to work in the gardens of Bochym Manor, near Helston. Or he may have stayed in Cornwall all the time, working both at Bochym Manor and in other gardens. What we do know for sure is that William was not actually employed by the Veitch nurseries, although he may have been known to James Veitch by then, in 1840, which is where we shall pick up the threads of the careers of himself and his brother, after bringing the Veitch story up to that date.

From the outset, the Mount Radford Nursery was James Veitch's responsibility while his brother Thomas stayed at Budlake. Exactly what happened to Thomas is something of a mystery. He never married, and since no mention of him was made in his father's will (old John Veitch died in 1839) the presumption is that he died before John. Long before that, though, with the typical Veitch skill at forward planning, they had transferred most of their stock of young trees from the borrowed land at Budlake to rented land nearby. But James was increasingly looking farther afield.

As a Fellow of the Horticultural Society, James was already benefiting from the supply of seed sent (or brought) back to England by collectors such as David Douglas. He also established his own network of contacts overseas, and through his connection with the Evangelical Christian movement he was in touch with missionaries who were more than happy to send back specimens from the remote regions that they visited. The coronation of Queen Victoria in 1837 came, with hindsight, to symbolize a period of expansion of the British Empire and the rise of a scientific industrial technology. In such heady times, it is hardly surprising that a man like James Veitch would want to have more control over the importing of new plants from abroad, and would decide to send his own collectors, responsible to nobody but himself, out into the field. Part of the phenomenon of the rise of the affluent middle class in Britain was a seemingly insatiable demand for new orchids—a demand which was to increase with the growth of new wealth and the construction of conservatories in large houses and middle-class villas. In James Junior, who had now completed a first-class training, the Veitch nurseries had just the person to cultivate such exotica. In 1837, when he was 22, James Junior married Harriet Gould, the daughter of a local farmer, and they settled in a house near the Exeter nursery, where their son John Gould Veitch (always known as 'John Gould', just as his father was always 'James Junior') was born in 1839. Soon afterwards, old John Veitch died at the age of 87. The old era had gone, the future of the dynasty was assured, and the following year James Veitch sent his first collector out into the world.

During the 1830s, as the nursery in Exeter became established as a smooth-running operation that no longer needed his daily supervision, James took every opportunity to visit the Horticultural Society's gardens in Chiswick, in the west of London, to see the latest specimens and get the latest news.[1] So he was one of the inner circle of Fellows who had early access to the discoveries made by Douglas and other collectors. As well as the contacts which the Veitch family maintained with William Hooker, James established another significant relationship with John Lindley (1799–1865), one of Joseph Banks's many protégés, who was Professor of Botany at University College, London, and successively Assistant Secretary and then Vice Secretary of the Horticultural Society, where he became the world's leading orchid expert. When Hooker became Director of the Royal Botanical Gardens in 1841, James effectively had a foot in both of the main botanical camps in London. Although there was some rivalry between the two camps, Hooker and Lindley were good friends, in spite of Lindley's initial hopes that he might have become the Director at Kew himself.

In 1840, the year before Hooker took over at Kew, he received a letter from James Veitch asking for information about sending a collector of his own out into the field. Frustratingly, the archives of the Veitch family were later destroyed, so our knowledge of how James came up with the plan is sketchy, to say the least; all we have to go on, as for the entire story of the collecting activities of the Lobb brothers, are the surviving parts of correspondence in the archives of the people, such as Hooker, that the Veitches and their collectors wrote to. Clearly, though, by August 1840, when James wrote to Hooker, the plan was already well formed. He refers to 'an application from a young man [William Lobb, actually then 31] desirous of going out as a Collector... either to Guatemala, Mexico, Chile or Peru', and says he is 'rather inclined to send him'. James asked Hooker about the likely cost of such an expedition, and the best place to send his collector, bearing in mind that 'we are growers of orchidaceous plants'. Significantly, he added that his aim was to send out a man who understood 'what to collect for a nurseryman rather than one who only appraised plants with a Botanist's ego'. He asked Hooker about the clothing and equipment his collector would need, what books and articles he should take with him, the best kind of paper for preserving dried specimens, the best time of year to travel, and even what kind of presents to give to 'Persons in Official situations to smooth the

Collector's way'. In all these areas, he told Sir William, 'your advice will be very acceptable'. Alas, no copy of Hooker's reply survives.

It is a moot point how much of the idea for the South American expedition was William Lobb's, and how much James Veitch already had in mind when he received Lobb's 'application'. What is certain is that in 1840 William was working in the gardens of Scorrier House, near the Cornish port of Falmouth, and had established a reputation not only as a competent gardener but as a keen amateur botanist whose collections had won prizes at county level. He had met sailors who told him tales of their journeys to exotic lands, and developed a longing to travel himself, which his brother was well aware of. Almost certainly, James Veitch discussed the possibility of sending out his own collector with his staff at the Exeter nursery, and 22-year-old Thomas Lobb, perhaps after turning down the opportunity himself, then suggested that his elder brother might be just the man for the job.

Once everything was agreed between James Veitch and William Lobb, James, always wary of letting rivals know his plans, wrote again to Hooker, urging that 'having decided on sending out a Collector, we would thank you not to name him' to anyone else, and confirming that although the expedition 'will be solely on our own account as regards plants and seeds', in return for all the advice and help Hooker had given 'we shall be most happy to afford every facility for his collecting for you such dried specimens as you require'. Lobb was duly booked on the *Seagull*, sailing for Rio de Janeiro on 7 November 1840 (two days after his brother's 23rd birthday). He had an allowance of £400 a year to draw on, and although largely left to his own initiative, was urged in particular to send back seed of the Monkey Puzzle tree (then known as *Araucaria imbricata*, now as *Araucaria araucana*),[2] whose seed had first been sent back to England from South America by Archibald Menzies in 1795. Only five saplings of the species had been introduced to England before Lobb's visit; he saw its commercial potential and sent back large quantities of seed to Veitch. As well as its value to gardeners, the Monkey Puzzle is of special interest to botanists as the only conifer from the Southern Hemisphere that will grow big enough to make timber in western Europe.

Neither William Lobb nor his brother Thomas kept journals of their travels, and their letters to the Veitch nurseries were lost when the archive was destroyed. So essentially all we know about their expeditions comes from the letters James wrote to third parties (in particular, Hooker) reporting on their progress at second hand. The rest has to be left to the imagination, aided by what we know of the hardships experienced by collectors such as David Douglas. It was March 1841 when the first package arrived from William, the fruits of a few weeks collecting in the Organ Mountains near Rio. Several of the specimens would prove commercially successful, including the shrub *Hindsia violacea*,[3] but James commented only that 'we are so far pleased with him', while waiting to see if the plants could be cultivated successfully in his hothouses.

Another package was delivered in May, in rather poor condition, and then nothing until January 1842. After leaving Rio, William had rejected the possibility of travelling round Cape Horn by ship, and had chosen the almost equally hazardous option of crossing the Andes by mule, over the Upsallata Pass and into Chile. In places the snow was five feet deep, and in the intense cold, sheltering only in rough huts by the side of the track, William had been taken ill and suffered several bouts of fever—possibly malaria contracted on his collecting in Brazil. But none of this prevented him from gathering thousands of seeds of the Monkey Puzzle, mostly by shooting the cones from the trees so that they would fall to be gathered by his porters. He then took the sacks full of seed to Valparaiso and put them on a ship for England, along with other specimens. He sent back more than three thousand seeds in this shipment alone, which Veitch sold at £10 per hundred. Originally 'discovered' on Captain Cook's second voyage (1772–5), the Monkey Puzzle had been introduced into cultivation In Britain in 1793; its exotic form led to huge demand from land and garden owners eager for novelty. From Valparaiso William travelled south by steamer, then inland towards the mountains, but failed to reach the snowline after an altercation with his porters. As James Veitch wrote to Hooker, 'I am *told* he is sometimes a little quick in temper'. With a modest collection of plants from the trip he sent back news that he now intended to sail from Chile north to the port of Lima, in Peru; but he was suffering from illness and exhaustion resulting from his arduous travelling, and nothing more was heard from him for some time. Tyler Whittle's assessment of all this is that 'in the pursuit of plants, [William Lobb] risked his personal safety to the point of lunacy', and it is easy to concur.

This was of no immediate importance to James and James Junior,[4] who throughout 1842 were busy raising the fruits of William Lobb's labour from seed. The successes far outweighed the failures, and by May the Exeter nursery was already offering the first examples for sale. By the summer, new arrivals were jostling for space in the hothouses, and James was able to reject all except the very best for propagation; several of the introductions, including *Hindsia violacea*, which has clusters of deep blue flowers and was a big hit with the Victorians, were awarded Silver Medals by the Horticultural Society. The Monkey Puzzle was also every bit as successful, and profitable, as James had hoped, although naturally it took longer to raise trees than hothouse flowers.

All of this made an impression on one of James Veitch's gardeners. By early 1843, Thomas Lobb, now 25 and having seen first hand what his brother had achieved, was itching to follow in his footsteps—at least, metaphorically. He had no wish to go to South America, not least since he had developed a passion for orchids, and the place to discover 'new' orchids was the Far East. It was time for James to seek Hooker's advice again, this time asking his 'opinion of Java as a place for a Collector'. Hooker's response was encouraging, and Thomas Lobb duly signed a contract with James Veitch & Son, which has survived. It spells out in no uncertain terms that he is 'to collect for the said James Veitch & Son and for no other person' and states that although his destination is intended to be China 'should that country be open to admit a botanical collector', he should use his own discretion as to what part of China to visit; if China was closed to him, 'the island of Java appearing to offer the greatest advantages to a botanical collector...he is directed to proceed thither'. Thomas sailed from Portsmouth in January 1843, giving James Veitch & Son two botanical collectors in the field at the same time, on opposite sides of the globe. They were payroll treasure seekers sent to discover and bring back plants, especially orchids, which could be sold by their employers at tremendous commercial gain. One surviving *Vanda caerulea*, a beautiful blue epiphytic orchid brought back by Thomas Lobb was sold for the enormous sum of £300.

In some ways, the timing of Thomas Lobb's trip was just wrong. At the end of the 1830s, relations between Britain and the Chinese were at a low ebb, because of local opposition to the British opium trade.[5] The first of the 'Opium Wars' was fought between 1839 and 1842, and although the British emerged triumphant and gained improved trading access to China through designated Treaty Ports under the Treaty of Nanking (now Nanjing), bad feeling lingered and Lobb was refused entry. Just six months later, however, one of the Horticultural Society's collectors, Robert Fortune, was, as we shall see in Chapter 6, allowed limited access to the country—and took advantage of this to travel well beyond the limits officially set. Following his instructions, Lobb moved on to Java, but found that his permit to travel in the Dutch-controlled island had not arrived. It was time to use the discretion allowed for in his contract, and Thomas went ashore at Singapore, heading into the jungle of the Malay peninsula and travelling as far north as the small island of Penang, off the western coast of Malaya. For more than a year, he travelled only with his native porters, keeping no record of his journey and meeting no Europeans (at least, nobody who has left any surviving record of the encounter) so that we are left to imagine the conditions under which he laboured to obtain his first collection of plants. But if we are frustrated by the lack of any record of those months, imagine how James Veitch felt, waiting anxiously on the other side of the world with no news at all from Thomas, who might, for all James knew, have died of a fever.

But at least James had some news of his other collector, Thomas's brother William. In April 1843, James received a lengthy account from William of his adventures in South America, which we know about because James described them in a letter to Hooker. After recovering his strength in Lima, William had continued slowly north to Panama. One of the reasons why so little had been heard from him in the intervening period now became clear. Four cases of plants collected in the lower Andes of Peru had been taken by boat to the port of Guayaquil, in Ecuador. There, William had entrusted the samples to a shipping agent for onward conveying to England, but had himself been evacuated with other Europeans to the island of Puna because of an outbreak of yellow fever. Once it was safe to do so, he had travelled by mule train inland to southern Colombia, gathering more plants with which he sailed from Tumaco to Panama, intending to complete the journey home with this collection himself. But in Panama William learned from the letters he received from James Veitch that the collections he had left in Guayaquil had never arrived in England, and that James hadn't even received any of the letters William had sent from Ecuador. It turned out, prosaically, that he had paid insufficient postage on the letters, but the saga of the missing collection was more depressing.

Gloomily, William sent off his latest collection from Panama and after mulling the setback over, resigned himself to returning south to find out what had gone wrong. Before he could do so, he suffered a bout of dysentery, which can hardly have improved his temper when he got back to Guayaquil to find that the agent had simply forgotten to send the cases on to England. Edward Michel, who was in Guayaquil, wrote a letter home, dated 15 November 1843, which survives in the Kew archive as testimony to the tragedy: '7 boxes of plants...were left by Mr. Lobb at the English Consul House...and were never forwarded...the boxes Mr. Lobb left on his first arrival... when he was last here he found, I believe, that the plants were in an unfit state to be sent forward and they were throw away as useless.'

That wasn't quite true. Ants had destroyed most of the specimens as they lay unnoticed in the warehouse, but William doggedly packed up the rest, sent them off to England, and waited for instructions. Veitch had been delighted with the specimens from Panama, which, he told Hooker, included 'a *clitoria* [butterfly pea] with beautiful azure blue flowers' along with 'a splendid specimen of the evergreen shrub *Befaria* and also seeds of several tropaeolum [nasturtium] and fuchsias'. But James was a hard taskmaster, and was so disappointed with the scrapings of the Peruvian collection that he ordered Lobb to retrace his steps back to the Andes. This took another four months hard travelling, and even when William made it back to England in May 1844, three and a half years after setting out, James told Hooker that 'I was disappointed at hearing William Lobb had left Peru', but acknowledged that he was 'pleased to hear of his safe arrival in England with many fine plants and seeds in good order'. We suspect the safe arrival of the plants and seeds meant more to him than the return of his collector.

The Veitch nursery in Exeter was by now being kept busy by both their collectors. A collection including orchids and pitcher plants had arrived from Thomas Lobb in the severe winter of 1843–4, but in spite of the care Thomas had taken with their packing, by the time they reached the nursery the frost had destroyed many of the plants, tantalizingly close to the safety of the hothouses. But in March 1844 another collection arrived, sent by Thomas from Singapore. This included the first of 'his' orchids to survive the journey, *Cypripedium barbatum* (Lady's Slipper), and many colourful, showy specimens— just right for the Victorian market. It was said that Thomas rarely gave a description of a plant, preferring to let the specimens speak for themselves, but that if he described one as 'very pretty' it was really something special. Many of the plants in this collection were, indeed, 'very pretty'.

By the time some of these specimens were on display, in May 1844, the collector himself had at last been able to work in Java, from where he sent back a huge variety of plants and seeds, and then moved on to Burma before returning home, eventually reaching England late in 1847. By then, William Lobb had already set out on his travels again.

It took William the best part of a year to recover from his exertions in South America, although he kept busy raising some of the specimens he had supplied in the hothouses in Exeter. But in April 1845 he set off again to South America, first revisiting his old haunts around Rio and then travelling by sea round Cape Horn to Valparaiso. After collecting in the Colombian Andes,[6] he journeyed south to Tierra del Fuego, collecting there and on the islands off the south coast of Chile, surveyed by Robert FitzRoy in the *Beagle* less than twenty years before. Although we do not have Lobb's own account of his travels, a little later another of Veitch's collectors, Richard Pearce, gave a dramatic description of the scenery of northern Patagonia:

It is of the most charming description—gently undulating meadows covered with a carpet of short grass, placid lakes reflecting from smooth surface the mountains around, foaming cataracts and gentle rivulets, deep gorges and frightful precipices, over which tumble numerous dark, picturesque water-falls reaching the bottom in a cloud of spray, high rocky pinnacles and lofty peaks, surround one on every side.[7]

One of the plants William Lobb sent back to England, where it was raised for the first time, was *Berberis darwinii*, now the most familiar of the 450 species of Berberis with its clusters of yellow flowers. It had been found by FitzRoy's companion, Charles Darwin, on the island of Chiloe on the second of FitzRoy's voyages in command of the *Beagle*. A report in the *Gardener's World* claimed that 'If Messrs. Veitch had done nothing else towards beautifying our gardens, the introduction of this single species would be enough to earn the gratitude of the whole gardening world'.[8] Happily, William also sent back seeds of the *Fitzroya cupressoides*, so Darwin's old captain was not entirely forgotten.

Although the Veitch nursery was going from strength to strength, in no small measure thanks to the introductions supplied by the Lobb brothers, James's immediate family wasn't faring as well. His daughter Anna died in 1845, and his son William, the one who had really wanted to be an architect, in 1847—both of them, probably, as a result of tuberculosis. Early the following year, William Lobb returned from South America, meeting up with his brother for the first time since 1840. The two of them worked alongside each other at the Exeter nursery for the best part of a year, propagating many of their introductions and gaining an appreciation of just how much their work meant to the gardening community. But neither William nor Thomas had any intention of resting on his laurels, and Thomas sailed again for the Far East on Christmas Day 1848.

Thomas Lobb's port of entry on this expedition was Calcutta, and in March 1849 he set about collecting in north-eastern India, overlapping with the territory already being investigated by William Hooker's son Joseph (see Ch. 9) on behalf of the Royal Botanical Gardens. When Joseph heard that Thomas Lobb was in India, he sent word via his father to James Veitch that Lobb would be welcome to make use of whatever facilities Joseph could offer him, but warned 'I travel as a poor man, and Lobb must not expect great tents and serv'ts'. Lobb was extremely reluctant to take advantage of this offer, probably because he feared that sharing knowledge with Hooker might give away commercially valuable secrets about the locations of exotic plants; but when their paths did cross by chance he must have wondered at Hooker's idea of poverty. Joseph travelled with a couple of dozen servants and his personal valet, carried in a litter while the porters carried the equipment. 'Lobb', he wrote home, 'passed us with his circus'—a ragged handful of men mounted on mules.

From India, Thomas moved on to Sarawak, sending back rhododendrons and the ever-popular pitcher plants, then to the Philippines
and back to India via Burma, where he found more rhododendrons,
including the species which became known as *veitchianum* after the
nurseryman himself. Rhododendrons were becoming eagerly sort
after and could command extremely high prices. Back in India,
Thomas did meet up properly with the Hooker expedition, but
initially at a time when Joseph himself was away in Calcutta. When
the two collectors did get together, three months later, Lobb managed
(the operative word) to make a very poor impression on Hooker, who
wrote in his *Himalayan Journals*:

He would not stay even a day with us . . . he talks very slightly of the plants
and seeds as usual and to judge by what he says he cannot be worth 6d to
Veitch & Co. His plants he says die en route to Calcutta and that it is almost
useless sending roots, bulbs or cuttings straight home from this.

This seems to have been a superbly successful piece of disingenuity on
Lobb's part, keeping all his secrets by making himself out to be
something of a Cornish country bumpkin, lost in the wider world.
If only he had kept a journal!

Among the secrets Thomas kept so well was that he had found a
new source of *Vanda caerulea* (the Blue Orchid) and sent back a load
of the plants to Exeter, where the Veitch nursery was selling cuttings at
up to £10 a time.[9] The flower was first shown at a meeting in London
on 3 December 1850, causing a sensation among the connoisseurs. All
this led to some bitterness from the Hookers; Joseph later complained
that he had been the person who told Thomas Lobb where to find the
Blue Orchid (which seems doubtful) and bemoaned the fact that a
'trader', rather than Kew Gardens, should be making so much money
out of botany. The bitterness was probably fuelled by the knowledge
that most of Hooker's own collection of Blue Orchids failed to survive
the trip back to Britain, and that the Kew gardeners were less adroit at
raising such delicate specimens than the mere traders at Veitch's. The

real point of his complaint was an attempt to obtain better funding and facilities at Kew.

But James Veitch had plenty more on his mind than a squabble about orchids. While Thomas was gathering orchids in India, William had set out on what would prove to be his penultimate expedition, this time to North America. The expedition was a direct result of the craze for conifers that had been stimulated by the introductions of David Douglas. Although it was now nearly twenty years since Douglas had travelled in California, there is a limit to how much seed one man (even Douglas) could send back to England, and with the introduced trees taking a long time to reach maturity and set seed themselves, there was a large unsatisfied demand for the fashionable conifers among Victorian gardeners. Veitch could be certain of commercial success by sending William Lobb to California to collect more seed of the popular species, with the anticipated bonus that he might come across species that Douglas himself had missed.

Lobb sailed for California in 1849, and arrived in San Francisco with the Gold Rush at its height. The harbour and bay were crammed with more than two hundred ships which had arrived in the course of their regular business, but had been abandoned by their crews, who had jumped ship in the hope of striking it rich. In the city itself, two thousand people, mostly men stricken by gold fever, were living in tents. But Lobb was made of more sober stuff, and went south to San Diego and Monterey to go about his botanical business. William's great achievement was to send back to England sacks full of viable seed from many species of pine—exactly what Veitch, and the British gardening public, wanted—in contrast to the way 'scientific' botanists such as Douglas, with their understandably different objectives, sent back smaller quantities of seed, or only herbarium specimens. Later moving north, Lobb travelled as far as the Oregon mountains (probably going north up the coast by ship, then returning overland through northern California) and collected seed from many species known to the gardeners back home, including the Douglas-fir itself, as well as finding several that were not known back home, including the Californian Red Fir (*Abies magnifica*) and the Californian Juniper (*Juniperus californica*).

In 1851, thanks to the initiative of Prince Albert, Victoria's Consort, Britain staged a Great Exhibition in the Crystal Palace, a specially constructed, iron-framed glasshouse, covering four times the area of St Peter's Church in Rome, built in Hyde Park. The Exhibition displayed the achievements of the Victorian industrial age, and wonders from the burgeoning British Empire. Taking advantage of the tide of visitors flooding into London for the Exhibition, many museums and art galleries staged special exhibitions; the Horticultural Society, not to be outdone, held its regular spring show, then at Chiswick, on an even grander scale than usual. The introductions of the Lobb brothers, featuring strongly in the Veitch contribution to the show, were among the most popular attractions, and won a Gold Medal (the Banks Medal) for James Veitch & Son. The collectors responsible for the success of the nursery were still toiling in the field, and neither was expected back for at least a couple of years. But in December 1853, shortly before Christmas, William turned up unexpectedly in Exeter. He had 'discovered' a tree so remarkable that he had cut short his stay in California and hurried home carrying with him as much seed and other samples of this one species as he could.

Of course, there is no sense in which William Lobb actually discovered this tree—even leaving aside the fact that it was already well known to the native Americans before Europeans arrived in California. It's a sign of just how rapidly civilization was developing on the Pacific Coast of North America that although stories of the 'Big Tree' were circulating in San Francisco in 1852, spread by a hunter called A. T. Dowd, who described how he had stumbled upon a grove of enormous trees in the foothills of the Sierra Nevada, Lobb got the details when he attended a meeting of the newly founded California Academy of Sciences in 1853. The Society dates its origins to a meeting of five doctors, a real estate agent, and a school superintendent on 4

April that year; in 1882, one of those doctors, Albert Kellogg, recalled how he had played his part in the story of the Big Tree: 'I, myself, took Mr. Lobb to the California Academy of Sciences, and showed him the first specimens he ever saw... this fact is well known to the old charter members of the Academy, several of whom are still living.'[10] Following Dowd's directions, Lobb hurried to the spot, now famous as the Calaveras Grove. For once, the details survive; what he saw was 'from 80 to 90 trees... all within [a] circuit of a mile, from 250ft to 320ft in height, 10–20ft in diameter'. There was also a recently fallen tree, which made gathering seed easy. It was 'about 300 feet in length, with a diameter, including bark, 29 feet 2 inches, at 5 feet from the ground'.[11]

Lobb knew he had to get the seed of the giant tree home before anyone else, and dropped everything to do so. In fact, a Scottish horticulturalist, John Mathew, had brought a few seeds from the tree home for himself and his friends in the autumn of 1853, but nothing on a commercial scale. The news of the 'new' tree spread like wildfire, and customers clamoured for specimens; within six months of Lobb's return to England, the Veitch nursery was selling seedlings at £3 2s each.

Such a big tree deserved a big name, and John Lindley pressed for it to be called *Wellingtonia gigantea*, in honour of the Duke of Wellington, who had died in 1852. In the Christmas Eve 1853 edition of the *Gardener's Chronicle*, Lindley declaimed that the name was apt because Wellington was 'the greatest of modern heroes, who stands as high above his contemporaries as this Californian tree', conveniently neglecting to mention that the redwood is actually taller than the Big Tree. This infuriated American botanists, who said that an American tree ought to be named after an American hero, and Kellogg proposed the name *Washingtonia gigantea* (he always claimed to have named the tree before Lobb even saw it). In the end, common sense prevailed and the species formally became *Sequoiadendron giganteum* (Giant Sequoia), recognizing both the native Americans

who saw it first and the tree's relationship with *Sequoia sempervirens,*
the California Redwood.[12] Nevertheless, in England the tree is still
sometimes referred to as the Wellingtonia. The Giant Sequoia is the
fastest growing tree in the world, increasing in height by half a metre
or so each year; although the California Redwoods are taller, they
are more slender and not so bulky. By some criteria, Giant Sequoia are
the largest living things on Earth—it depends on whether you regard
the Honey Mushroom (*Armillaria ostoyae*) as a single organism; the
largest known example of this fungus, living a metre below ground,
covers an area of more than two thousand acres of the Malheur
National Forest, in Oregon.

Thomas Lobb also returned to England around this time, to find
the Veitch business taking a big leap forward. In 1852, James Veitch
purchased the site of the long-established Exotic Nursery on the King's
Road in Chelsea, converting it into the 'Royal Exotic Nursery'. This
opened in the spring of 1853, with James Junior in charge of showing
off the best examples of their wares, while the cultivation of new
plants continued to be based in Exeter (there is no evidence, by the
way, that the Veitches had Royal permission for the new name of their
Chelsea nursery!). The nursery was attached to a splendid residence,
Stanley House, which had been built for the Stanley family, from
which came the Earls of Derby. This now became the home of James
Junior and his family.

While the first year of the new nursery proved a roaring success, the
brothers who were ultimately responsible for that success were for the
last time briefly working alongside each other in the hothouses in
Exeter. By the spring of 1854, both of them were ready to travel again,
and in August Thomas was sent on what proved to be a rather
unsatisfactory trip to Java and Borneo, which was curtailed when
political difficulties and civil disturbances made it impossible for him
to travel as he had wished. Although William had not been in the best
of health for some time, he had, as James Veitch said to William
Hooker, 'a sort of restlessness about him … a sort of excitability and

want of confidence'. The evidence suggests that both the symptoms of ill-health and the excitability were the result of syphilis, which William seems to have caught during his time in South America. Not knowing this, James sent him back to California in the spring of 1854, on a three-year contract; but there were no more big discoveries to come from him, just more supplies of seed of the now-familiar conifers. By January 1857, James was telling Hooker that 'Lobb has been ill, his writing appears shaky and I am inclined to think it probable he will soon return'. But he never did.

After the end of his contract with Veitch, William Lobb stayed in California, occasionally sending seeds and specimens back to private collectors in Britain, and even to William Hooker at Kew. The only letter we have in Lobb's own hand, dated 4 February 1858, refers to a larger shipment of seeds and plants, urging that 'should this reach you before the arrival of the Steamer at Southhampton due March 15th probably it would be advisable that some person should see the Cases opened at the customhouse and the contents carefully handled'. James expressed astonishment when he heard the news from Hooker: 'We thought [Lobb] had given up collecting plants, for Californian gold', he wrote.

Although Lobb was out of contract and free to act as he pleased, Veitch was anxious to avoid the precious shipment falling into the hands of any of his competitors, and after some sticky negotiations bought five cases of this material from the Royal Botanical Gardens for £250. They were the last samples William Lobb ever sent back to England. His name appears in various directories as a resident of San Francisco after 1858, and he died there, in St Mary's Hospital, in the spring of 1864. The cause of death was officially given as 'paralysis', a common euphemism at the time for syphilis. This was very much the end of an era, for James Veitch had died almost exactly a year earlier, in May 1863. Thomas Lobb, who long outlived both of them, had meanwhile made one last expedition of his own, again to the Far East.

Like his brother's last expedition, though for different reasons, this too was something of an anticlimax.

In 1859, Thomas set off to look for more orchids and ferns, travelling through northern Borneo and Burma. In horticultural terms, the trip was a great success, and resulted in many new introductions for the Veitch nurseries to propagate and promote. One of them, the scarlet-flowering *Rhododendron lobbii*, was even named in honour of the brothers. But somewhere along the way, in an accident of which no details are known, Thomas injured his leg badly, and he had to return home in May 1859. He was well enough to show his new introductions at the summer gathering of the Horticultural Society, but his leg had not healed properly and immediately after the show he went back to Cornwall, initially to live in the household of his married sister, Jane Mitchell. He spent the next three decades in quiet retirement. The leg eventually became so bad that at some point (we don't know precisely when) it had to be amputated—the operation was carried out on the Mitchell's kitchen table, quite a normal procedure in those days, and was completely successful, although Lobb, who had been only 41 when the accident happened, never worked again; happily for Lobb, though, anaesthesia had been developed in the late 1840s and was routine by the time he lost his leg. He received no pension or other financial support from the Veitch family that he had served so well and for whom he had generated so much income.

The last meeting between Thomas Lobb and James Junior (himself then in his mid-fifties and suffering from heart trouble) took place in 1869, when James Junior, in failing health, asked his old collector to come to London to discuss the possibility of yet another orchid-gathering expedition. Lobb travelled up by train for the meeting, which took place in Stanley House, James Junior's residence, on 9 September that year. It degenerated into a shouting match, no doubt related to the ostentatious wealth of the surroundings, built upon the work of the two Lobbs, in contrast to the humble circumstances Thomas was reduced to. Lobb left in a huff; James Junior retired to bed and died of a heart attack, for which his family blamed Thomas, deepening the rift between the Veitch family and their former employee.

Lobb became something of a recluse. He lived alone in the village of Devoran, in a cottage that he called, with heavy irony, Stanley Villa. There, he looked after his garden, and had supplies brought to the cottage by his nephew, scarcely leaving his own home except to visit his sister. He died in May 1894, at the age of 76, surviving both of the next two collectors whose tales we have to tell.

The achievements of the Lobb brothers were summed up succinctly by James Herbert Veitch, the family historian and great grandson of James Veitch, in his *Hortus Veitchii*. Of William, he wrote: 'The singular success which rewarded his researches is, perhaps, unparalleled in the history of botanical discovery; the labours of David Douglas not even forming an exception.' And of Thomas, even more succinctly, he said: 'His efforts were not short of that of his brother.'

IN THE GARDEN

William and Thomas Lobb made fortunes for their employers by helping to feed the Victorian passion for gardens, conservatories, and hot (stove) houses. These became far more affordable following the ending of the Glass Tax in the 1840s. By the late 1860s the price of glass had fallen sufficiently to make exotic plants and flowers a powerfully attractive hobby for those with the money to indulge it. The 1851 Exhibition, housed under a vast and magnificent glass roof, ignited the passion for glass houses and the social cachet that could be achieved through owning an orchid house. A very rare orchid could command as much then as a rare car could today; perhaps the most prized was the iconic Blue Orchid (*Vanda caerulea*). The rain forest was a rich source of orchids. Java supplied beautiful *Phalaenopsis* (Moth) orchids and from Burma came many striking *Dendrobiums*, the tree-perching orchids that thrived so well in the new greenhouses. Thomas Lobb also found the vast and strange Pitcher Plant which reeks of rotten fish—this was definitely a curiosity rather than a popular money-spinner. The *Nepenthes* (Pitcher Plant) species spotted by Thomas Lobb were later to fascinate the intrepid botanical artist Marianne North.

Alongside the orchids, the Rhododendron *veitchianum* was a vastly popular, income-generating introduction. The Jasmines sent back by Thomas Lobb are still huge garden favourites.

William is now remembered more for the trees he introduced than the flowers. His expeditions to the forests of North America enabled him to send back enough healthy seed to enable Veitch & Son to grow and sell thousands of healthy, and extremely expensive, seedling trees which were eagerly snapped up by British landowners. As well as the conifers 'discovered' by David Douglas he sent back the Red Cedar, *Thuja plicata*, and the Colorado White Fir (*Abies procera*) as well as the nurseryman's money-spinner—the Monkey Puzzle. William Lobb's greatest tree 'discovery', in every sense of the word, is, of course, the Giant Redwood (*Sequioadendron giganteum*), which can live for thousands of years and grow to a height of ninety metres.

But William Lobb brought colour as well as form into our landscape. The brilliant blue bush *Ceanothus* so loved by butterflies; the yellow-flowered *Freemontodendron* (Flannel Bush), and the passionately coloured fire red, yellow, and orange of *Tropoleums* (nasturtium) all add a blast of colour to the garden.

6

ROBERT FORTUNE

(1812–1880)

R OBERT FORTUNE WAS the first plant collector to enter China after the signing of the treaty of Nanking. He wasn't a plant *hunter*, in the sense of a David Douglas or one of the Lobb brothers, entering unexplored territory to find plants previously unknown in the civilized world; China was, after all, already civilized, even if its culture was rather different from that of Europe. As far as the collecting went, much of Fortune's work simply involved purchasing plants from Chinese nurseries. But the trick was to get himself into a position where the Chinese were willing to trade with him, which often involved hazards of one kind or another as well as an ability to fit into the culture. Fortune did this so well that eventually he was able to carry out his trick on a massive scale, and became chiefly responsible for the development of the black tea industry in India, using plants and experts obtained in China.

Fortune's career was so adventurous that it is frustrating how little is known about him as a person or his private life. His letters and journals were burned by his family after his death, and almost all we have to go on are the books that he published describing his travels. These are a rich source of material, but there must always be a nagging thought that they cannot be the whole truth, since most authors tend to present themselves in as favourable a light as possible. We know the story told in the books is at best incomplete, since it focuses on Fortune's travels to such an extent that they never even mention that during his years abroad he left a wife and family back home—a wife and family about whom we know absolutely nothing except for the fact of their existence.

We know scarcely more about Robert Fortune himself. Although his date of birth is firmly established as 12 September 1812,[1] even the exact location of that event is a matter of debate. Several places in the Scottish border county of Berwickshire lay claim to the 'local hero', but all we can say with reasonable confidence is that he was born in a cottage somewhere in the parish of Edrom, watered by the rivers Blackadder and Whiteadder, and given the same sort of basic Scottish education in a local parish school as many of his botanical compatriots. He first appears on the record as an apprentice in the gardens of a Mr Buchan at Kelloe, a town in Berwickshire, and then as a gardener at Moredun, near Edinburgh. The step that would change his life for ever came in 1840, the year he turned 28, when Fortune took up a post at the Botanic Garden in Edinburgh, under William McNab, following in the footsteps of David Douglas. It was McNab who, two years later, recommended Fortune for the job of Superintendent of the hothouse department at the Horticultural Society's garden in Chiswick. This was the year (1842) that the Treaty of Nanking was signed, and the Society immediately sought to benefit from the opening up of China, even to a limited extent, to Westerners.

The speed with which the Horticultural Society responded to this opportunity was largely thanks to one man, John Reeves. Born in 1774, Reeves worked in China as a tea inspector for the East India Company (a very important post) from 1812 to 1831, when he retired and returned to England, living until 1856. Reeves was interested in all the plants of China, not just tea, and his position allowed him more opportunity to travel than most Westerners. He corresponded with

Banks, Sabine, and Lindley, taking advantage of his post to send back many specimens on the East India Company's ships. When he retired to England, Reeves became one of the most powerful figures in the Horticultural Society; although the Treaty of Nanking was signed only on 26 August 1842, and it took several weeks for news of the signing of the treaty to get back to England, before the year was out Reeves was presiding over a 'Chinese Committee' of the Horticultural Society, making urgent plans to send a collector out to seize the opportunity. The man they chose was Robert Fortune, who must have made a good impression during his short time in Chiswick.

In the absence of any contemporary descriptions of his character, some modern accounts describe Fortune as a stereotypical 'dour Scot', lacking in humour or any appreciation of the finer things of life. But as we shall see, his own writings give the lie to that image. He mixed well with people from all walks of life, enjoyed a joke,[2] and the nearest his books come to waxing lyrical is when he expresses his delight at the beauties of nature. Just because Fortune took his work seriously, and was prepared to suffer hardship where necessary, didn't make him a humourless philistine. He could, though, be obstinate—and just as well. When the Society proposed to send him off armed only with a 'life preserver' (a kind of cosh, weighted with lead) he demanded, and got, a shotgun and a brace of pistols. Never ones to miss an opportunity for profit, however, the Society instructed Fortune to sell the firearms in China, where they would fetch a higher price than in England, before his return.[3] With equal parsimony, they paid Fortune the same salary, £100 per annum, that Francis Masson had received from Kew seventy years earlier. He was also provided, rather more generously, with an allowance for expenses of £500. The 30-year old Fortune sailed for China on board the *Emu* on 26 February 1843, six months to the day from the signing of the treaty of Nanking, and that is where we can pick up his own account of his adventures in China. But before we do so, we want to make a small digression to explain a technological advance which sounds prosaic to modern ears but was revolutionary for plant collectors in the 1840s, and which was instrumental in Fortune's success.

As we have seen, one of the major difficulties facing plant hunters before the middle of the nineteenth century was getting the plants they had found home in good condition. They were at the mercy of wind and weather, the whim of eccentric ships' captains and inefficient shipping agents, and even if all of those factors worked out well, the plants might die from having too much or too little water, too much or too little sunshine, or (most likely) from the effects of salt spray. Even the advent of steamships only slightly eased the problem. You might think that it would have been easier to send seeds back to Britain, rather than living plants. But seeds have to be collected at the right season, which might not be when the collector is around. They come in all kinds of shapes and sizes, from tiny dust-like particles to avocado 'pips' and coco-de-mer. And, crucially, many kinds of seed (including, as it happens, those of the tea plant) do not remain viable for long; they might be shipped back to Britain, but they would refuse to germinate when planted there. What was really needed was a secure way to transport living plants without them being subjected to outside stresses. The solution was found, by accident, by a physician practising in the East End of London, the splendidly named Nathaniel Bagshaw Ward.

Ward had been born in London in 1791, and may have lived in Jamaica as a teenager, which could explain his interest in plants. In the late 1820s, approaching his fortieth birthday, he was living and working in the docklands area of London, then a rough working-class area prone to the infamous 'Pea Soup' fogs that often choked a city in which smoky coal fires were the chief means of providing warmth for houses and power for industry. Even the more affluent few, like Ward, who had a garden could not expect to get much to grow there except a few bedraggled ferns. But Ward was interested in entomology as well as botany, and one day in 1827, not for the first time, he placed the pupa of a caterpillar in some mould at the bottom of a sealed glass jar and left it to develop into a butterfly. On this occasion, he put the jar to one side and forgot about it. When he remembered to look at it some time later, he was surprised to find a tiny fern and a blade of grass growing in the mould (history does not record the fate of the butterfly). Keeping a close watch on the sealed jar, Ward tells us that: 'I observed the moisture which during the heat of the day rose from the mould condensed on the surface of the glass and returned whence it came, thus keeping the earth always in the same degree of humidity.'

Ward wasn't the first person to notice the phenomenon—something similar can be seen in poorly ventilated hothouses. But he was the first person to realize the full implications. Plants that couldn't grow in the polluted atmosphere of his garden could grow in the sealed jar because they had 'a moist atmosphere free from soot or other extraneous particles', as well as light from the Sun. And if the trick would work in the grimy East End of London, why not on the spray-soaked deck of a ship?

Ward left his original jar undisturbed while he carried out further experiments—the plants inside it thrived for four years, until the lid rusted and let the polluted air of East London in. Meanwhile, he designed and had built larger versions of the jar, the forerunners of cases called terraria, a bit like fish tanks for ferns, which became extremely popular as indoor gardens among the middle classes of Victorian Britain.

But Ward had a bigger vision. In 1834 he sent two sealed glass cases stocked with ferns and grass on a ship to Australia, where, six months later, the cases were opened and the healthy plants removed. The cases were then restocked with Australian plants, chosen from the species that it had proved most difficult to get to survive the rigours of a long sea voyage, and sent on the journey round Cape Horn back to England. They left in February 1835 and took eight months on the journey, experiencing temperatures ranging from $-7°C$ to $50°C$. The plants made it safely to London, and from then on the work of the botanical explorer was transformed. In 1842, when he was 51, Ward published a book describing his discoveries and the technique of growing and transporting plants in 'closely glazed cases', and lectured on the subject to the Royal Society, but made no further contributions to horticulture; he died in London in 1868, having lived to see just how important his work had been.

The use of what became known as 'Wardian cases', which eventually came in a variety of sizes from something like a shoe box to something like a mini-greenhouse, was pioneered on a large scale by Joseph Hooker, of whom more later, and by Robert Fortune, whose story we can now pick up on 6 July 1843, when he arrived at Hong Kong, recently leased to the British under the terms of the Treaty of Nanking. We can put the importance of Ward's terraria in the precise context of the hazards of obtaining plants from China, thanks to a letter written by John Livingstone, a surgeon and plant collector based in Canton, to the Horticultural Society in 1819. He said, based on his personal experience, that:

I am of the opinion that one thousand plants have been lost for one which survived the voyage to England. Plants purchased at Canton, including their chests and other necessary charges, cost six shillings and eight pence sterling each, on a fair average; consequently every [Chinese] plant now in England, must have been introduced at the enormous expense of upwards of £300.

Two decades later, the situation had been transformed by the Wardian cases, and Fortune and his employers were among the first beneficiaries.

On the voyage out to Hong Kong, Fortune took with him a selection of British plants for the infant colonial base, travelling in his Wardian cases. They arrived in good health, which was more than could be said for the state of the colony itself. When Fortune arrived at the island, Hong Kong was in what he described as a 'lamentable condition', with fever rife, while the township of Victoria, he wrote, 'swarms with thieves and robbers'.[4] The hills of the nearby mainland offered no attractions for a plant hunter, having 'a scorched appearance with rocks of granite and red clay showing all over their surface:

the trees are few, and stunted in their growth'. The only advice the doctors could give was to move on to escape the fever, advice which Fortune was happy to take. He sailed for Amoy on 23 August, but it was already too late; he carried the fever with him, and lay 'in a very precarious state' for several days before recovering. 'The sea air probably did more for me than any thing else, and, under Providence, was the means of saving my life.'

Amoy was as much of a disappointment as Hong Kong, except that it was free of fever. It was 'one of the filthiest towns which I have ever seen, either in China or elsewhere'. Overall, during his first visit Fortune, who had expected to find a sophisticated Chinese civilization, was shocked to find instead an agricultural society living to no small extent on past glories, 'retrograding rather than advancing. Many of the northern cities, evidently once in the most flourishing condition, are now in a state of decay...'. But at least Amoy provided a base for Fortune's first plant-gathering trips—they hardly justify being called expeditions—travelling inland up rivers before landing and 'prosecuting my botanical researches in the adjacent country'.

On most occasions, he found the people away from the coast friendly and curious about the stranger, 'as if I were a being from another world'. On the rare occasions he encountered signs of hostility, he found that the best response was to put on a bold front and march into the village (with his ever-present servant) and make friends. Soon, he would have 'boys running in all directions gathering plants for my specimen-box, and the old men...offering me their bamboo-pipes to smoke'. His interest in plants often led the Chinese to assume that he was some kind of medical man, which did no harm for his status; but they were particularly intrigued by Fortune's lack of a pigtail. On one occasion, he delighted the villagers simply by taking tea and cakes with the head man:

'He eats and drinks like ourselves', said one; 'Look', said two or three behind me who had been examining the back part of my head rather attentively, 'look here, the stranger has no tail;' and then the whole crowd, women and children included, had to come round me, to see if it was really a fact, that I had no tail.

On this occasion, he jokingly suggested that if the owner of a particularly fine pigtail, 'rather a dandy in his way', were to cut it off, Fortune would wear it, like a wig, in his honour. The joke went down well; but eventually a similar idea would become more than a joke.

In these early months, what Fortune was learning about Chinese culture and how to get on with the locals was as important as his plant collecting, which was as yet on a relatively modest scale. Not all the lessons were enjoyable. At the end of September Fortune left Amoy and sailed north, heading for the island of Chusan (Zhou Shan, a large island part of an archipelago off the mouth of the Ningpo river[5]); but the ship he was on encountered a severe storm, and had to put in to a bay just fifty miles north of Amoy for repairs. To pass the time, Fortune went ashore to take a closer look at a pagoda on the top of the highest nearby hill. In spite of warnings that the region was notorious for its bandits and robbers, Fortune set out on foot, accompanied only by his servant, gathering plant specimens as they went. Although they were surrounded by 'three or four hundred of the Chinese, of both sexes, and all ages, looking down upon us with wonder painted in every countenance', there was no trouble until some of the men 'took a great fancy' to a silk handkerchief that Fortune was wearing around his neck. It was only with difficulty that Fortune convinced them he would not trade the neck cloth, and avoided the crowd by climbing uphill towards the pagoda—'a plan which I always adopted when I wanted to get away from the Chinese, as they are generally too lazy to follow far'.

The pagoda proved a disappointing ruin, so after admiring the view Fortune took care to descend back to the plain by a different route, hoping to avoid his former acquaintances. The ruse failed, and he was soon surrounded once again by 'natives'. Worse, while Fortune took wide detours from their route to gather plants, his servant plodded in a straight line back towards the shore, so they became separated. In the close press of people around him, Fortune felt a hand in his pocket, and although the thief ran off when discovered, several valuable items had been stolen. Looking around, Fortune saw his servant being threatened by eight or ten ruffians with knives, 'endeavouring to rob and strip him of every thing of the slightest value, and my poor plants collected with so much care were flying about in all directions'. Fortunately, the robbers ran off when Fortune raced to the aid of his servant. Badly shaken, they gathered up what specimens they could and made straight for the boat, arriving 'with my opinion of the Chinese considerably lowered by the adventures of the day'. But the day had not been wasted—among the plants that survived were several roots of *Campanula grandiflora* (Bellflower) and a 'new' species of the ornamental shrub Abelia, *Abelia rupestris*, all of which made it safely back to England and flourished in the garden of the Horticultural Society.

Fortune eventually reached Chusan in the autumn of 1843, and was delighted with the contrast to the barren lands around Hong Kong:

The first glance at the vegetation convinced me that this must be the field of my future operations, and I had then no doubt that my mission would end most successfully...few can form any idea of the gorgeous and striking beauty of these azalea-clad mountains, where, on every side, as far as our vision extends, the eye rests on masses of flowers of dazzling brightness and surpassing beauty.

As a base of operations, Chusan, about twenty miles long and twelve wide, was ideal. The nearby rivers gave access to the mainland (not that Fortune travelled far from any Treaty Port on his first trip to China) and in the islands themselves there were hills tall enough to provide a variety of environments for different kinds of plants, and ravines deep enough to be in an uncultivated state of nature. Among the plants Fortune found there were several palms, including the species that became known as *Trachycarpus fortunei*, or the Chusan Palm, now a popular plant in frost-free gardens. Fortune later sent several young palms back to William Hooker at Kew, including one as a gift for the garden of Queen Victoria and Prince Albert at Osborne House on the Isle of Wight. The tree was planted[6] to mark the Queen's thirty-second birthday in May 1851, and still stands there today.

The British presence on Chusan centred around the town of Tinghae, where Fortune was amused to discover that the Chinese regarded the English as members of one of three ranks. The term *Mandarin*, originally a Portuguese introduction to denote a Chinese official, was applied to British government representatives and officers in the army and navy; *Sien-sang*, a Chinese term meaning master, used in the same way as the English 'sir', was the term used for merchants; and 'common soldiers, sailors, and the rest of the lower orders, were all classed under the head of *A-says*'. This term, Fortune was delighted to discover, was a corruption of the affectation 'I say', then 'a very common expression amongst our soldiers and sailors'.

The key feature of Fortune's travels in China was that he got to know the Chinese way of life—and state of mind—by travelling through the countryside, usually accompanied by one servant, sleeping in the temples like Chinese travellers, eating Chinese food with Chinese people (using chopsticks), learning enough of the language to get by, and on occasion dressing in Chinese clothes. Even near the coast, where Europeans were regarded as the Devil's Children (Kwei-tsz), he made friends; when he later travelled farther inland, as we shall see, he was accepted as a civilized foreigner from 'beyond the Great Wall'. An early sign of Fortune's assimilation of Chinese culture, and another example of his broad sense of humour, came in the late autumn of 1843 when he visited the town of Ningpo, on the east coast of China, almost due west of Chusan and about twelve miles upriver. There, he met an American medical missionary:

dressed *à la Chinoise*, tail and all complete, but truth compels me to state that his dress was rather a ludicrous one...The large flowing gown which he wore was almost too fine for a mandarin, while the hat was one commonly worn by servants and coolies. The English reader, if he wishes to understand the strange sort of appearance the doctor presented, must imagine a London judge clothed in his fine black flowing gown, and wearing the hat of a dustman...I soon found that he in his Chinese dress was a greater object of attention than I was in my English one. How the Chinese laughed and enjoyed the joke!

Although he didn't obtain a great deal in the way of botanical specimens on this trip to Ningpo, Fortune learned about the technique of growing dwarf trees (bonsai) and saw fishermen using tame cormorants to catch fish. As winter set in (a particularly severe one, when Fortune, lodging in a draughty house with paper windows, tells us he 'never felt so cold in England as I did during this winter in the north of China') he moved on to Shanghae (as he spelled it), about a hundred miles north-west of Chusan and the most northerly of the five Treaty Ports, where foreigners were then permitted to trade with the Chinese.[7] There, he found a rich agricultural plain ('by far the richest which I have seen in China') and by perseverance managed to make a fine collection of plants, not so much by going out into the field himself, but by cultivating the acquaintance of Chinese gardeners and buying plants from nurseries.

At first, this was not as easy as it sounds. There were plenty of interesting plants in the city, because Shanghai was rich, a centre of trade, and had many nurseries which contained species brought in from other parts of the country. They stocked ornamental plants unknown in England and therefore potentially of great value to the Horticultural Society, but the difficulty was first finding the nurseries and then persuading the owners to do business. Fortune found that the flower shops in the city were eager to sell him plants, but that, anxious not to lose their profit, they were reluctant to say where the plants came from. 'Give us the names of the things you want, and we will get them for you.' But of course, he didn't know the names! Although the shopkeepers told him the nurseries were far away, Fortune knew this not to be the case from the fresh state of the plants.

The first step out of the impasse came when some local boys were impressed by Fortune's gun (the one the Horticultural Society had been so reluctant to supply him with), which he had been using to shoot birds; in exchange for showing them the weapon, he asked for directions to the nearest nursery. But every time he approached the place, each day by a different route, the gates were shut in his face by the owners, who feared that the foreign devil wanted to seize their stock and make off without payment. In the end, he had to obtain the help of the British Consul, who sent one of the Chinese officials attached to the Consulate to explain that the foreigner was willing to pay good money for the plants he wanted. Once the ice was broken, the first nurserymen introduced Fortune to other nurseries. Over the following weeks he became firm friends with the entire horticultural community, and by treating them fairly received a wealth of botanical specimens. Equipped with these plants, he headed back south, first to Chusan then on to Hong Kong to pack the collections in Wardian cases and ship them back to England in three separate ships, to guard against disaster.

Before returning to Chusan, Fortune spent a few weeks visiting Canton and Macao, including the celebrated Fa-tee gardens, near Canton, where the spectacular displays of tree peony, camellias, roses and in particular azaleas reminded him 'of the exhibitions in the gardens of the Horticultural Society at Chiswick, but the Fa-tee exhibitions were on a much larger scale'. Less happily, after his enjoyable time among friendly folk farther north, when Fortune took a walk alone out of the centre of Canton on a quiet road among fields and gardens, he was once again attacked by robbers, this time beaten and stripped of everything valuable, left without even a hat as protection from the hot Sun. He was ever afterwards convinced that the southern

Chinese were uncouth ruffians, while those farther north were hospitable and friendly.

So Fortune was happy to set sail again for what he called 'the northern provinces' at the end of March 1844, basing himself once again on Chusan. During the summer of 1844, and also in 1845, he visited the islands of the archipelago and made several small excursions on the mainland, travelling in comfort but able to visit places which had formerly been closed to Europeans, and meet people who 'had never seen an Englishman before'.[8] These included a visit to the green tea district near Ningpo, a foretaste of his later adventures. Travel was often by boat, but in the mountain regions Fortune took advantage of the traditional travelling 'chair', carried by two men: 'It consists merely of two long bamboo poles, with a board placed between them for a seat, and two other cross pieces, one for the back and the other for the feet; a large Chinese umbrella is held over the head to afford protection from the sun and rain.' He also astonished the locals by sometimes getting out of the boat to walk along the side of the canal—'a Chinaman never walks when he can possibly find any other mode of conveyance'.

It was on the trip to the green tea district, travelling with the British Consul and two other gentlemen, that Fortune nearly emulated the fate of David Douglas. As usual, they stayed in temples, and at one of these the priests were plagued by wild boars which came down from the mountains at night and destroyed the young bamboo shoots. For protection, the priests had dug deep pits on the hillside, narrow at the top but widening out below, covered with sticks and grass; the pits then naturally half-filled with water. Once, when coming out of dense brushwood, Fortune:

stept unawares on the treacherous mouth of one of them, and felt the ground under my feet actually giving way; but managing to throw my arms forward I caught hold of a small twig which was growing near, and by this means supported myself until I was able to scramble on to firmer ground... The fate of my predecessor, Mr. Douglas, who perished in a pit of this kind on the Sandwich Islands, must still be fresh in the recollection of many of my readers, and his melancholy end naturally coming to my mind at the time, made me doubly thankful for my escape.

This was, though, a rare alarm in almost two years of relatively comfortable travelling and collecting, in which, among other things, Fortune learned about the methods of tea production and was surprised to discover that green tea and black tea were made from the same kind of plant, the difference arising solely from the way the leaves were processed and dried. He also had interesting views on opium, acknowledging that it had 'a most pernicious effect' on some individuals, but adding that in his experience 'in the great majority of cases it was not immoderately indulged in', and suggesting that it ought to be legalized and taxed to provide income for the Chinese government.

In the spring of 1844, Fortune again visited 'Shangae', and made his first successful foray a little way into the interior in his Chinese disguise, to visit the city of Soo-chow-foo, which was closed to foreigners but reputed to have many flower gardens and well-stocked nurseries. He wore the proper Chinese dress (unlike the American missionary who had afforded him such amusement), with shaved head and 'a splendid wig and tail, of which some Chinese in former days had doubtless been extremely vain'. Although he obviously could not pass as a local, China was so big, and the differences between populations of different regions were so great, that by behaving like a Chinaman he was able to pass himself off as a visitor from a distant province. Even the fact that he did not speak the local language was no problem, since he wouldn't be expected to and had a servant to translate and explain that his master was a visitor from a far province who only spoke the Court dialect, the Kwan-hwa; and, of course, he was helped by the fact that the people of Soo-chow-foo had never seen a European. Although it turned out that the nurseries were nowhere near as splendid as he had been led to believe, Fortune was able to obtain some valuable plants unknown in England, including 'a fine new double yellow rose,[9] and a *Gardenia* with large white blossoms, like a Camellia'. He is also credited with introducing Forsythia (named after the Scottish horticulturalist William Forsyth) to Britain around this time, although the specimens probably did not come from Soo-chow-foo.

Fortune's travels may have been easy compared with those of, say, David Douglas; but there were enough 'routine' alarms to put modern travel in perspective. He suffered bouts of fever, storms at sea, and a typhoon—fortunately, while on land. But the most dangerous encounter came almost at the end of his first visit to China.

In the summer of 1845, Fortune spent most of his time revisiting places he knew, gathering the best specimens he could of the best plants he had 'discovered', in order to pack them carefully in Wardian cases and take them home to England under his own supervision. With most of this work completed, Fortune left his latest collections in Shanghai while he travelled south to the region of the Min river, almost due west of the northern tip of Taiwan, and nearly halfway from Shanghai to Hong Kong. The region proved a disappointment in botanical terms, so he soon took passage on a junk sailing as part of a convoy north to Ningpo. Struck by another bout of fever, Fortune was lying down below, alternately sweating and shivering, when the captain arrived in an agitated state to tell him that five pirate vessels were making for the craft. Fortune loaded his shotgun and pistols and staggered on deck, where the crew and other passengers were in a state of panic, attempting to hide their valuables and exchanging their usual clothing for rags in the hope that they would not be held for ransom. Everyone assumed that the junk would be taken by the pirates, and the two helmsmen only remained at their post when Fortune threatened to shoot them if they ran off. When the first pirate ship, confident of victory, was only twenty yards away, Fortune let fly with both barrels of his shotgun, loaded with ball on top of the shot:

'They were so completely taken by surprise, that their junk was left without a helmsman; her sails flapped in the wind; and, as we were still carrying all sail and keeping on our right course, they were soon left a considerable way astern.' Another attacker was beaten off in the same way, after which the pirates left Fortune's vessel alone and concentrated on easier prey. Fortune was hailed as a hero by the crew, and his status increased further when another pirate attack was beaten off the following day. One unfortunate consequence of this, however, was that the captain decided he wanted the protection of Fortune's gun all the way to Ningpo, and attempted to renege on a promise to drop his passenger off at Chusan; it was only when Fortune threatened to turn his guns on them that 'the trembling varlets landed me safely at Chusan'.

In spite of the fever, Fortune was able to 'crawl on board' an English vessel that was fortuitously just leaving for Shanghai, where he recovered from the fever and everything was packed and ready by 10 October, when he left for Hong Kong with the finest plants in his collection. There, 'eight glazed cases of living plants' were despatched to England, while Fortune himself moved on to Canton and took passage on 22 December 1845 on the *John Cooper*, with eighteen Wardian cases 'filled with the most beautiful plants of northern China'. He arrived safely at anchorage in the Thames on 6 May 1846, with the plants 'in excellent order'.

As a reward for his efforts, Fortune was appointed Curator of the Chelsea Physic Garden, but found time from his duties to complete his first book, *Three Years' Wanderings in the Northern Provinces of China*, by the end of October 1846—it was published the following year. Unable to settle at a routine job, however, when the East India Company asked him to go back to China in 1848 to collect tea plants to grow in India Fortune leapt at the chance, even though this was a far riskier expedition than his first visit to China. The Chinese authorities jealously guarded the secrets of their tea industry, which was a major source of revenue, and would not take kindly to the prospect of their near-monopoly being broken by a rival tea industry in India.[10]

Fortune's commission from the East India Company was 'for the purpose of obtaining the finest varieties of the Tea-plant, as well as native manufacturers and implements, for the Government plantations in the Himalayas'. As this suggests, there were already tea plantations in India, but these were very inferior both in size and quality of their product to those in China, not least because it had proved very difficult to transport tea plants, while their seeds were among those that didn't survive long enough to be viable after the journey. Fortune, with his experience of travelling in China in disguise and his skill at handling and propagating delicate plants, was the ideal man for the job; he left Southampton in the P&O steamship *Ripon* on 20 June 1848, scarcely two years after his return from China, and arrived back in Hong Kong on board the same company's steamship *Braganza* on 14 August 1848.

He found the island itself and the town of Victoria transformed since his first visit, already becoming densely covered with houses:

When it is remembered that six years before Hong-kong was but a barren island, with only a few huts upon it, inhabited by pirates or poor fishermen, it is surprising that in so short a time a large town should have risen upon the shores of the bay, containing many houses like palaces, and gardens too . . .

The town of Shanghai, which Fortune moved on to in September, was an even greater revelation. What was virtually a new town of English and American houses 'now occupied the place of wretched Chinese hovels, cotton-fields, and tombs. The Chinese were moving gradually backwards into the country, with their families, effects, and all that appertained unto them.'

But this Western influence was restricted to the Treaty Ports. The tea district Fortune was initially interested in, Hwuy-chow, lay more than 200 miles inland from Ningpo, and was closed to foreigners. In Ningpo itself, Fortune found two men from the Hwuy-chow district who were willing to accompany him into the forbidden region, stipulating only that he should—as he already intended—disguise himself as a Chinese visitor from a far province.[11] Dressed in Chinese clothes, and with the pigtail that he had worn before 'nicely dressed by the barber' and placed on his shaven head, Fortune encountered remarkably little difficulty on his travels, mostly by boat and the kind of mountain chair described earlier. There were, of course, difficulties enough to overwhelm most European travellers—bribes that had to be paid, relatively minor acts of dishonesty by the servants and the chair-carriers, occasions when the disguise only just passed muster, and so on. But Fortune applied the precept 'take things coolly and never lose your temper', and came through unscathed. One mark of the success of his disguise came, far inland, when he was crossing a river by ferry:

Amongst the ferry-boat passengers were two very pretty and handsomely dressed young ladies, with whom I was greatly amused. When they came into the boat they seated themselves quietly by my side, and began chatting to each other in high spirits. I could not help contrasting their conduct with that of any of their countrywomen at the five ports where foreigners are permitted to trade. Respectably dressed females always fly from foreigners as they would do from a wild and ferocious animal. Had these pretty damsels known that a 'barbarian' was seated at their side, how astonished and frightened they would have been!

Fascinating though Fortune's traveller's tales are, however, the importance of his expedition lay in the tea seeds and plants that he was able to obtain, and the expert tea makers to go with them to India.[12] He found that the seeds are ripe in the month of October, when they were gathered and put in a basket, mixed with damp earth and sand, where they were kept until planting in spring. Without these precautions only a few viable seeds would survive the winter, and their viability was reduced by any sudden changes in temperature or moisture. Fortune obtained 'a good collection' of young plants and seeds, as well as information about how the plants were cultivated, and added to this when he visited Silver Island, in the Chusan archipelago, another green tea region. Young tea plants were then carefully packed in Wardian cases and despatched via Hong Kong to India, where they arrived in good order. But all but a few of the seeds sent in the same shipment, some loose and some mixed with dry earth, failed to germinate.

All of these specimens came from green tea regions, but on a further expedition in the north Fortune also visited the black tea districts (around Woo-e-shan) and confirmed his earlier suspicion that the plants were identical, with the different teas being produced by different methods of treating the leaves. He also saw just how labour intensive the process of cultivating the tea shrub for commercial use was, and pointed out that this made it impractical as a crop in places like the United States and Australia:

Were it merely intended as an ornamental shrub, there could be no objections to its introduction into those countries. But [we must inquire] also into the price of labour. Labour is cheap in China. The labourers in the tea-countries do not receive more than twopence or threepence a day. Can workmen be procured for this small sum either in the United States or Australia? And if they cannot be hired for this sum, nor for anything near it, how will the manufacturers in such places be able to compete with the Chinese in the market?

The labour problem might have been alleviated if there had been any truth in the widespread belief that in some regions tea could be gathered conveniently by throwing stones at monkeys in the trees, who would respond by tearing off leafy branches of the tea plant and throwing them back. Always careful to test hypotheses in the true scientific method, Fortune wrote: 'I should not like to assert that no tea is gathered by...monkeys, but I think it may be safely affirmed that the quantities produced in such ways are exceedingly small.'

In the autumn of 1849, Fortune, now based in Shanghai, had a large supply of tea seeds and plants to be packed and sent to India, and came up with what he called 'a sure and certain method' of transporting these delicate seeds 'to foreign countries in full life'. Even better, the technique would work for all such short-lived seeds. Essentially, the trick was to sow the seeds in Wardian cases soon after they were gathered—but there was a little more to it than that.

Fortune's first experiment with tea seeds involved planting mulberry plants in a Wardian case in well-watered soil, waiting for a couple of days for the soil to dry, then sprinkling a large quantity of tea seeds over the surface and adding a layer of soil half an inch deep. With a few crossbars on top to keep the soil in place, the case was fastened in the usual way and despatched to India. 'When the case reached Calcutta the mulberry-plants were found to be in good condition, and the tea-seeds had germinated during the voyage and were now covering the surface of the soil.'

Encouraged by this success, the next year Fortune developed the technique for the cases which he was planning to take to India in his own care. Jumping ahead in our story a little, at the beginning of 1851 he prepared fourteen cases using essentially the same technique, but with tea seeds planted between the rows of young tea plants, rather than mulberry plants. This still left him with about a bushel of seeds, which he was reluctant to leave behind. But there were two more of the glazed cases that had been set aside to take camellias to the Botanic Garden in Calcutta. Fortune simply took the extra seeds, mixed them with soil in the proportion one part earth to two parts seeds, and laid the mixture in the bottom of the cases. The camellia plants were gently lifted from their pots with earth still around their roots and placed on top of the mixture, before the spaces between the plants were filled to the proper height with the rest of the mixture of soil and tea seeds. A little soil was sprinkled on the top, everything well watered, bars nailed across the surface to keep the soil/seed mixture in place, and the cases secured.

Before these final preparations for the journey to India, in 1850 Fortune had another chance to see the azaleas in bloom in their natural habitat:

Nature plants and rears with no sparing hand; her colours are clear and brilliant, and she is not confined to greenhouses and flower-tents in which to display her productions, but scatters them with wild profusion over the sides of the hills. It is here that she is inimitable, and it is thus that she produces effects which, once seen, can never be forgotten.

Among the plants introduced to Britain by Fortune was an azalea which he named *Azalea amoena*, with a profusion of small, semi-double pink flowers. But his task for the summer of that year was to find men from the tea district willing to emigrate to India, with their tea-making implements, to give a boost to the emerging Indian tea industry by teaching Chinese methods of production. While he concentrated on this, now that he knew the country and the people so well Fortune was able to despatch trustworthy men to collect the plants and seeds which formed the contents of the sixteen Wardian cases referred to above. The recruiting of tea manufacturers, which Fortune had feared would be a 'difficult and uncertain task', was accompanied with relative ease, and eight of the Chinamen duly arrived in Shanghai, with all their equipment, ready to embark with Fortune and his sixteen glazed cases on board the steamship *Lady Mary Wood*. They left Shanghai on 16 February 1851, and arrived in Calcutta on 15 March.

When the cases containing tea plants were opened in Calcutta, the young plants themselves were in good condition, and the seeds sown between the rows were just beginning to germinate. As there was enough space for them to grow, they could be left undisturbed until the cases reached their final destination. But the camellia cases were a different matter:

The whole mass of seeds, from the bottom to the top, was swelling, and germination had just commenced. The camellias, which had now arrived at their destination, were lifted gently out and potted, and appeared as if they had never left their native country. Fourteen new cases were got ready, filled with earth, and these germinating seeds were sown thickly over the surface, and covered with soil in the usual way. In a few days the young plants came sprouting through the soil; every seed seemed to have grown; and by this simple plan about twelve thousand plants were added to the Himalayan plantations.

Fortune, the plants (now in a total of twenty-eight large cases), his Chinese tea manufacturers, and their equipment went on by river steamer to Allahabad, arriving on 14 April, and then overland to the plantations. They had enough baggage to fill nine wagons on the journey to Saharunpore, thirty miles from the foot of the Himalayas, but with only enough bullocks available to pull three wagons at a time the journey had to be made in three stages. Altogether, 12,838 plants survived the journey, with many more seeds germinating in the cases.[13] 'They seemed as green and vigorous as if they had been all the while growing on the Chinese hills.'

There were already extensive tea plantations in the region, and Fortune stayed on to inspect them and report on their condition and prospects to the Government and the East India Company (itself effectively a branch of government). By his own account, some of these plantations already had hundreds of thousands of plants, derived from stock brought from China in the previous decade, which puts the image of Fortune as the 'father' of the Indian tea industry in perspective. But the existing plantations all used an inferior variety of tea plant from the southern region of China, where it had been easy to obtain. Fortune's mission had been to obtain the best varieties and expert manufacturers to improve the quality of Indian tea, and in this he succeeded admirably. His most important contribution, though, was to realize that black tea could be made from the same plants as green tea (the plants already in cultivation in India) and to introduce to India experts in the technique of making black tea. It is in no small measure thanks to Robert Fortune that in England the term 'Indian tea' became synonymous with 'black tea'. After some time travelling in the mountains and a detour to visit Delhi and Agra, he arrived back in Calcutta on 29 August 1851, ready to catch the next steamer home to England.

Once again, though, Fortune didn't settle back in England. In 1853, after writing his second book, *A Journey to the Tea Countries of China*, he was off to China again to collect more tea seeds and plants—and, crucially, to recruit more experts in the art of black tea manufacture for the plantations in India. Although he did not return home until 1856, and the trip was successful in its main objective, Fortune's opportunities for more widespread travel and botanizing were limited, because China was in the grip of a conflict known as the Taiping Rebellion, which lasted from 1851 to 1864. The conflict affected most of southern China, and the rebels, under Hong Xiuquan (1812–64), took Nanking in 1853 and for a time controlled much of southern China; but they were eventually crushed.[14] Although Fortune was unable to do much exploring (and once again suffered the indignity of being robbed), it was on this trip that he found a beautiful plant named in his honour, *Rhododendron fortunei*, which played an important role in the development of hybrid rhododendrons in England. The enthusiasm generated for rhododendrons changed the face of the gardens of many great houses whose soil (and the wealth of the owner) made it possible to plant them en masse to form romantic groves.

After once again spending less time at home than he had been away, in 1858 Fortune made his fourth, and last, visit to China, this time acting on behalf of the United States Government, which (in spite of his comments about the cost of labour) intended to start a tea industry of its own. By this time the rebellion had lost momentum, and although parts of the country were still dangerous for travellers Fortune was able to complete his mission the following year and see more than thirty thousand plants established in America. It is unlikely that the American tea project would have succeeded anyway; but the

American Civil War, which started in 1861, disrupted the embryonic scheme and it was never revived.

Although Fortune had returned to England only in 1859, the year he was 47, in 1860 he was off again, this time on a self-financed private expedition to Japan. Just as China had been forced to open up to Westerners to some extent by the Opium Wars, Japan, previously a closed society, had been forced to allow some access by Westerners by American intervention in the mid-1850s (although the process of opening up the country only really got rolling with the Meiji Restoration in 1868). John Gould Veitch arrived in Japan in the same year as Fortune, and they both had a relatively easy time collecting plants unknown in Europe by the simple expedient of buying them from nurseries. Fortune spent only a week in Nagasaki and a few months in Tokyo (then called Yedo) and Yokohama. His 'collections' included many kinds of chrysanthemum, which caused a sensation when they reached England, and the variegated bamboo *Pleioblastus variegates*. It's hardly surprising that the chrysanthemums were a sensation; in his book *Yedo and Peking* (1863) Fortune describes varieties:

Quite distinct from any of the kinds at present known in Europe. One had petals like long thick hairs, of a red colour, but tipped with yellow, looking like the fringe of a shawl or curtain; another had broad white petals striped with red like a carnation or a camellia; while others were remarkable for their great size and brilliant colouring.

Veitch, meanwhile, collected many conifers, magnolias, and other species. Inevitably, there was some overlap between their collections, and since it happened that both collections went back to England in the same ship, in many cases it is impossible to say who should have the credit for introducing a particular species to England.

While Veitch went on to the Philippines in search of orchids, Fortune returned to England (via Shanghai and Peking; giving him material for another book) on 2 January 1862. At last, in his fiftieth year, he settled down, initially in Kensington—in the nineteen years from 1843 to 1862, he had spent just nine years at home. With a comfortable income from his books, and money from the sale of Chinese and Japanese collectibles that he brought back, Fortune was able to take what amounted to early retirement, and soon moved with his family back to Berwickshire, where he took up farming and wrote the occasional article for *The Gardeners' Chronicle*. He died in 1880, when our next subject was setting out on what would be her second journey around the world.

IN THE GARDEN

Robert Fortune was responsible for bringing us plants of great economic importance—British tea drinkers certainly have much to thank him for. Indeed, he has been regarded as the creator of the black tea industries of India and Sri Lanka (Ceylon), which ended China's natural monopoly on tea production. He was also the first European to discover that black tea and green tea are both produced from the same plant. But as well as enriching our lives with tea he helped fill our gardens with Viburnums, Forsythias, Weigelias, Honeysuckles, Wisterias, Magnolias, Bamboos, Cornus, Reeds, Peonies, Azaleas, Chrysanthemums, and Rhododendrons. One of Fortune's introductions, the lovely *Jasminium nudiflorum* (Winter Flowering Jasmine), helps to tide gardeners over during the dark days of winter. Many plants bear his name, including the vein-leaved *Cytomium fortunei*, *Eunoymous fortunei* (the Spindle Tree), *Hosta fortunei* (Plantain Lilies), and the garden favourite *Mahonia fortunei*. Perhaps the prettiest, most delicately evocative plant that Robert Fortune introduced into our gardens is *Dicentra spectabilis*, romantically known as Bleeding Heart.

Plants brought back by Robert Fortune helped to trigger a passion in Victorian gardens for all things Japanese. Japanese Anemone (*Anemone japonica*), *Mahonia japonica*, and other anemones formed part of themed Japanese gardens which brought a hint of the mysterious East to the gardens of Britain.

7

MARIANNE NORTH

(1830–1890)

B ARELY A HUNDRED years after Joseph Banks's voyage around
the world with Captain James Cook, the world was a place where
a woman (admittedly, a wealthy woman with connections in high
places) could travel twice round the globe, once in each direction,
visiting every inhabited continent and many of the major islands.
Marianne North did this not out of idle pleasure-seeking, but as a
self-imposed task: to paint all the flowering species she could in all the
tropical regions of the globe, and whatever other plants she encountered along the way. The result, still housed in a special gallery she paid
for at Kew, was a spectacular benefit to botany. She received some
lessons from Valentine Bartholomew, who was Flower-Painter-in-
Ordinary to Queen Victoria; although her pictures are not as detailed
as those of a professional botanical artist, they are always accurate—
which is far better than being highly detailed but inaccurate. She
visited and painted in the Horticultural Society's gardens in Chiswick,
and on one of her visits to Kew met Sir William Hooker, who gave her
some blossoms of *Amherstia nobilis*.

The vast majority of North's botanical paintings were carried out
during her foreign travels. Since many of the plants she painted were

barely known at all in Europe—and a few were completely un-known—her work formed an invaluable contribution to botanical science. North's travels did not involve the hardships suffered by explorers such as her predecessor David Douglas, or her contemporary Richard Spruce who we meet in the next chapter; but they were gruelling enough to ruin her health and lead to her early death, and truly remarkable for a well-brought-up Victorian lady. Not least, the story is remarkable because she did not start on her quest until she was over forty.

North's background was distinctly aristocratic. She was directly descended from Roger North, who was the youngest son of the fourth Baron North (Lord North of Kirtling), and Attorney-General during the reign of James II. Her father, Frederick North, inherited an estate at Rougham, in Norfolk, and later had a house built for him in Hastings, in the constituency he served for many years as a Liberal Member of Parliament. Born in 1800, he had experienced a conventional upper-class education at Harrow and Cambridge, spent time in Switzerland learning French, and intended to study law, but on his return to England fell in love with Marianne's mother, whom she describes only as 'the beautiful widow of Robert Shuttleworth...and eldest daughter of Sir John Marjoribanks', the MP for Berwickshire. Sir Robert Shuttleworth had died in a road accident, after the coach and four he was driving overturned. His pregnant wife was a passenger in the coach; her daughter, Janet, was born afterwards. As well as a daughter, she brought an estate in Lancashire into the marriage, and soon provided Frederick with children of his own. In addition to her half-sister, Marianne had a brother, Charles, who was born in 1828 and a sister, Catherine, born in 1837. Marianne was born in Hastings on 24 October 1830, the year her father was first elected as an MP. On that occasion, before the electoral system was reformed, there were just ten voters in the constituency, one of whom was Frederick North himself. She was always her father's favourite child, although that doesn't seem to have caused any jealousy among her siblings.

As a girl, Marianne was not educated for much except the life of a gentlewoman—'Walter Scott or Shakespeare gave me their versions of history, and Robinson Crusoe and some other old books my ideas of history'. She had a fine singing voice when young, and took music lessons, but although she showed skill at drawing and painting in watercolours had little or no formal training in art. Winters were spent in Hastings, spring in London, and summers divided between the estates in Lancashire and Norfolk. When Marianne was 12, to her astonishment her sister Janet married the educational reformer James Kay, who was in his late thirties, more than twice Janet's age, and bald; he adopted Janet's surname when she came into her inheritance, and is known to history as Sir James Kay-Shuttleworth. Her father had to give up his seat for a time because of ill-health brought on by overwork, and in 1847 the two remaining girls and their parents set off for Heidelberg, where they stayed for eighteen months at the start of what became a three-year sojourn on the Continent. These were troubled times in Europe (1848 is known as 'the year of revolutions') but Marianne's only comment is that often they were 'too close for comfort to the civil disturbances and wars'.

When they returned to England in 1850, Marianne had a few 'lessons in flower-painting from a Dutch lady, Miss van Fowinkel'; the following year she attended the Great Exhibition, but apart from that led a quiet life until everything changed in the mid-1850s. Frederick North had been re-elected as MP for Hastings again in May 1854, but his wife died, after a slow but pain-free decline, on 17 January 1855. Before she died, she made Marianne promise never to leave her father, and true to her word Marianne, now in her twenty-fifth year, took charge of the household and remained her father's companion for the rest of his life. The house in Hastings was let, and they took a flat in London, giving Marianne the chance to visit Chiswick Gardens and Kew, developing her skill as a flower painter, meeting Sir William Hooker, and seeing exotic plants that made her 'long more and more to see the tropics'. When her brother married, he was given the estate in Norfolk (the Kay-Shuttleworths had the one in Lancashire), and Frederick North and his two daughters would spend their summers travelling in Europe, where their combined luggage was 'nicely calculated under the 160 lb allowed on Continental railways', and on pleasant mountain walks they took 'just enough of necessaries to be easily carried on an Alpine porter's back'.

Over the years, these journeys took in Italy, Hungary, and Greece, and a long talked of trip to Egypt became possible in 1865, when Frederick lost his seat in a General Election. By then, Catherine too was married. While in Switzerland in 1863, the girls had met 'two nice young Oxford lads', one of whom was the 22-year-old John Addington Symonds, already known as a promising poet.[1] After formally asking Marianne's permission, Symonds successfully wooed Catherine and married her in Hastings on 10 November 1864.

Travelling just with her father, Marianne found Alexandria to be 'a nasty, mongrel, mosquito-ish place', but delighted in Karnack, Abu Simbel, Jerusalem, and the Holy Land. It was their last major expedition together. After a couple of short Continental holidays, the Hastings seat became vacant again, and although Frederick North was elected in November 1868 after a hard-fought and ill-tempered campaign, the opposition tried to have the election declared invalid because of bribery. Although the case was thrown out by the courts in April 1869, North was now nearly 70 and his health had been broken by the bitterness of the campaign and its aftermath. In August, Marianne and her father set out for Germany for him to recuperate, but although he seemed at first to recover, soon both his strength and his health declined and he had to return home, where he died on 29 October—five days after Marianne's fortieth birthday. 'He had been my one friend and companion, and now I had to learn to live without him, and to fill up my life with other interests as best I might. I wished to be alone.'

The principal 'other interest' with which Marianne tried to fill up her life was painting. After returning from Egypt, she had been introduced to the use of oils by the artist Robert Dowling (1827–86), who stayed with the Norths in Hastings. Although born in England, Dowling had moved to Tasmania with his parents in 1834, but returned to England in 1857, where he achieved considerable success. After lessons from Dowling in oil painting, Marianne never used any other medium, 'oil-painting being a vice like dram-drinking, almost impossible to leave off once it gets possession of one'. A holiday on the Riviera, accompanied only by her maid Elizabeth, restored Marianne's physical strength, although not her spirits. Then it was on to Pisa, Leghorn, and by steamer to Sicily, with North, a seasoned traveller, discovering that even without her father she encountered no difficulty with customs officers or other arrangements, as she was used to the idea of providing small gifts of tobacco to encourage the efficient processing of her trunks. Although the first weeks were 'full of pain and suffering', the surroundings and her painting gradually revived North, the only fly in the ointment being the 'constant complaints and weariness' of her servant. When the heat reached southern Italy in May 1871, she returned to England, after briefly meeting up with Catherine and John Symonds in Italy, wondering what to do next.

North's long-held dream of travelling to some tropical country to paint the vegetation was triggered into reality when a friend she had made on her visit to Egypt (a 'Mrs S'.) invited North to spend the summer with her in the United States. This seemed like a step in the right direction, because 'people in England have but a very confused idea of the difference between North and South America'. So with the house in Hastings sold and armed with letters of introduction from, among others, Charles Kingsley, she set off with her friend from Liverpool on the Cunard steamer *Malta* on 13 July. She was not quite 41 years old. Whether or not she was really confused about the difference between North and South America, this first modest adventure was ideal preparation for what was to come. Canada and the United States would provide North, like David Douglas before her, with a gentle introduction to independent travel in foreign lands in search of interesting plants, which would stand her in good stead in the years ahead.

The early weeks gave no indication of the kind of hardships North would encounter later. They landed in Boston, and settled into the house Mrs S. had rented in West Manchester, enjoying a holiday and socializing with the quality. This included the wife of Louis Agassiz, the Swiss-born naturalist and Harvard professor who had been the first person to promote the idea of Ice Ages, and the family of Henry Wadsworth Longfellow, who personally showed North round the colleges in Cambridge. A trip to Canada with 'an enormous quantity of luggage' belonging to Mrs S. included a visit to the Niagara Falls; but the independent North was soon travelling on her own, mostly by rail, visiting some of her father's old servants who had settled in America, then on to New York and Washington, always armed with introductions from friends to friends of friends.

After a party at the home of 'diplomatic people', North was invited to the White House, where she met President and Mrs Ulysses Grant. They got on so well that the following evening North was guest of honour at dinner in the White House, and 'wondered if Gladstone or Dizzy would have taken as much trouble for the daughter of an American M.P. who brought a letter from the Secretary of an English embassy'. It was only much later that she learned to her intense amusement that she had been taken for the daughter of Lord North (1732–92), the British Prime Minister chiefly responsible (rather than King George III) for the loss of the American colonies. 'I always knew I was old', she wrote, 'but was not prepared for that amount of antiquity.'[2]

Returning to New York as autumn turned to winter, and now having a clear idea of the relationship between North and South America, North made arrangements to travel next to Jamaica, departing by steamer on 15 December, soon after the first snows. She arrived in Kingston 'alone and friendless' on Christmas Day 1871, but soon made friends and found a house she could rent for 4 pounds a month, surrounded by 'the richest foliage' including bananas, rose-apples, breadfruit (how Banks would have rejoiced!), mangoes, dates, and coconuts. The brightly coloured flowers ran wild like weeds in the neglected garden. For a month, North painted in peace all day while the light was good enough and the rain held off, until 'people began to find me out'. Then, she began to visit them, often irritated by the socializing but happy to be shown even more exotic locations in which to paint. Later, she travelled farther afield, visiting a sugar plantation plagued by rats where they had 'introduced the mongoose from India to eat the rats, but they preferred chickens, and rather liked sugar too, so were, on the whole (like most imported creatures), more harmful than beneficial'. This astute observation highlights that North did more than just paint what she saw, but observed it in context; her writings clearly show her as an early conservationist, much more aware than most of her contemporaries of the damage humankind was already doing to the planet.

At the end of May, North left Jamaica for England, landing at Liverpool on 16 June. But after seeing what the island of Jamaica had to offer she was more than ever eager to see the real tropical vegetation of South America, and two months enjoying the society of her friends in London was enough; on 9 August she was at sea again, this time bound for Brazil via Lisbon. North had a letter of introduction to the captain of the ship, the *Neva*, so was assured of a good cabin and the best attention; on the voyage she became friends with a Belgian merchant, who helped her find accommodation in Rio, where they landed at the beginning of September. At first, North painted the flowers in the Botanical Gardens, making many friends, including a Mr Gordon, the manager of a mining company, and his daughter. They invited North to visit their home on the high plains. Seeing a good opportunity to paint in the real country, she suggested staying for a fortnight; 'they laughed, and with reason, for I stayed eight months!'

Those eight months were the heart of North's South American adventure. Just getting to the Gordon property provided her first real taste of hard travelling, after crossing the bay by boat and un-healthy marshes by train to the foot of the Petropolis hills. From here, it was in a carriage dragged by mules to Petropolis itself, 'a bad imitation of a second-class German watering place', and a rendezvous with the Gordons. For much of the rest of the journey the party travelled in the company of the self-styled 'Baron' Antonio Marcus, an important local figure who did a great deal to help North in the months that followed; but in spite of these well-connected travelling companions, the journey through mud and rain involved overnight stops as varied as a pleasant inn serving an English dinner to a cigar manufacturer's mansion and a grocer's shop.

Where the 'road' became impassable for wheeled traffic, the party joined a train of thirty-seven laden mules heading up into the mining country, forming 'a party which would not have shone in Hyde Park, but was admirably adapted for riding through Brazil in the wet season'. North rode 'Mueda, the steadiest and most calculating of mules', but even she was troubled by a road in which the mud often reached above the knees of the mules. The consolation for her rider was the scenery—tall trees draped with bougainvillea, orange-flowered cassia, *Araucaria braziliensis*, and as they gained altitude, bamboo. 'Every bit of the way was interesting and beautiful'. Eventu-ally they reached the high country and their destination at the Casa Grande of Morro Velho, about a thousand metres above sea level; 'the only drawbacks to the journey left were blistered lips and slightly browned hands'.

Welcomed into the Gordon family home, North found a garden full of flowers, including *Magnolia grandiflora*, gardenias, heliotropes, and 'great bushes of poinsettia with scarlet stars a foot across'. Beyond lay bananas, palms, and the wild flowers she had come to paint, where she saw how at noon the banana leaves 'shut themselves up tight like sheets of folded letter-paper, so as to keep their moisture in, and appear mere knife-like edges to the sun's scorching rays'. In her eight months with the family, North made several excursions, including one through virgin forest in a party led by the Baron and a trip to the Caves of Corvelho with Gordon and his daughter. There, she met the elderly Danish palaeontologist Peter Wilhelm Lund (1801–80), who in 1843 had discovered the caves and the fossils they contained, including human remains some 25,000 years old—at the time the oldest human remains known in the Americas. Lund stayed near the site, at the village of Lagoa Santa, for the rest of his life.

At the beginning of July, North started on the journey home. 'I took away the hope of seeing my kind friends again in England; but in spite of this it was hard to say goodbye to dear Mrs Gordon'. Back in Rio, North met the Emperor of Brazil, introduced to him by 'a letter from my father's old friend Sir Edward Sabine'.[3] She found him to be a gentleman 'full of information and general knowledge on all subjects', who questioned her closely about her activities and told her the names of all the plants in her paintings; he was 'a man who would be worth some trouble to know, even if he were the poorest of private gentlemen'. Although increasingly homesick, North had one last ambition to fulfil in Brazil—a visit to the Organ Mountains. She was surrounded by people who thought it rather shocking and dangerous for a woman to wander in the hills alone, and warned that the way was so difficult and dangerous that she would never succeed; but she persevered, hired a guide, and found 'a quaint and lonely house on the sierra', where 'every rock bore a botanical collection fit to furnish any hot-house in England'. It was 'a spot for an artist to spend a life in', but she had only four days before it was time to head for Rio and her boat home; she arrived in Southampton on 14 September 1873. During her travels Marianne North had developed a style so swift that she could complete a picture during the course of one day. She would start by making a rapid sketch of her subject in pen and ink on strong paper and would then paint the finished sketch in oil paint squeezed straight from the tube. Her aim was to make a lasting record of 'plants in their homes'. The result was vibrant, bold images of plants, especially flowers, in their natural, ecological settings.

During the winter of 1873–4, which was unusually cold in England, North spent much of her time learning to etch on copper. A sociable summer was pleasant enough, but she was beginning to suffer from rheumatism, and couldn't face the prospect of another English winter, so sailed on 1 January 1874 'in a wretched little steamer in unpleasant squally weather' to spend the season in Tenerife. She had, of course, a letter of introduction to the manager of the local Botanic Gardens from the Director of Kew Gardens (by now, William Hooker's son Joseph, who features in Ch. 9), and spent much of her time painting. She was back in England on 8 May, and joined in the pleasures of a London season, including weekend visits to various country houses. It was at one of these weekend gatherings, in the middle of July, that she fell into conversation with 'some people I had never met before, Mr. and Mrs. S'. After listening to North's traveller's tales, they asked where she planned to go next. 'Oh', said North, plucking a name more or less out of the air, 'Japan'. 'You had better start with us', they said, 'for we are going there also, on the 5th of August.' North implies that the offer was not entirely serious, but 'to their surprise, I said I would'. Two and a half weeks later she was on her way.

The journey took them by sea to Quebec, train to Chicago and Salt Lake City, and on by stagecoach—'a horrible springless machine'—in which they were jolted for fourteen hours at a stretch. The Yosemite valley provided a chance to rest for a few days and paint, before pressing on to San Francisco and the comforts of the Occidental Hotel. Not that North spent much time enjoying those comforts. With time to spare before her ship departed, she was soon off again by train for a week in the Nevada Mountains, painting around Lake Taho and Lake Donner. Her last expedition there was a journey of a couple of hours by rail to see some of the remaining redwood forests. 'They were gradually sawing them up for firewood, and the tree would soon be extinct...It is invaluable for many purposes, and it broke one's heart to think of man, the civiliser, wasting treasures in a few years to which savages and animals had done no harm for centuries.'

Then back to San Francisco and a rendezvous with the *Oceanic*, 'one of the finest steamers afloat', which sailed on 16 October. The ship followed a northern route, 'too cool for pleasure', and North 'suffered much from an attack of my old pain', being grateful for the heat from the open fireplace roaring away in the corner of the ship's great saloon. Crossing the International Date Line, they jumped from 28 October to 30 October, and after three weeks without seeing land reached Japan at the end of the first week in November. While North settled in to her hotel in Yokohama, Mr and Mrs S. set off on their own travels. But as usual, North had her letters of introduction, and soon set out to Kobe to pay her respects to the British representative in Japan, Sir Harry Parkes, and his wife. Parkes, who had been born in 1828, was near the end of a long diplomatic career during which he had witnessed the signing of the Treaty of Nanking. After the Second Opium War he was for three years effectively the Governor of Canton, a city with a million inhabitants; he had been Minister in Japan since 1865 and would stay until 1882, three years before he died of malaria. North travelled by train to Yedo, staying for a few days at the British Legation and seeing the sights. She then travelled onward by steamer to Kobe, where Lady Fanny Parkes, eager 'to make me an excuse for escaping its heavy lunches and dinners', took her off to Osaka by rail and sent her on by jinricksha, 'a kind of grown-up perambulator' dragged by men who trotted thirty miles in a day, to Kyoto and a rendezvous with Sir Harry on a diplomatic visit to the governor.

Although the temple area of Kyoto was closed to Westerners at that time, still only half a dozen years after Japan opened up to the West, North was given special permission to go where she liked and paint anything she wanted for three months, 'provided I did not scribble on the public monuments'. Although suffering severely from rheumatism in the cold (not helped by sleeping in a room with paper walls), she held out until 19 December before making her way by boat and train back to Yokohama, where 'I was in the doctor's hands for ten days with rheumatic fever'. The remedy was to travel south, sailing for

Singapore with brief stops at Hong Kong and Saigon. North landed in Singapore, just three degrees north of the equator, on 19 January 1876, still so stiff she could 'barely hobble from the office of the hotel to my rooms', but found one of her windows almost blocked up by a great breadfruit tree, which she immediately began to paint.

Once again, North's network of contacts came to her aid. Friends of friends insisted on putting her up at their home for a fortnight, before, much recovered, she was invited to stay at Government House with Sir William and Lady Jervois. A 'gorgeous tree of *Poinciana regia* (blazing with scarlet blooms)' provided a subject for painting, but once she was well Singapore could not provide enough subject matter, and North was soon making plans to travel farther afield. After just two weeks at Government House, she was off, armed with letters from Sir William, to Sarawak, in Borneo, in a steamer commanded by 'good old Captain Kirk'.

From a botanical point of view, it was here that what became North's first circumnavigation really began to bear fruit. At first, she stayed with the Rajah and Rani (an English couple, Sir James and Lady Margaret Brooke) in some comfort. 'Every one collected for me as usual', and the only problem was what to paint first. But when an official envoy came to visit the Rajah, North persuaded her host to send her off to a remote farm in the mountains. 'The Rajah lent me a cook, a soldier, and a boy, gave me a lot of bread, a coopful of chickens, and packed us all into a canoe.' In the mountains, there were 'caladiums, alpinias, and the lovely climbing plant *Cissus discolor* of all manner of colours, creeping over everything'. North stayed until she had eaten all the chickens and 'the last remains of my bread had turned blue', then descended back through the swamps, 'my soldier using his fine long sword to decapitate the leeches which stuck to me by the way'.

On another journey into the interior, to Tegoro, accompanied by the manager of the Borneo Company's mines and the Rajah's treasurer, a young man from the west of England, North stayed in a house where 'we had our morning tea at half-past six on the verandah, and a plum-pudding in a tin case from Fortnum and Mason'. At a stop on the return journey (made partly by canoe, in which they 'shot the rapids for many miles'), North painted 'the largest of all pitcher-plants ... my picture afterwards induced Mr. Veitch to send a traveller to seek the seeds, from which he raised plants and Sir Joseph Hooker named the species *Nepenthes northiana*'. In all, North had four species and a genus (*Northea seychellana*) named in her honour.

From Borneo it was back to Singapore in Captain Kirk's little steamer, then off to Java in a steamer with only one other English passenger. He turned out to be Arthur Coke Burnell (1840–82), an expert on Sanskrit, with whom she became firm friends and maintained a correspondence until his early death. Batavia proved to be 'a most unpleasant place to sleep in, full of 'heat, smells, noise, and mosquitoes'; but it was no longer the death trap it had been at the time of the *Endeavour*'s visit, and North soon escaped to Buitenzorg, a few hundred feet above sea level, where it was cool enough to sleep. She found Java 'one magnificent garden of luxuriance, surpassing Brazil, Jamaica, and Sarawak all combined'. Everything in Java was well ordered, and 'in spite of the strong rule of the Dutch, the natives have a happy, independent look one does not see in India'. The Botanic Garden, only a quarter of an hour's walk from her hotel, proved a delight; there was a huge variety of species, which had been there so long that 'they grew as if in their native woods', and North had no need to look farther afield for material for more than a month. Then she was off on her travels round the island, armed with a letter from the Governor General instructing all officials 'to feed me and lodge me, and pass me on wherever I wished to go'. Her diaries record the now familiar mixture of some hard travelling and some almost banal 'normality'—taking tea and biscuits with a 'gentlemanly chief, who wore a very stiff stick-up collar and cuffs under his jacket', before heading on horseback up into the volcanic mountains, walking on narrow paths across a bubbling, sulphurous sea of mud where 'it was all rather horrid, and the cold caused me such suffering that I determined to get down the shortest way to warmth again'.

After Java, North returned to Singapore to catch the French ship *Amazon*, 'with a good cabin but unpleasant people', for the voyage to Ceylon (now Sri Lanka). 'I much missed the neat mat and bamboo houses of Java. In Ceylon they were mud-hovels, and everything was less neat.' But there was plenty to paint, and she based herself in Kandy to make the most of the opportunity. Apart from the botanical delights of the island, the highlight of North's visit was a meeting with the photographer Julia Cameron (1815–79), with whom she stayed in Kalutara. Cameron was a pioneer of portrait photography, who has left us a legacy of pictures of nineteenth-century celebrities, ranging from the astronomer William Herschel to the poet Alfred, Lord Tennyson. She was notoriously hard on her subjects, bullying them into the poses she wanted, but North found her 'oddities' to be 'most refreshing':

She dressed me up in flowing draperies of cashmere wool, let down my hair, and made me stand with spiky cocoa-nut branches running into my head, the noonday sun's rays dodging my eyes between the leaves as the slight breeze moved them, and told me to look perfectly natural (with a thermometer standing at 96°)!

Hardly surprisingly, the portrait was not a success.

North left Kalutara on 21 January 1877 and caught the French steamer *Sindh* three days later, travelling via Aden to Naples, where she arrived on 11 February, then on via Rome and Cannes to London, arriving at midnight on 25 February. She had completed her first journey round the world, but would spend only six months in England (the highlight being a visit to her flat by the Emperor and Empress of Brazil) before setting out on her travels again. She had time to put her 500-odd paintings in order and catalogue them for an exhibition at South Kensington Museum, but found that most of those who admired her artistry were woefully ignorant—'nine out of ten of the people to whom I showed my drawings thinking that cocoa was made from the cocoa-nut'.

On 10 September 1877 North left England again to pick up her travels where she had left off in January—initially in Ceylon (where 'I found Mrs. Cameron much as I left her'), then on to India. In Madura, 'starvation, floods and fever were all around', the railway washed away, and the gardens all flooded. In the hope of staving off fever, 'every one was taking opium, so I followed the fashion, prevention being better than cure'. North escaped from the floods on 'a long chair on the shoulders of four coolies' and found a train to Tanjore, the home of Dr Burnell, which she reached on 24 December. It was 'like living with a live dictionary', but with the arrival of the hot season she moved on, visiting the hills where many Europeans went to escape the heat; but finding her limbs and ankles beginning to stiffen and swell, soon descended to the warmth she loved. Her travels took her across a swathe of India that would make an impressive trek even today—to Bombay, to Agra and the Taj Mahal ('bigger and grander even than I had imagined'), to Amritsar and the Golden Temple, to Lahore, Simla, Calcutta, and Darjeeling. From Darjeeling, she painted the distant view of Mount Kanchenjunga, the region where Joseph Hooker botanized and explored. She enjoyed solitude, and abhorred most of the English women she met, 'unthinking, croqueting-badminton young ladies' who 'always aggravated me... I had not met a single person at Darjeeling who had seen the great mountain at sunrise, and few of them had seen it at all that year. Kinchinjanga did not keep fashionable hours.'

One of North's objectives on her tour of India was to build up a collection of paintings of the sacred plants of the various religions of the subcontinent, which are now displayed together at Kew. She also saw the downside of religion in Jaipur, where the sacred bulls were 'a great curse', wandering through the market and eating up food needed by the poor. 'In the famine time it was quite scandalous the amount that was consumed by the idle beasts.'

After another Christmas in India, North sailed from Bombay on 24 February 1879. 'Cold was the one enemy I dreaded, and I met it in the steam-launch which took us up Southampton Water.' Although she enjoyed the luxury of being home, she tired of the tedious task of showing her Indian paintings to friends and friends of friends, and eventually hired a room in Conduit Street for them to be exhibited for the summer. The shillings taken at the door covered two-thirds of the expenses, and 'the remaining third I thought well spent in the saving of fatigue and boredom at home'. Among the enthusiastic reviews of the exhibition, one, in the *Pall Mall Gazette*, suggested that North's paintings ought to be on permanent display at Kew. She wrote to Hooker asking if he would indeed like to take the pictures, if she provided a gallery to put them in. Her wish was to combine the gallery with a tea-house. 'A rest house for the tired visitors', possibly with a cottage attached where a gardener's wife could serve 'tea or coffee & biscuits (nothing else) in the gallery at a fair price'. Hooker 'at once accepted the first part of my offer, but said it would be impossible to supply refreshments to so many', so the tea-house was abandoned. North decided to show her paintings grouped geographically to show the plants of the world, chose the site for the gallery, and picked the architect, James Fergusson, who worked to her direction. Fergusson was a renowned authority on Indian temples, an interest he had pursued during the ten years in which he had been manager of an indigo business. Marianne had enjoyed life in India and was much taken with Fergusson's gallery design with its striking similarity to the verandahed colonial bungalows favoured by members of the British Raj. Fergusson was also fascinated by the problem of providing enough light to show off the unconstrained colours of Marianne North's paintings. He solved this problem by large clerestory windows set high above the paintings, which were to be hung in geographical order above a dado made up of 246 vertical strips of different timbers. At Miss North's request floral sprays decorated the gold painted door surrounds. But the geographical layout of the gallery soon had an unanticipated consequence.

After the wheels had been set in motion, early in 1880 Henrietta Litchfield, one of the daughters of Charles Darwin and an acquaintance of North, passed on a request from her father for the artist to visit him. Darwin was now over 70, and had barely two more years to live; he was too much of an invalid to cope with a visit to North's flat, so she made an agreeable visit to the person she regarded as 'the greatest man living, the most truthful, as well as the most unselfish and modest'. So when, after talking botany for some time, Darwin gently suggested that North's gallery representing the flora of the world would not be complete until she had seen and painted the plants of Australia (which he had seen first-hand on the *Beagle* voyage), 'I determined to take it as a royal command and to go at once'. In her fiftieth year, after various illnesses (largely glossed over in her books) and increasingly affected by rheumatism in cold weather, North set out on what would turn into her second journey round the world, this time from west to east. She joined a party including the Rajah of Sarawak on board the *Sindh* at Marseilles on 18 April 1880, and arrived at Singapore on 15 May.

After ten days in Singapore, the party left for Sarawak in the Rajah's gunboat *Alarm*; North describes Sarawak as 'a country about the size of Scotland' where the population was some 200,000, a 'strange mixture of races' that 'submitted cheerfully to the mild despotism of one simple Englishman'. Once again she travelled upriver by steam launch and pony into the forest to paint, returning by canoe with two Dayak paddlers, 'shooting the rapids lying on my back and looking at the tangled branches overhead'. Fortunately, she was back in the launch when she encountered 'a water-snake full twelve feet long, with its head held nearly a foot out of the water'. On 10 July North left Sarawak, returning to Singapore to catch the *Normandy* ('the very smallest of comfortable ships'), departing for Australia on the 19th.

Brisbane, where she landed on 8 August, was a disappointment. 'A most unattractive place—a sort of overgrown village, with wide empty streets full of driving dust and sand, surrounded by wretched suburbs.' She was happy to escape into the hills, staying with farmers, painting, and soon encountering her first kangaroos. Over the next few months, North travelled by train and stagecoach through much of the habitable part of Australia—down the eastern side via Sydney to Melbourne ('by far the most real city in Australia'), across the south by boat to Adelaide and on to Perth, and over to Tasmania. For part of the journey she travelled with a companion, a 'Miss B.'; the two of them were apparently the first unaccompanied ladies to travel on the route of one of the stage companies, Cobbe and Co., who treated them as minor celebrities.

North's keen eye noted the changes being wrought by the settlers—'it is curious how we have introduced all our weeds, vices and prejudices into Australia, and turned the natives (even the fish) out of it'. Botanical highlights included the wild flowers of the Blue Mountains of New South Wales, the bottlebrush *Callistemon speciosus,* and hakeas. North 'screamed with delight' when she saw the eucalyptus in flower—'every leaf and stalk was pure floury white, and the great flowers (as big as hollyhocks) of the brightest carnation, with gold ends to their stamens'. The biggest disappointment was Tasmania, where much of the countryside was 'too English, with hedges of sweet-brier, hawthorn, and blackberry, nettles, docks, thistles, dandelions'. One rich bit of countryside 'might have been a bit of Somersetshire'. But in Hobart North acquired some travelling companions—'three little opossum-mice, the smallest of all marsupials'. They were with her on the next leg of her journey, across to the southern island of New Zealand. The little marsupials, looked after by friends she had made on the voyage, continued by sea north to the warmer climate of Wellington to await her arrival, while North travelled overland to see more of the country.

For a while, she stayed in the lake country around Queenstown, but the weather there suited her scarcely more than it did opossum mice: 'I felt I could never rough it in such a climate, and my aching limbs could not crawl fast enough to warm me. I sat and wondered if I should ever get home to England and see my gallery finished... I longed to be there without the trouble of going.' But there was a reason for North to be in New Zealand, quite apart from the botanical attractions. She had a cousin there, and had promised his mother to call on him and report back to her how he was getting on. On 1 March 1881 she left Queenstown, travelling via Dunedin to Christchurch, where she took comfort in its 'well-regulated and extra-English hotel'. By then 'I was sick of everything belonging to that cold, heartless, stony island'.

A visit to the farm of her cousin, John Enys, did nothing to change her opinion. Four hours west by train and then by horse-drawn buggy through 'dreary, burnt-up hills', he lived in such primitive conditions that taking breakfast involved leaving the house and scurrying through the yard to the separate kitchen house. Her fingers too stiff to sketch outside, North sat and painted at the window, making only one lengthy excursion with her cousin. By the time she got back to Christchurch she was ill and miserable, and didn't fully recover even in Wellington. She sailed from Wellington for Auckland on 27 March, and then on to San Francisco: 'the Equator nearly cured my rheumatism'.

It's a sign both of how easy travelling was becoming in the 1880s and how exciting North's travels had been to date that her second crossing of the United States, although it provided plenty of material for her painting, was essentially routine. She was back in Liverpool on 13 June 1881, and spent the next twelve months getting everything ready for the opening of her gallery at Kew on 7 June 1882. But in the summer of 1881 she also found time to visit an old family friend who lived at Bromley Common. The family drove her over to Down to meet Darwin once again; he 'seemed no older than his children, so full of fun and freshness', as they sat under a shady tree for hours talking and looking over the Australian paintings. Less than eight months later, on 19 April 1882, he died, forestalling North's hope that he might open her gallery.

There was, though, still one continent not represented in the gallery—Africa. Undaunted by her troublesome time in New Zealand and her recurring ill health, in August 1882 North sailed for Cape Town to correct the omission. Although the nine months she spent in South Africa provided the material she needed to plug the gap, North was often ill, tired, and homesick, frustrated because she could not paint fast enough, and increasingly irritated by the demands of society. In May 1882 she decided enough was enough, and went back to England to take a rest; 'three months at home were delightful, and gave me fresh strength and courage for the task I had still set myself to do', which was to paint in the Seychelles, which had been described to her as a kind of island paradise. She sailed from Marseilles on 27 September, landing in Mahé on 13 October. The climate was right, the flora superb; but in terms of her health it was probably one trip too many.

The islands themselves were everything she had dreamed, the hospitality was excellent, and the flora provided an abundance of subjects for her to paint. Her own account gives little detail of exactly what went wrong, but before she could return home she had to be held in quarantine with a group of would-be fellow travellers because of an outbreak of smallpox in January 1884. During this period she seems to have suffered a nervous breakdown brought on by overwork, developing paranoid delusions of persecution and fearing for her life, imagining that her companions were plotting to murder her and steal her money. 'The same troubles followed me till I reached England, when I was again among friends, and able to enjoy finishing and arranging my paintings in the new room at Kew.'

Stubbornly, as soon as her health seemed to recover North determined to complete her set of paintings with one last journey, to the western part of South America. Her particular objective was to paint the Monkey Puzzle Tree, *Araucaria araucana,* in its native Chile—the only big tree of the world not already represented in her Kew gallery. She set out in November 1884, and 'till we reached Bordeaux all was enjoyment. Then my nerves gave way again...and the torture has continued more or less ever since.'

By now also deaf in one ear, North struggled on, her ship rounding Cape Horn (by now routine for steamships) and landing her at Valparaiso before she travelled on to Santiago. She had by no means lost her sense of wonder at the beauties of nature, marvelling at the view from the mountains 'with blue sky overhead, and a mass of clouds like sheets of cotton-wool below me', and she wryly commented on the oddity of the Monkey Puzzle's name, 'as there are no monkeys in Chili to puzzle'. The work was done as she had planned, but by now it *was* work, no longer a real pleasure, and although she made a modest (by her old standards) excursion into the country, after spending Christmas and New Year at Santiago she sailed to Lima and then on to Panama. Too ill to make a planned visit to Mexico, she crossed to the Caribbean coast (this was long before the opening of the Panama Canal) and sailed for Jamaica, where 'quiet and much good feeding did me real good' before returning to England for the last time early in 1885. A small studio for her use and that of other bona fide artists had been added to her Kew gallery in 1883. The gallery, with its two double-height gallery spaces, housed 832 paintings and delineated more than 900 species of plants. The paintings are arranged oddly to modern eyes, jostling together like a patchwork, but everything is kept in accordance with Marianne North's wishes and it is still a fitting memorial to a redoubtable woman.

Marianne North spent her final years quietly at a house in Gloucestershire, making a new garden and entertaining visitors such as Joseph Hooker and Francis Galton, Charles Darwin's cousin. But she became ill in the winter of 1887–8, and although she made a partial recovery, died on 30 August 1890, just short of her sixtieth birthday. Given the times she lived in, it is by no means disparaging or patronizing to say that she achieved remarkable things for a woman. Not that she didn't experience real hardships—she just doesn't tell us much about them. As Anthony Huxley has commented:[4]

There is practically no hint anywhere [in her writings] of the immense amount of planning her journeys must have involved, while scorching sun, drenching rain, fearful road conditions, travel sickness, leeches and giant spiders, and unsalubrious accommodation are all dismissed in a few airy words.

Few modern English gentlewomen (or men) would put up with that; all hardships are relative. But some are less relative than others. Those endured by our next subject, Richard Spruce, were as extreme as those of any of the botanical explorers, including David Douglas.

IN THE GARDEN

Four species and one genus have been named after Marianne North: a tree in the Seychelles, *Northia seychellana*, which, prior to being painted by North, was unreported outside the islands; a relative of the Amaryllis, *Crinium northianium*; a Feather Palm, *Areca northiana*; and the one most likely to adorn a garden, the African Torch Lily or Poker Plant (*Kniphofia northiana*).

A Marianne North Garden would be a passionate mix of heat, light, and colour. Plants popularized by her paintings are often wildly vibrant and exotic, plants of the jungle rather than the garden. Her paintings feature the wild colours of Bougainvillea, Poinsettia, and Azaleas. North America gave her the Large Yellow Lady's Slipper Orchid and Solomon's Seal, wild Geraniums, black Huckleberries, and *Aquilegias* (Columbine).

Jamaica was a tropical delight, from the opulent orange and black *Blighia sapida* (Akee) and the Nutmeg tree (*Myristica fragrans*) to delicate Gardenias, Lilies, and a 'close, waxy pink creeping ivy'. As well as the wild flowers, Marianne North painted the flowers of domestic gardens—the showy red *Passiflora quadriglandulosa, Brugmansia sanguinea* (Red Angel's Trumpet), and *Lagerstroemia speciosa* (Pride of India).

Brazil was a wonderland of flowers and plants, wild Bromeliads, Ferns, Orchids, Daturas, and Lilies. In the Botanic Gardens of Rio de Janero Marianne North painted huge red and white Water Lilies. As well as flowers she painted an avenue of tall *Roystonea regia* (Royal Palms) and the strange Strangler Fig tree that grows around another tree, finally destroying it. The flowers of the high plains delighted her: 'The flowers on these high campos were lovely campanulas of different tints, peas, mallows, ipomoeas creeping flat on the ground, some with the most beautiful velvety stalks and leaves: many iris, gladioli and sweet herbs.'

8

RICHARD SPRUCE

(1817–1893)

ALTHOUGH RICHARD SPRUCE was much more of an explorer than Robert Fortune, and didn't have the luxury of purchasing his specimens from nurseries, they played similar roles in the commercial development of the botanical world for the benefit of the British Empire. Fortune took tea from China to India; Spruce, in South America, obtained seeds of the tree that produces quinine, and other drugs used in treating malaria, for new plantations in India. But although Fortune seems to have been intended for a horticultural life from boyhood, Spruce came to his vocation by a more devious route.

We know rather more about Spruce's early life than we do about Fortune's, partly thanks to the notes, letters, and diaries that he left, and most accessibly from the biographical introduction that his friend Alfred Russel Wallace wrote for a book that he edited based on Spruce's notes. Richard Spruce was baptized on 10 September 1817, almost exactly five years after the birth of Robert Fortune, in the little village of Ganthorpe, near Castle Howard, in Yorkshire. He was the only son and eldest child of the local schoolmaster (also named Richard), whose own father (yet another Richard) had been a farmer, from a long line of farmers and shepherds. Young Richard's mother, Ann Etty, was said to be a distant relative of the Yorkshire painter William Etty (1787–1849), who painted many nudes in honour of 'God's most glorious work'; some can be seen in the York City Art Gallery. Richard's sister Anna was born in 1819, and another sister, Mary Ann, in 1822. But Mary Ann lived for only two weeks, and Anna died in January 1828. When Ann Spruce (née Etty) died a year later, at the age of 38, Richard, not yet quite 12 years old, was left alone with his 47-year-old father.

Richard barely had time to adjust to the situation before his father married again, in 1832 when he was 50. His second wife, a local girl called Mary Prest, was just 24—less than half his age. In a letter written years later Spruce said that his relationship with her was 'no more cordial than usually exists between stepmother and stepson'.[1] Over the following years, Richard's stepmother produced eight daughters, starting with Hannah in 1833.

All of this may well have played a part in developing Richard's interest in botany. Already bitten by the botany bug, he increasingly spent long periods roaming the countryside, probably in part because of a wish to get away from a house run by his stepmother and filled with an increasing brood of half-sisters. He had the freedom to do so because he seems to have been almost entirely taught by his father, supplemented, Wallace tells us, with 'lessons in Latin and Greek from an old schoolmaster named Langdale'. He excelled both academically and with his botanizing, and was also very musical—in later life he played the bagpipes. By the time he was 16, Spruce had made a list of 403 species found near Ganthorpe, and when he was 19 he listed 485 flowering plants in the Malton district. But there was no hope of him developing his obvious talent through further education. A schoolmaster's modest pay and the needs of an expanding family meant that Spruce's father could do no more than assist his son to become a tutor at a school in Haxby, four miles north of York. There, he did well enough to be able to move on at the end of 1839 to a post as mathematics master at the Collegiate School in York.

Spruce disliked the work, hated being indoors, and was almost continually ill during his time in York. The one good thing about schoolmastering, though, was that it gave him long holidays in which to botanize. Taking advantage of every such opportunity, Spruce began to develop a passion for bryophytes (mosses and liverworts), to publish modest papers, and to develop contacts with other botanists by correspondence. In 1841, he discovered a previously unknown British plant, the rare sedge *Carex paradoxa*, and in 1842 he spent two months in Ireland botanizing and studying bryophytes in the herbarium of Thomas Taylor, then in his mid-fifties and an acknowledged expert on the subject.

Things might have continued like this indefinitely (or until, as Spruce was convinced, schoolmastering and ill-health combined to send him to an early grave), but in the summer of 1844 Spruce's life was set on a new path when the Collegiate School was closed and the premises purchased by a rival school, which moved in. Although he was soon offered another teaching post, Spruce decided that the enforced break gave him an opportunity to try to make a career in botany. He applied for several posts, and wrote to his botanical contacts, including William Borrer, in Sussex, to ask their advice. Borrer introduced Spruce to William Hooker, at Kew. After discussing several possibilities, at the end of 1844 it was decided among the three of them that the best plan would be for Spruce to travel to the Pyrenees as a private collector, financing his trip by selling sets of the plants he collected to wealthy patrons. This was hardly likely to provide financial security, but it would involve proper botanizing and the mountain air might be good for Spruce's health. After much deliberation, he decided to give it a try. The initial expenses of the expedition would be paid for by Borrer, in exchange for the first set of Pyrenean plants that Spruce collected.

With all the arrangements for the trip completed, in March 1845 Spruce was visiting his father's family in Welburn, a village a couple of miles from Ganthorpe, where Richard Spruce senior was now teaching, when there was an outbreak of scarlet fever. Four of the eight Spruce girls caught the disease, and three of them—first Sarah Jane, aged 7, then Diana, aged 2, and lastly Mary Ann, aged 4—died by the end of the first week in April. In addition, Spruce's father was severely ill with the skin infection erysipelas, and Spruce had to take over the schoolmastering duties for a few weeks. So it was not until the end of April, doubtless with a sense of relief, that he was able to leave Yorkshire and set off through France for the Pyrenees.

Although the Pyrenean expedition was a great success in its own way, it was no more than an apprenticeship for Spruce's life's work in South America, and we shall not go into details of it here. To put it in perspective, though, around this time a leading French authority on bryophytes, Léon Dufour, published a list recording 156 mosses and thirteen liverworts from the area; Spruce found 386 mosses and ninety-two liverworts. Returning to England in April 1846, Spruce had to prepare his herbarium specimens for sale, organize his huge collection of bryophytes, and write up his discoveries in a scientific paper, which ended up 114 printed pages long. In both 1847 and 1848 he also had to take time out from these labours for weeks to stand in again for his ailing father, now in his mid-sixties. Spruce also had his own health problems, which had been much less severe while he was in the Pyrenees, and in July 1848 he told Borrer in a letter that he had been in bed for ten days 'suffering at times the most excruciating pains from the passing of gall stones'. But by September that year he was in London again, discussing his future with Borrer, William Hooker, and another botanical acquaintance he had previously corresponded with, George Bentham.[2] The hot topic of botanical conversation that autumn was South America, where two young naturalists from England had arrived in May, and were sending back glowing reports of the opportunities open there for botanizing.

The two men were Alfred Russel Wallace (1823–1913) and his friend Henry Walter Bates (1825–92). Wallace and Bates were both, like Spruce, keen self-taught naturalists—Wallace more interested in botany, Bates more interested in insects. Also like Spruce, they came from the layer of nineteenth-century English society with enough education to dream of following in the footsteps of the likes of Charles Darwin, but not enough money for a university education. Darwin was a direct influence on both Wallace and Bates, as well as Spruce. His book about the voyage of the *Beagle*,[3] which included his inland excursions in South America, had been published in 1839 and eagerly devoured by all amateur naturalists, most of whom could do no more than dream of following him. In this case, though, the dream came true, thanks to the Victorian railway boom.

After a succession of jobs (including a spell as, he admitted himself, a second-rate teacher) Alfred ended up in February 1845 taking over his brother William's surveying business in South Wales when William died of pneumonia. The work he got surveying for the new railway lines provided him with a modest nest egg which he used as seed money for the two-man expedition to Brazil. Once in South America, they intended to finance their investigation of the plants and insects by selling specimens to wealthy collectors back in England—mostly rich dilettantes, but including serious naturalists like Darwin. The specimens they sent back, the glowing reports they gave of the climate, the friendly people, and the abundance of flora and fauna convinced Spruce and his colleagues that the Amazon was the place for him.

With better contacts than Wallace and Bates, even before he left England Spruce was able to find eleven 'subscribers' who agreed to buy his collections. Once his material started arriving back in England and was seen to be of high quality, this was increased first to twenty and then to thirty subscribers. This was largely thanks to the efforts of Bentham, who acted as Spruce's agent, receiving the material from South America, sorting it out, and passing it on to the subscribers. The income, though modest (just £2 per hundred specimens!) was welcome; but it did mean that in addition to his own scientific work Spruce had to collect thirty perfect examples of everything for his patrons (in fact, 31; like Borrer with the Pyrenean material, Bentham was paid with the first complete set that Spruce sent back).

After spending the winter of 1848 and the spring of 1849 preparing for the expedition by studying the material at Kew, Spruce left for South America:

I embarked at Liverpool on the 7th of June 1849, on board the brig, *Britannia*, Edmund Johnson, commander, with a crew of twelve men. My fellow passengers were Mr. Robert King, a young man who agreed to brave the wilds of the Amazon as my companion and assistant,[4] and Mr. Herbert Wallace, who was going out to join his elder brother.

The *Britannia* arrived at Pará (now Belém), near the mouths of the Amazon, on 12 July. Spruce was 31 years old; he would not return to England, his health broken, for fifteen years—and he would never see his father again.

Spruce spent three months collecting around Pará, acclimatizing and learning Portuguese. A natural linguist, he had already got a good grasp of French and Spanish, and would soon add a working knowledge of several native tongues to his repertoire. One of the first lessons he had to absorb was the sheer immensity of the rainforest, and the modest scale of any impact that he could make on it as an individual.[5] Life in the jungle is most prolific high in the trees, in the canopy, where there is access to sunlight, a hundred feet or more above the ground. At first Spruce was reluctant to destroy such mighty trees to obtain specimens, but:

The conviction was forced upon me that the best and sometimes the only way to obtain the flowers or fruits [of the many plants thriving in the canopy] was to cut down the tree ... By little and little I began to comprehend that in a forest which is practically unlimited—near three millions of square miles clad with trees and little else but trees—where even the very weeds are mostly trees, and where the natives themselves think no more of destroying the noblest trees, when they stand in their way, than we the vilest weeds, a single tree cut down makes no greater a gap, and is no more missed, than when one pulls up a stalk of groundsel or a poppy in an English cornfield.

In October 1849, Spruce travelled up the Amazon in the brig *Tres de Junho* to the town of Santarém, 475 miles from the sea. Even there, where the Rio Tapajós joins the Amazon, the river is thirty miles wide, which gives some inkling of just how big the Amazon really is. Santarém was the base used by Wallace and Bates, and it was there that they first met Spruce. Wallace and Spruce formed an instant rapport, and became firm friends. The friendship lasted until Spruce's death, and afterwards, as we have seen, Wallace edited Spruce's *Notes* for publication. He also wrote the obituary of Spruce which appeared in the journal *Nature*.

Spruce spent a further year of relatively easy collecting in the region of Santarém. In October 1850 he left Santarém, heading upriver to Manaus, where the Rio Negro pours into the Amazon, arriving in December. By now, Spruce had formed a clear impression of the 'civilizing' influence of Europeans on the natives. 'Civilized' natives wore shirts, had probably been converted to Christianity, and had picked up other European habits. The natives who had been largely (or completely) untouched by civilization went without. They turned out to be much more trustworthy and hospitable than their civilized cousins, in spite of scary stories about headhunters in the jungle. 'God save me from Indians with shirts', Spruce commented.

At each stage of Spruce's journey upriver, the opportunities for the botanist increased, as did the hardships and the danger. But the hazards of life anywhere on the Amazon were brought home in 1851, when yellow fever broke out in Pará. Its victims included Herbert Wallace, and Alfred Wallace never forgave himself for encouraging his brother to join him in South America. The news took a long time to reach Spruce, whose real adventure began after a further eleven months botanizing. He left Manaus on 14 November 1851 to head up the Rio Negro in a large canoe (large enough to have a cabin) with six paddlers—none of them 'shirts'.

Little more than a month into the journey, Spruce received news that his friend Wallace was desperately ill with 'fever' (in fact, malaria) at the settlement of São Joaquim, where the Rio Uaupés flows into the Rio Negro. This was on his route, and Spruce was close enough to hurry to the village and attend his sick friend, who was cured with the aid of quinine, possibly brought by Spruce, who certainly carried a supply with him. At that time, malaria (or the ague) was thought to be caused by 'bad air' (hence the name, from the Italian *mal'aria*) associated with swamps and stagnant water; nobody knew that it was carried by some kinds of mosquitoes.[6] But quinine, obtained from the bark of trees found (at that time) only high in the Andean rainforest, had long been known to cure the disease. Those trees would eventually feature large in Spruce's life; but not until he had spent nearly another ten years in South America.

The epic journey which had been interrupted by tending the sick Wallace took Spruce up the Rio Negro and the Rio Uaupés, and into the region where the borders of Brazil, Colombia, and Venezuela meet. One of the hazards of this trip was an encounter with tiny blood-sucking bats, which operated by night, attacking any exposed extremities of a sleeping person: they 'do not stop at the toes, but bite occasionally on the legs, fingers' ends, nose and chin and forehead, especially of children'. But Spruce avoided their attentions: 'As I wear stockings of a night, wrap myself well in my blanket, and often cover my face with a handkerchief, I have hitherto escaped being bitten, but they often come into my hammock in search of a vulnerable point.'

Collecting as he went, and sending his collections back downriver whenever the opportunity arose, to be forwarded to England, it took him a year and a half to reach San Carlos del Negro, in Venezuela, where he arrived on 11 April 1853. The journey was as uneventful as any trip up these rivers by canoe could be—that is, apart from the usual jungle hazards there were no particular risks to Spruce's life—and his notes give very little detail of his day-to-day life. He made San Carlos his base until November 1854, taking several long collecting trips into the jungle, particularly to the north and east. Some idea of the 'normal' hazards of life at that time and that far from the centres of civilization, even in a settled community, can be gleaned from a letter Spruce wrote to Hooker on 27 June 1853:

We think ourselves well off at San Carlos when we can eat once a day...A country without priests, lawyers, doctors, police, and soldiers is not quite so happy as Rousseau dreamt it ought to be; and this in which I now am has been in a state of gradual decadence ever since the separation from Spain, at which period (or shortly after) the inhabitants rid themselves of these functionaries in the most unscrupulous manner.

The lawlessness was highlighted a week later, when the Feast of St John was an excuse for the natives to get drunk and rampage through the settlement. Most Europeans, anticipating what was to come, left for the duration of the festivities; but Spruce and two young Portuguese men he was sharing a house with decided to stay. At the height of the rioting, Spruce stood in the open doorway of the house, a revolver in each hand, keeping guard. Six feet two inches tall, thin to the point of gauntness and heavily tanned, with long blond hair and a wild beard, he made an impressive sight, and none of the drunken revellers came near the house.

In August, Spruce experienced his worst encounter with the wild-life—not a big cat or a venomous snake, but stinging ants, known as tucandéra. Accidentally disturbing a nest of these creatures, he was 'dreadfully stung about the feet, for I wore only slippers without heels and these came off in the struggle [to escape]'. Although only five minutes' walk from the house he struggled to get there:

I was in agonies and had much to do to keep from throwing myself on the ground and rolling about as I had seen the Indians do when suffering from the stings of this ant. I had in my way to cross a strip of burning sand and then wade through a lagoon, partly dried up and not more than two feet deep. Both these increased the torture: I thought the contact with water would have alleviated it, but it was not so.

The only relief he found was to rub the afflicted portions with a little hot oil—curiously, though, when the pain began to subside three hours later, the parts that had been rubbed took longest to recover. 'The stings that caused me most suffering were four close together among the fine veins below the left ankle', and a slight numbness persisted in his feet the next morning; but 'nothing was visible externally more than would be caused by the stinging of an ordinary nettle'.

A year later, Spruce had his own first encounter with malaria. He had been on a long trip away from San Carlos, north up the Rio Casiquiare to the Orinoco. This was where the great German explorer Alexander von Humboldt (1769–1859) had shown, at the beginning of the nineteenth century, that there was indeed a connection between the Orinoco river system and (through the Rio Casiquiare and the Rio Negro) the Amazonian river system. Humboldt's *Personal Narrative* was one of the books (another was Darwin's *Journal of Researches*) that Spruce carried with him on his travels, and he was particularly delighted to be following in the great man's footsteps. The richness of the flora was also a delight; but the process of collecting specimens was a torment.

On this expedition, Spruce came to a tiny settlement called Esmeralda, intending to collect on the slopes of the nearby Duida mountain. He arrived on Christmas Day 1853 to find what seemed like a ghost village—just a few houses, doors closed tight in spite of the heat, and no sign of human or animal life. But:

If I passed my hand across my face I brought it away covered with blood and with the crushed bodies of gorged mosquitoes. In this you have the key to explain the unearthly silence. The apparently tenantless houses had all the inhabitants in them who, bat-like, drowse away the day and only steal forth in the grey of the morn and evening to seek a scanty subsistence.

Spruce had no choice but to work during the daytime, in spite of the mosquitoes. He couldn't sit down to eat, but to obtain slight relief from their attentions had to walk about with his plate in his hand; even then, the food was crawling with the creatures:

I constantly returned from my walk with my hands, feet, neck and face covered with blood, and I found I could nowhere escape these pests. If I climbed the cerros, or buried myself in the forest, or sought the centre of the savannahs, it was the same, but it was worst of all on the river.

In the light of modern knowledge, the surprise is not that he became ill with malaria, but that he lasted so long before succumbing to a severe attack.

Plagued by mosquitoes all the time, Spruce continued collecting, travelling north up the river system. In the summer[7] of 1854 he was at a mission post called Maipures, near the border between Colombia and Venezuela, when the fever began to set in. By the time he reached his temporary base at the township of San Fernando, right on the border, he was 'nearly helpless' as the fever struck with full force. For some reason, at first Spruce failed to dip into his supply of quinine, perhaps hoping that the fever wasn't malaria and would soon pass. In fact, he came very close to death over the next two weeks. Anticipating the event, his native porters exchanged all the equipment he had with him on the trip for rum and got paralytically drunk; a so-called nurse hired to look after him was no better, and Spruce recalled her sitting on the verandah shouting 'Die, you English dog, that we may have a merry valorio [watch night] with your dollars'.

After fifteen days, Spruce at last began dosing himself with quinine, and by 5 August, thirty-eight days after collapsing, he was cured. On the 28th, he had made it back to San Carlos and the junction with the Amazonian river system, although he was still far from being his old self. As he wrote to Bentham a couple of weeks later, 'Even yet at the end of three months from the first attack, I am very far from having regained my strength, and I am unable to work continuously on anything'. But at least he was alive.

What was this quinine that had saved Spruce, Wallace, and un-counted numbers of other people from the clutches of malaria? In the second half of the seventeenth century, a romantic but completely untrue tale circulated in Europe about a beautiful woman, the Con-desa de Chinchón, wife of the fourth Count to hold that title, who was said to have been struck down by malaria in Lima, then part of Spain's South American empire. She was allegedly cured by a native remedy prepared from the bitter bark of a tree found growing in the Andean rainforests, and known in the local Quechua language as *quina quina*, meaning 'bark of barks' (shortened by Europeans to *quinquina*). According to the legend, the Condesa recovered, returned to Spain, and introduced the cure for malaria to Europe. In fact, the Condesa, whose husband kept a detailed diary from which we know a great deal about her life, never had malaria, never returned to Spain, and died of yellow fever in 1641. It was actually the Jesuits who learned about the bitter bark and its almost miraculous powers, and who first took the powder made from the bark back to Rome. But one person who lapped up the romantic story was Linnaeus, who got it from an Italian source, where the Condesa's name was spelled 'Cinchón', because in Italian the 'ci' is pronounced the same way as 'chi' in Spanish. So in honour of the Condesa, in 1742 he gave the generic name '*Cinchona*' to the trees from which quinine is derived, and *Cinchona* they have been ever since.

By the middle of the nineteenth century, demand for quinine was soaring as European countries extended their empires around the world. But it had never been 'farmed' in any sense, and the *Cinchona* of South America were being cut down for their bark at such a rate that there was a real risk that the supply would run out. The British and Dutch in particular needed a steady supply of quinine for their colonies—and in both countries politicians realized the commercial potential if they could cultivate quinine in their colonies and sell it worldwide. An opportunity to make money while doing something that could be presented to the world as altruism was too good to be missed, so it was inevitable that someone would soon rise to the challenge of taking *Cinchona* from South America to India and the Far East. The person who was in the right place to organize this 'rescue' of the fever-curing tree was Clements Robert Markham, an ex-Royal Navy officer fascinated by South America, and the person who was in the right place to obtain the seeds and young plants required on Markham's behalf was Richard Spruce.[8]

Clements Markham was born (on 20 July 1830) in the same part of Yorkshire as Spruce; but there the similarities in their circumstances ended. Markham's great-grandfather had been the Archbishop of York and a tutor to two royal brothers who both became kings—George IV and William IV. The connection was not forgotten, and in the reign of George IV Markham's father was appointed Canon at Windsor, one of the principal royal residences. Brought up among the most privileged members of society, Markham was also a bright and eager student who might have become an academic or a lawyer if not for a chance encounter when he was 13. Dining at the house of an aunt who happened to be the Countess of Mansfield, Markham fell into conversation with another guest, Rear-Admiral Sir George Seymour, who was soon to depart on a voyage to the Pacific in *HMS Collingwood*. Perhaps not expecting to be taken seriously, Seymour asked if the boy would like to come along; Markham said 'yes', and joined the navy as a cadet. The ship sailed less than a month later, on his fourteenth birthday.

From Markham's point of view, the geographical aspects of the voyage were a great success, and he fell in love with South America. He also coped comfortably with most of the navy life, and showed signs of becoming a good officer—perhaps even, in due course, an admiral himself. But he abhorred the harsh naval discipline meted out to the common sailors, still enforced by punishments such as flogging forty years after the death of Nelson, and wanted no part of it. For that reason, he decided to resign from the Navy on his return to England; but his father felt that he had not given it a fair trial, and at his behest Markham stayed in the service. In 1850 the young man was posted to *HMS Assistance* as a midshipman. The *Assistance* was part of an expedition sent to seek traces of John Franklin's earlier expedition, lost in attempting to find a north-west passage from the Atlantic to the Pacific through the ice of the Arctic north of Canada. The new expedition found no trace of the Franklin expedition, and was itself stuck in the Arctic ice through the winter of 1850–1. But at least this gave Markham the opportunity to read and reread, until he almost knew them by heart, two books he had brought with him—one on the history of Peru, and one on the Quechua language he had heard on his earlier travels. Although promoted to lieutenant on his return to England, Markham, now 21 and legally his own man, resigned his commission in September 1851; the following summer, with reluctant support from his father, he set out for Peru. His travels were, however, cut short in the (northern) spring of 1853 by the death of his father, which meant that Markham had to find a job.

He ended up in the Civil Service, stuck in an office of the Board of Control, a government department closely involved with the East India Company. In his spare time, Markham wrote papers for the Royal Geographical Society about his experiences in South America, becoming known as an expert on Peru. He also found time to meet and marry Minna Chichester, the daughter of the Rector of Arlington. Throughout the 1850s, both the need for quinine and the appreciation of its value had increased, and in 1857 Forbes Royle, the splendidly titled 'Reporter on Indian Products' to the East India Company, wrote that the British had a 'duty to humanity' to save the *Cinchona*. 'The subject is yet of such great importance, both in an economical and a philanthropic point of view, that every exertion should be made to ensure its accomplishment.' But 1857 was also the year the Indian Mutiny began,[9] one result of which was that the British Government finally took over the running of its colony from the East India

Company, and no immediate action was taken on Royle's *crie de coeur*. Late the following year, William Hooker lent his weight to the proposal, and the wheels began to turn in 1859. Markham, one of their own men and someone with experience of Peru, was asked by the India Office to take on the task. He was formally appointed to the job on 8 April 1859, still a few months short of his 29th birthday.

The thoroughness of Markham's preparations for the task, including giving himself a crash course in the relevant botany, is shown from his notebooks, which are now in the archive of the Royal Geographical Society, and his correspondence.[10] Although the original proposal was to send just Markham and a skilled gardener to Peru to gather the plants and seeds, he pressed hard for four separate expeditions to operate simultaneously. In the end, he was given funding for three. As Markham explains in his book *Travels in Peru and India*:

In employing several agents in districts widely removed from each other, my chief object was to effect the introduction of as many valuable species as possible; but I also reflected on the extreme difficulty of the undertaking, and the overwhelming chances against success which confronted a single-handed attempt.

Why the rush to send these expeditions simultaneously? Because:

I considered that it was essential that the proceedings should be completed during the first year if possible, in order to give as short a time as was practicable for the awakening of that narrow-minded jealousy in the people of the South American Republics, which I was well aware would sooner or later be aroused.

In other words, it was to be a smash and grab raid, before action could be taken to stop the 'export' of the valuable *Cinchona*.

Markham himself left to explore the forests of Bolivia on 17 December 1859, accompanied by his wife, Minna, and a gardener, John Weir, recommended by the Veitch nursery. To collect in the Huánuco province of Peru, Markham 'procured the services of Mr. Pritchett, a gentleman who had passed some years in South America'; and from Kew another skilled gardener, Robert Cross, was sent out to assist Markham's third collector, Richard Spruce, in the *Cinchona* forests of Ecuador.[11] On the voyage out, Markham took with him thirty Wardian cases, fifteen for himself and fifteen for Spruce, built to the best specifications after he had consulted Robert Fortune, who happened to be in England in 1859.

For various reasons, but rather proving the wisdom of making several simultaneous attempts to secure *Cinchona* for the British Empire, only the plants and seeds collected by Spruce survived to take root and flourish in India, so we shall say little about the other two expeditions. But don't just take our word for it; Markham, never a self-effacing man, was fulsome in his tribute to Spruce, whom he described as 'an excellent botanist and most intrepid explorer', continuing:

Of his qualifications there could be no doubt, but I could scarcely have ventured to hope that the service which he undertook to perform would have been done so completely and so thoroughly, and would have been crowned with such undoubted success. It is perhaps invidious to make distinctions, where all have worked so zealously; but it is due to Mr. Spruce to say that by far the largest share of credit is due to him, and that his name must take the most prominent place in connection with the introduction of these precious plants into India.

Spruce first became aware of the *Cinchona* situation in 1856, when he travelled overland to Ecuador. Ecuador is a small country (by South American standards) on the Pacific side of the continent; as its name suggests, it straddles the equator, which runs just north of the major city of Quito. The easiest way to get there would have been to go down the Amazon to Pará and round Cape Horn by ship. But by 1855 Spruce had followed the Amazon and its tributaries so far west that he was collecting around Tarapoto, a pleasant, if remote, town fifteen hundred feet above sea level on the eastern side of the Andes in Peru.[12]

It was at least possible to get to Ecuador partly by river and partly on foot through the jungle—and if a journey was possible, Spruce was up for it. To reach the town of Ambato, not far from Quito and an ideal base from which to go botanizing, would then involve further travel through the mountains; but Ambato offered a climate that might be beneficial to Spruce's health as well as a chance for more collecting and an opportunity to work quietly on his collections. There would also be a chance to pick up money sent out by Bentham.

About this time, Spruce began a correspondence with Daniel Hanbury, a 'druggist' (pharmacist) based in London, who wrote to draw his attention to the importance of *Cinchona* and urged him to collect specimens. Hanbury's original letter has been lost, and there is no direct evidence that at this stage Spruce was thinking about the commercial potential of *Cinchona*, even though he was, as always, very short of cash. He may simply have decided to go to Ecuador, in the words of the mountaineer George Mallory, 'because it's there'. Whatever his motives, the journey Spruce set out on on 23 March 1857 proved his most arduous yet.

Spruce was accompanied by two traders, twelve natives, and his dog, Sultan. Even the first stage of the journey, along the Huallaga River, proved too much for the dog. The open dugouts had to pass under waterfalls, survive rapids, and were tossed around in whirlpools. 'The horrid roar of the waters', wrote Spruce, drove the dog mad, and he refused to eat for six days, snapping at anyone who came near him. 'I saw all hope of saving him was vain, and was obliged to shoot him.' This inauspicious beginning set the tone for the journey. Travelling up the Pastaza river to the border with Ecuador, then on the Bobonaza up towards the Andes, they spent dreary days pestered by insects, usually hungry, and on one occasion passing through a village struck by leprosy. Heading up the Bobonaza, the climate improved, but they had to work against the strong current in the narrow river. On the evening of 21 May, with the dugouts tied up for the night and everyone on board, a sudden storm caused a rise in the river 'in a roaring surge which broke under the canoes in whirlpools'. The natives climbed into the trees to fasten the mooring ropes (actually lianas) of the canoes higher up, but before they could do so the surging current increased further, and all they could do was cling to the lianas attached to the boats while also maintaining their grip on the trees. Spruce, in his canoe, expected at any minute to be swept away to his death. 'I shall ever feel grateful to those Indians who, without any orders from us, stood through all the rain and storm of that fearful night, relaxing not a moment in their efforts to save our canoes from being carried away by the flood.'

In spite of this experience, Spruce stayed in the region, based at a village called Puca-yuca, for three weeks, collecting and recovering from the trials of the journey so far. From here onwards, the journey would have to be by foot,[13] and he set off on 14 June, accompanied by eight natives. His immediate destination was the town of Baños, known for the hot springs that gave it its name, lying under the Tungura-hua volcano; but to get there would be a struggle across steep ravines and fast-flowing streams, ploughing through mud in almost constant rain. The consolation—a real one for Spruce—was that this climate made the region the mossiest place he had ever seen. Not just the branches of the trees but the topmost twigs were, he recorded, 'shaggy with mosses...whenever rains, swollen streams, and grumbling Indians combined to overwhelm me with chagrin, I found reason to thank heaven which had enabled me to forget for the moment all my troubles in the contemplation of a simple moss'.

Spruce eventually reached Baños on 1 July 1857, 102 days after leaving Tarapoto and a few weeks before his fortieth birthday. The higher altitude (6,000 feet) did little good for his health—he found it too cold after his years in the jungle, and suffered 'a cough so violent as often to bring up blood from both nose and mouth'. But he made Baños his collecting base for the next six months, before moving on to Ambato, on the high sierra on the route to Quito. It was a miserable journey over cold, windswept mountain passes, with Spruce, muffled inside several ponchos, seated on a mule; but Ambato, enjoying a warm mountain climate like perpetual spring, was worth the discomfort of getting there. Ecuador was in a state of political turmoil (most South American countries were in a state of political turmoil most of the time in the nineteenth century), but in Ambato Spruce made a friend who would prove invaluable in these troubled times—a physician, James Taylor, who had been a doctor for the former President of Ecuador, General Juan José Flores, and knew his way around the political scene; it also helped that he was married to the daughter of one of the generals who had liberated much of South America under Simón Bolívar. Spruce also met the American Ambassador, Philo White, and the British Consul in Quito, Walter Cope, who seems to have been the person who first impressed Spruce with the political and commercial importance of *Cinchona*.

Ambato remained Spruce's base for the next two and a half years. Even though, as he wrote to Bentham, he felt 'unequal to the painful mountain ascents, exposed at the same time to a burning sun and a piercingly cold wind', the fear of a penurious existence in England, 'a contingency not to be reflected on without dread', stopped him from going home; he pleaded in vain for 'some consular appointment here, were it only for £150 a year', on which to get by.

In September 1858, Spruce wrote to the Chief Clerk at the Foreign Office in London, George Lenox-Conyngham, offering to collect *Cinchona*. He said that he could 'speedily' travel to the *Cinchona* forest, where 'the bark trees are rapidly verging to extinction, and it is therefore of the first importance that steps should be taken for their cultivation on a large scale, in some country where there is no lack of industrious hands'. He went on to point out that if the Government took up his offer they would have 'the advantage of a person already on the spot, and familiar with the country, the people and the language[14] and (what is of more importance) with the plants whose products are sought'.

This letter reached London in December 1858, just at the time when Hooker was reviving the interest of the powers that be in the idea of transplanting *Cinchona* to India, and the Foreign Office were quick to check Spruce's credentials with Hooker. He wrote to them in January that 'I will venture to say without hesitation if the Government ever makes an attempt of the kind there is no man so competent to the work as Mr Spruce'. So in April 1859, when Markham was given the task of organizing that attempt, it is no surprise that with this information to hand (he refers to it in his first 'Cinchona Notebook') one of his first acts was to recruit Spruce. Spruce was so delighted when Markham wrote to him to negotiate terms, and so used to poverty, that he seriously undervalued himself, only asking for £30 a month to undertake the task. Not surprisingly, his terms were accepted. As we have seen, it would be early 1860 before the Wardian cases would arrive in South America with Markham and the collecting could begin. While Markham made his preparations in London, Spruce was finding the best source of *Cinchona* in Ecuador and making his own arrangements. He had no illusions about the difficulties he faced; to his fellow-botanist John Teasdale he wrote 'I have been entrusted by the India Government with the charge of obtaining seeds and young plants of the different sorts of cinchona (Peruvian Bark) found in the Quitonian Andes for transporting to our Eastern possessions... This task will occupy me (if my life be spared) the greater part of next year.'

Not the least of the difficulties faced by Spruce was the fact that at the time he was collecting *Cinchona* Ecuador was in the grip of full-blown civil war, with rebels controlling the port of Guayaquil and the lowlands, while the Government, based in Quito, controlled the high sierra. In August 1859, in spite of these difficulties, Spruce visited the *Cinchona* forests around Lucma, in the western Andes, but was unimpressed with the opportunities the sadly depleted forests offered for his task. Back in Ambato, he learned that in the opinion of the locals the best bark came not from Lucma but from the western foothills of the Chimborazo Mountain, at over 6,000 metres one of the highest in the world. The forests, which flourished between about 3,500 and 7,000 feet (roughly 1,000 to 2,000 metres) above sea level, covered five thousand square kilometres, and were owned by two men. One was General Flores—the same General Flores whom Spruce's new friend James Taylor had served as a doctor. Although Flores had been living abroad for fifteen years, he had just been called back to Ecuador to help the government forces against the rebels, and through Taylor's good offices Spruce was able to get the General to agree to rent his forest to Spruce for the months the collecting would require. With Flores on board, the other owner, a notary named Francisco Neyra, agreed as well. The fee was four hundred US dollars, which were supplied by the British Consul in Guayaquil. This successful bargaining, which covered Spruce's activities with a cloak of legitimacy, was just as important as the collecting itself, and a great tribute to his skill with people, as well as with plants.

Now came the real work—collecting seeds and preparing plants for transportation to India. But first, Spruce had to get to the forests. As part of Markham's plan to obtain as many kinds of *Cinchona* as possible, Spruce persuaded Dr Taylor to gather one kind, *Cinchona officinalis*, from one part of the forest, while he collected *Cinchona succirubra* (the 'red-barked' *Cinchona*, also known as 'roja-roja') in another part of the forest—one man couldn't collect both in one season, since it was a fifteen-day trek between the locations of the two kinds of tree.

While making the final preparations for his own expedition in Ambato in early April 1860, Spruce suddenly became deaf in his left ear. But the dry season and the opportunity it provided to collect seeds wouldn't wait, and the deafness was only an inconvenience, so he continued with his preparations anyway. Less than three weeks later, however, he suffered an illness so severe that the entry in his journal for 29 April is simply headed The Break Down. He woke up that day paralysed in his legs and back, and although he eventually made a partial recovery, he later added a note to that diary entry:

'From that day forth I was never able to sit straight up, or to walk about, without great pain and discomfort, soon passing to a mental exhaustion.'

For a time, Spruce seriously considered giving up his mission, and delegating it to Taylor; but by the second week in June, tended by Taylor (but probably to little effect over and above nature taking its course) he was sufficiently recovered to set out, initially with Taylor and the usual native assistants, for the western slopes of the Andes. Although he managed to get around on horseback, or by mule, and complete his far from easy task, he would never be fully mobile again.

The early part of the journey involved trekking along narrow mountain trails across a saddle rising as high as four thousand metres. On the journey down the other (Pacific) side of the mountain, the trails were so difficult that instead of mules the Ecuadorians used small Andean bulls as pack animals, because their cloven feet made it easier for them to maintain a grip on the slippery slopes. Those trails took Spruce back down into the jungle and its all too familiar hardships. Spruce wrote that although he did not intend to fill up his journal with 'the continual groanings of an invalid' he would set down 'once and for all' that 'I was but too often in that state of prostration when to lie down quietly and die would have seemed a relief'. And all for £30 a month.

Spruce made his base for the collecting at a settlement called Limón, where he would stay for three months. He first had to identify good specimens of mature *Cinchona* in full flower, then wait for the seeds to ripen, paying the locals to leave the trees and their seeds alone. As if he didn't have enough problems, government forces moving down from the sierra to attack the rebels in the lowlands chose a route through Limón. 'For six weeks we were kept in continual alarm by the passage of troops, and it required all our vigilance to prevent our horses and other goods being stolen.' The need for vigilance, and for Taylor's local political knowledge and contacts, meant that Spruce's companion could not, after all, be sent to collect *C. officinalis*, so the entire success of the mission depended on their efforts at Limón. But before the seeds were ripe, an exhausted Robert Cross arrived, after an arduous journey up river from Guayaquil. He had suffered the inevitable illnesses, and been so hampered by the difficulty of travelling through a war zone that he had had to leave the Wardian cases, knocked down in a 'flat pack' state for ease of conveyance, at Aguacatel, a village downriver, for safe keeping.

On his arrival at Limón Cross set to work taking cuttings from the *Cinchona* trees, and planting them out in a makeshift nursery, shielded by a roof made of palm leaves. By August, there were a thousand seedlings to be tended, watered by hand from bamboo buckets and kept safe from a plague of caterpillars by what Spruce called Cross's 'unremitting watchfulness'. The first seed pods ripened in mid-August, and eight seeds planted by Cross as an experiment all produced healthy plants. By mid-September, Spruce had gathered 2,500 seed pods, each containing, on average, about forty seeds. With those and the plants, they were ready to leave. Fortuitously, by this time the troops under the command of General Flores had taken Guayaquil, and there was no military impediment to travel to the coast. Spruce travelled by horse and steamer to the port, completing an overland journey across South America from the mouth of the Amazon to the Pacific, and sent off two packages of seed by steamer, one to Hooker and one to the Botanic Garden in Jamaica, on 14 October. That was the easy part of the job.

Spruce now returned to Aguacatel and spent two days putting the fifteen Wardian cases together. He hired a large balsa-wood raft made from the trunks of twelve trees, ranging from 63 to 66 feet long and a foot or so wide, loaded the cases aboard, and waited for Cross to arrive with the plants. With the seedlings, individually wrapped in wet moss, packed in bamboo baskets on the backs of Andean bulls, Cross made the difficult journey, arriving on 13 December with 637 plants intact. They set off together on Christmas Eve 1860, with the rainy season having begun and the river running, in Spruce's words, 'like a sluice'. The river 'narrowed in places to 30 yards, and the navigable channel is further straitened by the trees (chiefly species of Inga) which hang far over the water'. With the winding river in flood, the run to Guayaquil was dangerous but quick; the three crewmen struggled to keep their craft in midstream, and on one occasion it smashed through the overhanging branches near the bank so that 'the heavy cases were hoisted up and dashed against each other; the roof of our cabin smashed in'. But none of the cases overturned. Most of the plants survived—just. It took only three days to reach Guayaquil, where Spruce saw Cross and his precious cargo safely on board a steamer, his poorly paid but patriotic duty to the British Empire completed. There was nothing illegal about any of this, because nobody in Ecuador had thought to pass a law making it illegal. When they found out what had happened, the Ecuadorian Government was furious, and in a classic example of shutting the stable door soon passed a law banning the export of *Cinchona* plants, cuttings, or seeds.

If it hadn't been for the political uncertainty caused by the civil war, Spruce would probably never have had a chance to complete his mission. As it was, Cross tended the plants all the way back to England, arriving at Southampton in February 1861, and then via Egypt and the Red Sea (this was before the completion of the Suez Canal) to India. For once, his job involved far more than just sealing the Wardian cases up and leaving the contents to fend for themselves. For such a long journey through different climatic extremes, being switched from one means of transport to another several times, the cases required regular attention. Sometimes they had to be exposed to benefit from whatever sunlight was available; sometimes they had to be protected from the heat in the Red Sea. But Cross was up to the task. His skill as a gardener saw 463 healthy plants, plus the viable seeds, landed at Ootacamund in April 1861. By 1866, there were more than two hundred and forty-four thousand young *Cinchona* in the Indian plantations.

The plantations established in India as a result of Spruce's skill in the field and Cross's skill on the journey were instrumental in establishing a supply of cheap, readily available medicine for the treatment of malaria—although not quite in the way that the British had intended. It turned out that the bark from the *C. succirubra* was not particularly rich in quinine itself, although it did contain other alkaloids, including quinidine, that were just as effective. The other great thing about *C. succirubra* was that it was hardy and proved relatively easy to cultivate. But while all this had been going on, the Dutch, Britain's colonial and commercial rivals in the Far East, had obtained seeds of another kind of *Cinchona*, *C. calisaya*, from an English adventurer based in South America, Charles Ledger. It turned out that the bark of this particular variety of *C. calisaya* had the strongest concentration of quinine of any *Cinchona*. After careful breeding, selecting the plants with the greatest concentration of quinine, the Dutch established plantations of the variety, which became known as *C. ledgeriana*, in Java. The big snag was that *C. ledgeriana* was difficult to grow and easily succumbed to attack by fungus. The solution was to graft young plants of *C. ledgeriana* onto *C. succirubra* rootstock. In this way, Spruce was responsible for the success of both the British and the Dutch *Cinchona* plantations. The person who benefited most from this success, however, was not Spruce, but Markham.

Markham became the Secretary of the Royal Geographical Society in 1863, helped to establish the *Cinchona* plantations in India and Ceylon (Sri Lanka) in the mid-1860s, was the Official Geographer on an expedition to Abyssinia (Ethiopia) headed by Robert Napier in 1868, was involved in the organization of the successful attempt by the British to smuggle seeds of the rubber plant out of South America in the 1870s, travelled to Greenland in 1875, was knighted in 1896, and became, as President of the Royal Geographical Society from 1893 to 1905, a powerful advocate of polar exploration—it was Markham who chose Robert Falcon Scott as leader of the British Antarctic Expedition at the beginning of the twentieth century. Markham lived long enough to learn of Scott's fate on his second Antarctic expedition in 1913, before he died, heaped with honours, at the end of January 1916, at the age of 85. His end was bizarre. Although his house had electric light, Markham was reading in bed by candlelight on 29 January and accidentally set light to his bedclothes. Although help came quickly in response to his cries, so that the fire was swiftly put out and Markham was not badly burned, he went into a state of shock and died twenty hours later without regaining consciousness.

And what of Spruce?

The *Cinchona* expedition was Spruce's last big adventure. Having fought ill-health since his breakdown in April 1860, almost as soon as Cross was safely on his way from Guayaquil Spruce suffered a nearly complete physical and mental collapse. He stayed in Guayaquil, struggling to write his report to the India Office, but by his own account he could sit upright only with difficulty, and spent the five months from May to September resting in a hammock. Before the collapse, he had deposited all his money in a Guayaquil bank, Gutierrez & Company. This amounted to a pathetically small £700, *including* the payments he had so far received from the British Government for his *Cinchona* work. But in October the bank went bust, and Spruce, now an invalid, was penniless.

He once again lobbied unsuccessfully for some kind of consular post, and wrote to Hanbury with justifiable bitterness: 'Had I worked as long in the East as I have done in the West, I might have reasonably calculated on a small [government] pension when I was disabled from working; but I do not suppose there is any hope of such a thing in my case.' Although out of sheer necessity Spruce did drag himself out of his hammock for a couple of modest collecting expeditions around Guayaquil on behalf of his sponsors, by the end of 1862 he had to admit defeat, and wrote in another letter to Hanbury:

I had never calculated on losing the use of my limbs, and yet nothing was more likely to happen, if the sort of life I led be considered. When after loss of health came wreck of fortune, simple though my wants be and modest as were my aspirations, I felt for a time completely prostrated. The fact is I have been far too constant to botany...exposed to thunderstorms, and pelting rain—sitting in a canoe up to the knees in water—eating of bad and scant food once a day—getting no sleep at night from the attacks of venomous insects...

The following year, Spruce managed to travel to Peru, hoping that the drier climate would be better for his health, and again managed a couple of modest collecting trips. But in 1864, the game was up. Rather than die in poverty in South America, having scraped up just enough money for his passage home, Spruce decided he might as well die in poverty in his homeland—the 'contingency not to be reflected on without dread' that he had referred to six years earlier. He arrived at Southampton on 28 May 1864; he was still only 46 years old, and had been in South America for nearly fifteen years—almost exactly a third of his life.

Like many travellers returning from the tropics, Spruce was struck by the grimness of an English winter. On 20 December 1864 he noted: 'It is an awful sight to see that the sun at noon barely rises as high as the weathercock on Kew Church steeple (seen from the opposite side of the green)—and the poor skeletons of trees! I have not seen trees without leaves for more than fifteen years.' Although still in pain, Spruce was at Kew because he had immediately set to work organizing the specimens he had collected and sent back (more than 30,000 plants). Spruce was renowned for the meticulous way in which he had sent back his specimens to Kew. On one occasion, Bentham wrote: 'The specimens are excellent...being so well packed they have arrived in admirable order. It is one of the best tropical collections as to quality of specimens that I have seen.' Joseph Hooker also had nothing but praise, commenting 'I can remember the arrival of one consignment to Bentham at Kew and marvelling at the extraordinary fine condition of the specimens, their completeness for description and the great fullness and value of the information regarding them inscribed on the tickets therein'. Now, he was sorting out vocabularies of the native languages he had learned, and beginning the writing of what would end up as a massive tome about liverworts, *Hepaticae of the Amazon and of the Andes of Peru and Ecuador*, describing hundreds of kinds of plants. In the midst of all this, around Christmas 1864 Spruce suffered a recurrence of malaria, cured by quinine but still a debilitating experience. But in 1865, things at last took a modest turn for the better.

Thanks to the efforts of friends and colleagues who appreciated the value of his work (including William Hooker, Charles Darwin, and Alfred Wallace, as well as Markham) after a few months living at Hurstpierpont in Sussex Spruce was able to retire to a cottage in Welburn, a few miles from his birthplace, provided by the Castle Howard estate. He was also awarded a government pension of £50 a year. Even in 1865, £50 a year was barely enough to keep a single man (Spruce never married) of modest needs in a cottage in Yorkshire, and Markham in particular lobbied vigorously for it to be increased. At first, all this produced was a one-off payment of £200 (even less generous than it might seem given that Spruce was still owed nearly £100 for his *Cinchona* work). Markham then managed to get the £97 owed by the India Office paid out as well, but it wasn't until 1877, when Spruce was 60, that Markham's continuing efforts got Spruce's pension increased to £100 a year.

Through all this, Spruce lived quietly, and painfully; too reticent to lobby on his own behalf, but expressing his bitterness about his treatment in letters. His condition was slightly eased by the Howard family (George Howard was the Earl of Carlisle), who in 1873 provided him with a different cottage with a tiny sitting room, twelve feet square, and an even smaller bedroom, at the village of Coneysthorpe, just outside the grounds of Castle Howard. There he spent his declining years, looked after by a housekeeper and a young village girl paid a pittance to nurse him, with the Howard family keeping a watchful eye over him. For the last twenty years of his life, he was barely able to walk, moving only between his bed, a chair, and a couch, and only occasionally able to venture out into his small garden. When he could, Spruce carried on with his botanical work, and 1885 saw the completion of his 600-page *Hepaticae*. He was a neat, meticulous man who kept everything in its place (just as well in such a small cottage), later described by Wallace as 'a man who, however depressing were his conditions or surroundings, made the best of his life'.[15] According to Wallace, 'whether in a native hut on the Rio Negro, or in his little cottage in Yorkshire, his writing materials, his books, his microscope, his herbaria, his stores of food and clothing, all had their appointed places in which they were always to be found'. Honours in recognition of Spruce's work came belatedly and sparingly—an honorary doctorate from the German Academy of Sciences in 1864, honorary Fellowship of the Royal Geographical Society in 1866, and election as an Associate of the Linnean Society only in 1893, and only just in time.

On 27 October 1892, Spruce had written to a friend: 'Last month I completed my seventy-fifth year, and am become almost a fixture. Only my eyes do not fail me. In the winter of 1889 I had a paralytic attack, accompanied by almost complete incapacity for two entire months. Since then I have only been able to write very little.' Having survived another year in spite of his various ailments, to see his 76th birthday in September 1893, at the end of December that year Spruce became ill with influenza, and he died on the 28th.

Even leaving aside his *Cinchona* work, Spruce was one of the greatest botanical explorers, traversing the South American continent from east to west nearly at its widest part, and discovering and classifying hundreds of 'new' species. Apart from his work east of the Andes, Spruce's success at obtaining *Cinchona* for the Indian plantations (and accidentally providing a rootstock for the Dutch plantations) was one of the great achievements of botanical explorers, directly responsible for saving millions of lives and opening up otherwise uninhabitable regions, including the heart of Africa. You might think that such a man would have been buried in a place of honour at Westminster Abbey, alongside his contemporary Charles Darwin. In fact, he was laid to rest in the churchyard at the village of Terrington, alongside his parents; the obituary in a local newspaper recorded that 'his name is commemorated by the moss *Sprucea*'. Perhaps Spruce, who loved bryophytes most of all, would have appreciated that.

IN THE GARDEN

S pruce wrote of coming upon a lagoon in which the dramatic Water Lily *Victoria amazonica* was flowering: 'The aspect of the Victoria in its native waters is so new and extraordinary that I am at a loss to what to compare it ... when viewed from the banks above it was that of a number of tea trays floating with here and there a bouquet protruding in between.' He also came across numerous plants and barks that were used as hallucinogens, ordeal drugs, and poisons with which to tip arrows or kill enemies. For those who have no access to rainforest conditions and who want to garden inside the law, however, perhaps the best way to honour the botanical legacy of Robert Spruce is to create an alpine garden reflecting some of the flowers that Spruce would have come across during his Pyrenean expeditions.

Alpines were one of the great passions of Victorian gardening. Their popularity reflected both the Victorian enthusiasm for gardening and the fashionability of Alpine travel. For the landed upper and middle classes wealthy enough to employ gardeners alpines were yet another opportunity to increase their social cachet. Alpines were notoriously difficult for amateurs to grow successfully, especially in polluted city air. They grow naturally in exposed rocky positions and flourish in clear air and plenty of sunshine—the blanket of snow covering them in winter helps give protection from extremes of air temperature.

Aubrieta Elsa Lancaster is an extremely pretty alpine which is easy to grow. Saxifrage works very well in an alpine garden—try *Saxifraga aspera, Saxifraga media, Saxifraga longifolia,* and *Saxifraga paniculata,* which all grow naturally in the Pyrenees. *Primula denticulata, Primula auricula, Rhodanthemum hosmariense, Viola biflora,* and the Spring Starflower (*Ipheion uniflorum*) are also widely recommended for use in a temperate alpine garden. For easy to grow spring flowering alpines choose *Phlox subulata* (Creeping Phlox) or *Pulsatilla* (Pasque Flower) and for lovely pink flowers in autumn plant *Sedum sieboldii* (Pink Stonecrop). For the superstitious, *Sempervivum* ('Hens and Chicks' or House Leek) are tough, freely growing alpines which, according to folklore, will protect property from lightning strikes.

9

JOSEPH DALTON
HOOKER

(1817–1911)

T HE LAST MEMBER of our first eleven would receive all the
recognition that Spruce missed out on—and although Joseph
Hooker had by no means as hard a life as Spruce, he deserved all the
recognition that came his way.

Joseph Dalton Hooker was born at Halesworth, in Suffolk, on 30
June 1817, just a couple of months before the birth of Richard Spruce;
but he outlived Spruce by almost exactly eighteen years, becoming the
only member of our first eleven to survive into the twentieth century.
Joseph was the second of five children, with an older brother, William
(born in 1816), and three younger sisters, Maria (born in 1819),
Elizabeth (1820), and Mary Harrietta (1826). His father, William
Jackson Hooker,[1] took up his post as Professor of Botany in Glasgow
in 1820, and Joseph showed early signs of following in his father's
footsteps, taking a great interest in the professor's herbarium and

going along to his father's lectures with his brother from the age of 7.[2] Like most small boys, he also enjoyed stories of adventure, and in later life remembered sitting with his grandfather looking at a copy of James Cook's *Voyages*; he also read Mungo Park's *Travels*, about the search for the source of the River Niger. As we have seen, he was also impressed as a child by the tales of adventure in the American North West told to him by David Douglas on his visits to the Hooker home in Glasgow. Joseph's formal education, with his brother, was at Glasgow High School, where he was remembered as a serious, hard-working student while William was brilliant but erratic. But the boys attended the school only from 1825 to 1828, when their father decided to employ a tutor to educate them at home, partly in the hope of getting William to concentrate more on his work.

In 1832, at the age of 15, Joseph formally became a student at Glasgow University, at the same time as his brother. This was not an unusual age to take such a step in those days, when students like Joseph Hooker could get a grounding in subjects such as the classics, mathematics, and moral philosophy before moving on to work for a degree in a subject such as medicine (still the obvious choice for a would-be naturalist in the 1830s), either at Glasgow or at some other university. During the vacations, and in any spare time he could snatch away from Glasgow, the young Hooker went on botanizing trips to the Highlands of Scotland, to England, and in 1838 to Ireland. His physical fitness and diligence are highlighted by a comment in a letter sent by his mother to her father after one of these trips: 'A fortnight ago, Joseph walked 24 miles—from Helensburgh to Glasgow—rather than wait for the steamer next morning, by which delay he would have missed a lecture.' His father described Joseph's 'steadiness and ardour' for botany as 'most gratifying', and in 1837, while completing his medical studies, Joseph demonstrated this again by taking an astronomy course so that he could gain 'The requisite knowledge, practical & theoretical, of working the different problems for time, longitude & latitude ... for travelling abroad as I hope I may in a few years. I can by means of a chronometer & sextant lay down bearings, &c. with much accuracy.'

Joseph's hopes of travelling abroad were realized even sooner than he could have expected. In the autumn of 1838, Sir William Hooker (as he now was) met Captain James Clark Ross, of the Royal Navy, at a friend's house. Ross, a nephew of Captain John Ross, was by that time the most experienced polar explorer in the world. Born in 1800, he had joined the Navy at the age of 11, and been on several Arctic expeditions (spending a total of eight winters in the Arctic), including unsuccessful attempts at finding the Northwest Passage (one led by his uncle) and a successful attempt to determine the location of the north magnetic pole. In 1838, he was preparing to lead an expedition, in two ships, to explore in Antarctic waters and search for the location of the south magnetic pole. Pressed by Sir William, Ross eventually agreed to take Joseph Hooker with him—provided that Joseph completed his medical studies satisfactorily and joined the Navy as an Assistant Surgeon.

Joseph was not entirely happy with the arrangement. He would have preferred to travel as a gentleman companion to Ross and his officers, an independent botanist like Charles Darwin, who had returned from his *Beagle* voyage in October 1836, and whose adventures were already an inspiration to the next generation. But Ross preferred a more formal arrangement, although he promised that Joseph would have every possible opportunity for collecting. The opportunity was too good to be missed, and soon after graduating in 1839 Joseph signed on. At 22 when the voyage began, he would be the youngest member of the expedition, serving on Ross's ship, the *Erebus*, as assistant to the surgeon Robert McCormick. McCormick was himself a keen naturalist with a special interest in birds. He was an experienced officer who had been the original surgeon on the *Beagle* when Robert FitzRoy set out on his famous voyage, but had left the ship in South America, officially on grounds of ill-health, but at least partly because Darwin's presence gave him little opportunity for his scientific sideline. There were no such problems on the Antarctic voyage. With McCormick and Hooker on the *Erebus*, and John Robertson and his assistant David Lyall occupying equivalent posts on her companion ship *Terror*, the expedition was equipped with four men who could between them investigate the geology, botany, and zoology of the territories they would visit, where there would be enough work to keep everyone happy.

Hooker had first come across Darwin's name through Charles Lyell (1769–1849), the father of Charles Lyell the geologist (1797–1875), who was a botanist friend of Hooker's father. He had a set of page proofs of Darwin's journal of the *Beagle* voyage, which his son had received from Darwin. The elder Lyell was given permission to lend these proof pages to the younger Hooker, who at the time was working hard to complete his medical studies and preparing for the voyage with Ross. Hooker later recalled, on the occasion of the unveiling of a statue of Darwin in Oxford in 1899, that: 'At that particular time I was engaged upon engrossing hospital duties, and I slept with the proofs under my pillow that I might at once, on awaking, devour their contents. They impressed me profoundly.'[3]

Before the ships sailed, Hooker chanced to meet Darwin himself. The first encounter was so brief that Hooker seems to have forgotten it. At the end of the 1830s, the American botanist Asa Gray (1810–88) was visiting England. While in London at the beginning of 1839 he bumped into Joseph Hooker and his father, down on a visit from Glasgow, at the herbarium of the British Museum, then still under the care of Robert Brown. The three botanists hit it off immediately, and spent a lot of time together during the two weeks the Hookers were in London; on 22 January 1839 Gray mentioned in his diary that after breakfast they all went to the College of Surgeons to see the museum: 'A magnificent collection it is, in the finest possible order; and the arrangement and plan of the rooms is far, very far better and prettier than any I have seen. I shall make some memoranda about it. We there met Mr. Darwin, the naturalist...'.

The first meeting with Darwin that Hooker himself recalled took place shortly before the *Erebus* and *Terror* left for the Antarctic, when Hooker was in Trafalgar Square with McCormick and they chanced to meet Darwin; this time, the pair were introduced by Darwin's old shipmate, which may be why the occasion stuck in Hooker's mind. Hooker later wrote that he had been impressed by Darwin's 'animated expression, heavy beetle brow, mellow voice, and delightfully frank and cordial greeting to his former shipmate'. Both Gray and Darwin became firm friends with Hooker and were involved in voluminous correspondence with him which has proved a treasure trove for historians.

The two ships, each with a crew of sixty-four men, sailed from the Medway at the end of September 1839. They were about as well equipped as any such expedition could be in those days, at a cost of over £100,000. The ships themselves were carefully chosen for the task ahead; they were designed and built as bomb ships, to fire large mortar bombs on high trajectories against their distant targets. In order to withstand the recoil from these weapons the ships were particularly strongly built, and capable of forcing their way through icy waters without suffering so much damage as conventional craft; they were further reinforced for the Antarctic voyage. Hooker's personal 'equipment' included a copy of the finished book of Darwin's *Journal*, a parting gift from the senior Lyell, 'and no more instructive and inspiring work occupied the bookshelf of my narrow quarters throughout the voyage', echoing the way Darwin had studied the younger Lyell's epic book on geology during the *Beagle* voyage.

Although the focus of the expedition was on Antarctic exploration, from the point of view of a botanist the main interest in the voyage lay in the time spent north of the Antarctic circle, visiting places where, unlike Antarctica, plants grew in profusion. There would be plenty of such opportunities, partly because as well as seeking the south magnetic pole Ross was instructed to set up magnetic observing stations at various sites around the globe. On the outward voyage, the ships called at Madeira and the Cape Verde Islands, from where Hooker wrote to Robert Brown that 'I first saw tropical vegetation'. At the end of January 1840, the ships arrived at St Helena to set up a permanent magnetic observatory, and Hooker was able to botanize in the footsteps of both Joseph Banks, who had called there in the *Endeavour* in 1771, and Charles Darwin, who had called there in the *Beagle* in 1836. From St Helena they sailed to the Cape of Good Hope to set up another observatory, arriving on 17 March 1840 and giving Hooker a chance to collect some 300 plants before they set out on 6 April to begin their exploration of high southern latitudes.

Sailing east from the Cape, the *Erebus* and *Terror* called at desolate Kerguelen's Island, in the southern Indian Ocean, where Ross made more magnetic observations en route to Tasmania (then still known as Van Diemen's Land). Although battered by gales, snow, and rain during the two months they were there, Hooker was particularly pleased at the prospect since Kerguelen's Island was one of the places he had dreamed of visiting since sitting on his grandfather's knee reading Cook's description of the place.

The expedition was not able to complete its observations and leave the island until 20 July, and the ships soon became separated in the continuing severe weather. In one storm all the sails of the *Erebus* were ripped from her masts, and the ship's boats (carried on deck) were smashed. But as Hooker reported to his father, 'she rides like a duck over the waves'. When the battered ship reached the port of Hobart in mid-August, they found that *Terror* had arrived just the day before.

There was also bad news for Hooker. His elder brother, William, had died of yellow fever in Jamaica, where he had gone in the somewhat forlorn hope of recovering from tuberculosis. The irony was that in childhood Joseph had always been regarded as the weaker of the two siblings, and throughout his life he suffered from palpitations and pains on his left side, which might indicate some kind of heart trouble, though he did live to be 94. Understandably upset by

William's death, but going a little over the top, Sir William Hooker wrote to Ross to tell him that he had heard from one of the other officers that Joseph was 'quite unfit to undergo the fatigues of such a voyage' as the one he now faced, and begged Ross to 'desire him to return or allow him to remain in Van Diemen's Land or New Zealand where he can be useful & not exposed to difficulties & privations for which his constitution is unsuited'. Ross would have none of it, and after checking with McCormick told Sir William there was nothing wrong with his son.

In order to carry out magnetic observations and repair and replenish the ships for their journey south, they stayed in Hobart until 13 November 1840, giving Hooker an opportunity to botanize extensively and develop his skills. 'My collections', he wrote home, 'improve as I go on.' In all this he had the support and approval of the Governor, Sir John Franklin (1786–1847), and his wife, who had established a natural history society in Hobart. Franklin was a naval officer who had served at the battles of Copenhagen and Trafalgar in the Napoleonic Wars, and also an experienced Arctic explorer. He had been appointed Governor of Tasmania in 1836; but he stayed in the post only until 1843, when he was called back to England partly because the authorities in England did not approve of his attempts to reform the running of the penal colony on the island. In 1845, at the age of 59, he would sail for the Arctic again in search of the Northwest Passage in command of a two-ship expedition—the veterans of the southern ocean, *Erebus* and the *Terror*. The two ships were last seen in Baffin Bay on 26 July that year; there were no survivors from the expedition, and its exact fate remains a mystery. But the intertwining of the fates of Franklin and the ships still lay nearly five years in the future when the *Erebus* and the *Terror* left Hobart for the far south on 12 November 1840.

There were still some opportunities for botanizing, as the ships visited the Auckland Islands, south of New Zealand, and Campbell Island before heading south across the Antarctic Circle into what became known as the Ross Sea. They encountered their first iceberg on Boxing Day, and crossed the Antarctic Circle (latitude 66.5 °S, about 1,650 miles from the South Pole) on New Year's Day 1841. This is not the place to go into details of the Antarctic explorations carried out by Ross, but the traces are scattered across the map of Antarctica in the form of the names of Victoria Land, Ross Island, the mountains Erebus and Terror, and lesser features named after the members of the expedition (Hooker had a Cape named after him). Our story focuses on Hooker the botanist—but there might have been no such story to tell. On 27 January 1841, Hooker was among the members of a party sent to land on an island at the edge of the pack ice, some fifty miles from the shore. Jumping from the boat to the land Hooker fell into the icy water and was almost crushed between the boat and the rocks. The island was claimed in the name of Queen Victoria and itself named after Franklin, but Hooker was hurried back to the ship to thaw out. Typically, he made no mention of the incident in his letters home.

The pack ice prevented the ships from reaching the mainland of Antarctica, but they penetrated to 78 °S, farther than anyone before them and farther south than any other purely sailing ships ever reached. With no safe harbour to provide a winter anchorage, they returned to Tasmania in May, after what Hooker described as 'a most glorious and successful cruise'. He wrote to reassure his mother that he was fit and well:

Except a slight cold and its concomitant discomfort, I have had nothing to complain of, and that has been since my arriving [in Tasmania]. During all the time I was in the Southward I did not know an hour's illness of any kind whatever; the cold is healthy in the extreme and an occasional ducking of sea-water proves rather beneficial. I always accustom myself to taking moderate exercise in hauling the ropes, setting sails, putting the ship about, &c. Thus my chest expands, my arms get hard, and the former *rings* almost when struck.

Hobart again provided a base for the ships to be refitted and replenished before they sailed for Sydney (Port Jackson) to make more observations and then on to New Zealand, where they arrived at the Bay of Islands on 17 August. New Zealand had only recently been claimed by the British, and was granted the status of an independent colony only in November 1840 (it had previously been technically the responsibility of the Governor of New South Wales). The political situation was still confused, and the number of British settlers was tiny, but the Bay of Islands gave ample opportunities for botanizing, once again in the footsteps of Darwin, who had called there on the *Beagle* voyage. Ross's plan was to complete the fitting out of his ships and continue eastward round the Antarctic continent more or less from the point where he had turned back the previous year; but among the flora of New Zealand the prospect of another voyage to the frozen south appalled Hooker. Unhappily, he wrote to his father: 'Could I with honor leave the expedition here, I would at once and send home my plants for sale as I collected them; but now my hope and earnest wish is to be able on my return home to devote my time solely to botany, and to that end the sooner we get back the better for me.' We can only speculate on how his life would have been changed if he had not been under naval discipline, but a 'gentleman naturalist' like Darwin, and had decided to leave the ship in New Zealand.

The voyage Hooker dreaded began at the end of November 1841, and on the following New Year's Eve the ships crossed the Antarctic Circle. But by then they were deep inside the pack ice, having been trapped in a region of open water that gradually shrank to nothing as the ice encroached. They escaped only with difficulty when the ice broke up under the influence of a gale and heavy seas which smashed lumps of ice against the vessels and damaged their rudders. But the sturdy bomb ships survived with their hulls intact, and were moored to a convenient ice floe where repairs were carried out. Now keeping well clear of the pack, they continued their voyage; but the ice was so extensive that there was no chance of approaching land. In March, with winter setting in and the sea beginning to freeze, Ross decided to go round Cape Horn and make for the Falkland Islands, where they arrived on 6 April 1841.

Although better than being crushed by ice, the Falklands were a much bleaker prospect as a winter base than the Bay of Islands or Tasmania. 'Kerguelen's Land', Hooker wrote soon after landing, 'is a paradise to it.' He later revised his opinion slightly, acknowledging that the Falklands were a slightly better prospect for botanists than Kerguelen's Land, and making the best of a bad job gathered interesting ferns and lichens among other plants during the short winter days. There was also the diversion of a trip to the nearby tip of South America, Tierra del Fuego, bringing back saplings and timber for the settlers on the treeless Falklands.[4] But his voyaging wasn't over yet.

Determined to make one more attempt at finding the south magnetic pole, Ross took his ships south again on 17 December 1842, this time heading into the Weddell Sea.[5] As in the previous year, however, there were no stretches of open water through which to reach the southern continent. The consolation, as far as Hooker was concerned, was that at almost 65 °S, on an island off the Arctic Peninsula, he found lichens and mosses growing in cracks in the rocks, 'in a situation much nearer the South Pole than vegetation had hitherto been supposed to reach'. How Spruce would have enjoyed that moment!

When Ross finally decided to set course for South Africa, Hooker wrote: 'I cannot tell you how rejoiced we are to be leaving [the Antarctic] for good, & all. Captain says he would not conduct another expedition to the South Pole for any money & a pension to boot. Nor would any individual of us join if he did; I am sure I would not for a baronetcy.'

Returning via the Cape,[6] the ships reached Folkestone at midnight on 4 September 1843 and were paid off at Woolwich on 23 September, almost exactly four years after they departed. Still with an 'earnest wish' to be able 'to devote my time solely to botany', the only career actually open to Hooker was to continue as a surgeon in the Royal Navy. Apart from that, he had no job, no prospects, no home, and no income. But one thing that would eventually make up for all that had happened while Joseph was away—in 1841 Sir William Hooker had been appointed Director of Kew Garden.

In discussions with his father and maternal grandfather Dawson Turner, Sir William's mentor, Joseph came up with the idea for a book, *Flora Antarctica*, presenting the botanical discoveries from the voyage, and with Robert Brown's support managed to obtain a grant of £1,000 from the Treasury to cover the cost of the planned 500 plates. His naval pay as assistant surgeon should have been £118 per year, but for the duration of the Antarctic expedition this had been increased, in line with increases for other officers, to £250; instead of reverting to the basic salary, Hooker was to receive £200 a year for the duration of his work on the book, being officially appointed as surgeon on the complement of one of the Queen's yachts, a sinecure with no duties. A base from which to work was, of course, provided at Kew by his father. It took Hooker until the autumn of 1847 to complete the two volumes of the book, during which time he established his friendship with Darwin and often visited Darwin's home at Down House in Kent. By the middle of the 1840s Darwin was already secretly developing his theory of natural selection,[7] and although still only in his thirties suffered poor health and worried almost obsessively about the fate of his work if he should die. In 1844, he left specific instructions for his wife that if anything should happen to him, Hooker, one of the few people who had seen Darwin's first written outline (what he called a 'Sketch') of his ideas on evolution, would be the right man to edit Darwin's work for publication.

Hooker knew nothing of this 'bequest' at the time, and, concerned about his own long-term future, in 1845 he accepted an opportunity to deputize, on an unpaid basis, for the Professor of Botany in Edinburgh—the same Robert Graham whose move from Glasgow had provided the vacancy filled by Joseph's father in 1820. Graham was seriously ill, and there was every chance that when he died his temporary assistant would be in line for the post. Graham did indeed die in August 1845, but the Chair went to John Balfour, from Glasgow University, and Hooker, who had not enjoyed lecturing, returned to London with mixed feelings. There, his father's contacts got him appointed as a kind of consultant on botany to the Geological Survey of Great Britain, making him one of the first palaeobotanists. Partly on the security of the extra £150 a year this brought in, in July 1847 he became engaged to Frances Henslow, the daughter of John Stevens Henslow, the Professor of Botany at Cambridge University who had himself been a major influence on Darwin when Darwin was an undergraduate. The Henslow and Hooker families knew each other well, and Frances was the best friend of Joseph's sister Elizabeth. In the same year, the 30-year-old Joseph was also elected as a Fellow of the Royal Society, and could have settled down to a career in England. But what he really wanted to do was to botanize in some far-flung land.

In Hooker's own mind the choice was between the Andes and the Himalayas. The Director of the Geological Survey, Sir Henry de la Beche, encouraged the idea of an Indian expedition, offering to keep Hooker on the payroll of the Survey as long as any fossils he found went to the Geological Museum. The Superintendent of the Calcutta Botanic Garden (Hugh Falconer, who happened to be an old friend of the younger Hooker) also offered his support. So the Andes were rejected. The next problem was, how to fund the expedition. An expedition to the mountains was not something the Navy were likely to support, especially when the First Lord of the Admiralty, Lord Auckland, was planning an official expedition to the Malay Archipelago, which could at least be reached by ship. Eventually, it was agreed that Hooker could remain in the Navy on half-pay while spending two years in India, on condition that he then joined the Navy expedition in Borneo.[8] Sir William Hooker, never one to miss a trick, then managed to get his son appointed as an official collector in India for Kew for two years at £400 a year. As if that were not enough, Hooker had a free passage to India with the entourage of Lord Dalhousie, travelling out to take up his appointment as Governor-General. This was a stroke of great good fortune; the fact that Dalhousie and Hooker got on well on the journey was to be crucial for the success of his mission in India.

They left Portsmouth on the frigate *Sidon*, powered by a mixture of sail and steam,[9] on 11 November 1847.

The first stage of the journey took them to Alexandria and Cairo, with a chance to visit the Pyramids and the Sphinx, and do a little botanizing. Then it was overland to Suez (the Suez Canal did not open until 1869), a journey of nineteen hours jolting in carriages, before getting back on board ship (the *Moozuffer*) for a hot and uncomfortable journey to Calcutta, where Hooker arrived on 12 January 1848. Hooker had been advised that the best place for him to explore would be Sikkim, then an independent statelet nestling in the Himalayas between British India to the south, Nepal to the west, Bhutan to the east, and the mysterious Tibetan plateau to the north. Although Sikkim was under British protection, this was not entirely from choice and its rulers only grudgingly admitted British travellers within its borders. Darjeeling lay to the south of the region, and most of Hooker's exploration would be carried out in the region around Kanchenjunga, at 28,169 feet (8,586 metres) the third-highest mountain in the world (and then thought to be the highest). But as it was not the right season to go botanizing in the mountains, after arriving in Calcutta, Hooker travelled and botanized in the lowlands for a couple of months, visiting among other things the poppy plantations where opium was produced for the Chinese market, and experiencing among other novelties his first journey by elephant.

At the end of winter, Hooker headed for Darjeeling, in the foothills of the Himalayas at an altitude of 7,000 feet. The British had acquired the region around Darjeeling from Sikkim in 1835, as part of the deal to protect Sikkim from its larger neighbours, in particular Nepal. The hill-station was a place for Europeans to rest and recover their health after exertions in and around Calcutta, at sea level 370 miles to the south; it was equivalent to the hill-stations of the north-west, such as Simla. Hooker arrived there on 16 April 1848, and after initially staying in the guest house, he was soon invited by Brian Hodgson, the former British Resident in Kathmandu, to share his bungalow. Hodgson was only 48, but had been forced to leave his post because the British authorities felt that he had become too involved in Nepalese politics; he had found it impossible to settle down back in England and had returned to India to enjoy his retirement. His advice and help were invaluable when Hooker began organizing his first expedition into the mountains.

More advice came from Archibald Campbell, the British Political Agent to Sikkim, also based in Darjeeling; he had previously been Hodgson's assistant in Kathmandu. Hooker and Campbell became firm friends, and Hooker was to become the godfather of one of Campbell's children, Josephine. It was just as well that Campbell liked Hooker, since one of his tasks as Political Agent was to obtain permission for Hooker to travel through Sikkim to the high northern mountain passes leading to Tibet. This was an extremely delicate matter. Sikkim was ruled by a Rajah, but this man was largely under the thumb of his chief political adviser, the Dewan (roughly speaking, his Prime Minister). The Dewan was suspicious of any British involvement in Sikkim, and although accepting that British protection was the least of several evils, was concerned that any excursion through the mountains into Tibet, which was then ruled by China, would provoke a hostile response from the Chinese, regardless of British protection. So excuses were found to delay granting Hooker permission to travel through Sikkim (though there was no outright refusal; that was not the oriental way) until it became impossible to carry out the journey to the northern passes in 1848.

This gave Hooker the opportunity to botanize on several lesser excursions around Darjeeling, which in the long run helped his preparations for the more arduous expeditions that would follow. He also noted, in a letter home, an interesting feature of the geographical distribution of the flora and fauna: 'In travelling N. you come upon genus replacing genus, Natural Order replacing Natural Order. In travelling E. or W. (i.e. N.W. or S.E. along the ridges) you find species replacing species, and this whether of animals or plants. Don't forget to send this to Darwin.'

The necessary permission to travel in Sikkim was granted only in September, when Lord Dalhousie insisted that the Rajah should give Hooker 'full leave to travel to the snowy passes' and grant him 'every assistance'. Perhaps Dalhousie would have intervened as forcefully even if he had not met Hooker; but the fact that he knew Hooker's character and personality from their journey out to India together certainly helped.

While all this was going on, through Hodgson's friendship with the Rajah of Nepal Hooker had been given permission to travel to the Tibetan passes in the east of that country, just across the border from Sikkim and to the west of Kanchenjunga. The Rajah even provided Hooker with an escort of Gurkha soldiers. Campbell wrote to Hooker's father that the planned journey was 'the most interesting that has ever been undertaken in this part of the Himalaya . . . the passes in this direction have never been penetrated by a European'.

The expedition set out at the end of the rainy season, on 27 October 1848. Hodgson was unable to go with them because he was ill, but Hooker had assembled a party of fifty-five people (plus himself) at a personal cost of £100. Although he had deliberately taken on more porters than he needed in the expectation that some would abandon the trek, this provides a striking contrast with the exploits of botanist explorers such as Spruce and Douglas, underfunded and setting off alone into the wilderness or accompanied by a couple of native guides. Hooker, though, would still suffer his fair share of hardship, and his unwieldy caravan was before too long reduced to a more manageable fifteen.

Travelling across country along narrow paths, Hooker and his party had to descend repeatedly into steep-sided valleys before climbing out of them onto ridges 5,000 feet or more above the valley floor, then heading down again into the next valley. The damp and lack of oxygen in the thin air made it difficult to light fires, Hooker suffered from altitude sickness, and as winter descended and they climbed higher dazzling sunshine reflecting off fresh snow hurt his eyes. Insects were a nuisance rather than a hazard, attracted in swarms to the candlelight of the camp at night. Collecting as he went, and sending specimens back to Darjeeling when the opportunity arose, Hooker reached the village of Wallanchoon, at 10,385 feet, on 23 November. Three days later he reached the Wallanchoon Pass, at 16,748 feet, where he recorded a temperature of 18°F (below −7°C). The nearby Yangma Pass was blocked by snow at 15,168 feet, and this late in the season there was no chance of Hooker carrying out his secret ambition to penetrate the Tibetan plateau, even without permission, and determine its altitude. He had the consolation of the many 'new' species he discovered, including a rhododendron that he named *hodgsonii* after his new friend. He had also been surveying and map-making as he went. He wrote to Sir William: 'During the greater part of my journey I saw not a single known object, and had to observe with the sextant. No map contains the name of a single place which I have visited! That I was poking in and out over the western base of Kinchin [Kanchenjunga] is all I can affirm.'

Hooker now had permission to return to Darjeeling through Sikkim, but had to travel south through deteriorating weather before he could find a pass that was open to the east, struggling through the damp, densely forested slopes at an altitude of about 10,000 feet. Here biting creatures were a problem—ticks that found their way through clothing to latch onto Hooker's limbs and body. With supplies running low, Hooker eventually made it to the Sikkim village of Lingcham, where he was warmly welcomed and found supplies that had been sent up from Darjeeling by Hodgson. The hungry Hooker celebrated by indulging in the luxury of eating a whole loaf for his breakfast. There was also news from Campbell, who was on his way to a formal meeting with the Rajah (a durbar) and invited Hooker to join them at Bhomsong. He left Lingcham on 20 December, and at one of the stops en route to Bhomsong purchased a black puppy, which he named Kinchin; the dog was his constant companion until meeting an untimely end a few months later.

The attempt by Campbell to improve the relationship between the British and the Rajah was unsuccessful, largely because of the hostility of the Dewan, and little was accomplished at the durbar; but Campbell did take the opportunity to tell (not request) the Rajah that Hooker would be making a major excursion through Sikkim to the Tibetan passes in the spring. With the durbar over, on Christmas Day 1848 Hooker and Campbell climbed the nearby Mount Mainom, a relatively modest 11,000-foot peak, just because (shades of David Douglas!) it was there. Hooker took his leave of Campbell at the beginning of January 1849, travelling by a circuitous route with a party of twenty-five men back to Darjeeling, where he arrived on 19 January. The collections he had sent back took six weeks to catalogue and pack before being sent on to Kew, and amounted to what he described as '80 coolie-loads'. After a month down on the Bengal plains with Hodgson, he returned to the comfort of Hodgson's bungalow to await the spring, and was ready to head for the mountains again on 3 May 1849, this time travelling to the passes east of Kanchenjunga.

For his second, and much more extended, major expedition into the mountains Hooker started out with a slightly more modest 'caravan' than before—only forty-two men, whittled down as the journey went on, but including only one personal servant, 'a Portuguese half-caste (John Hoffman by name), who cooked for me'.[10] They travelled up the Teesta river and beyond to the mountain passes leading to Tibet, hampered as much by the actions of the Dewan as by the terrain. Although the local villagers were friendly, the Dewan sent 'guides' who directed Hooker through the most difficult terrain, and interfered with his line of supplies so that for days on end he was reduced to eating nothing but boiled rice flavoured with chilli vinegar; the Dewan even sent agents who sabotaged the bridges, which were no more than rope and log or plank (or even just cane) affairs strung over the ravines and rivers. As a result, a journey that should have taken thirty days, from Darjeeling to the Kongra Lama pass at an altitude of 15,745 feet, actually took eighty-three days, and saw Hooker's party whittled down from forty-two to fifteen. But, Hooker wrote, 'I had attained the object of so many year's ambition' by reaching the border with Tibet.

Whatever the Rajah of Sikkim and his Dewan might say, Hooker had no intention of stopping at the border, which was in any case ill-defined, and on 24 July, still suffering from altitude sickness, briefly crossed over into Tibet. Triumphantly, he wrote: '[I] stood on the Table-land of Thibet, beyond the Sikkim frontier, at the back of all the snowy mountains, alt. 15,500 feet.' There, as well as determining the altitude and surveying the landscape, he noted that on the Tibetan side of the mountains the snowline was at 16,000 feet, compared with 15,000 feet on the Indian side, and collected specimens from the sparse patches of vegetation that survived the harsh conditions on the plateau.

The natural hazards of the journey had been bad enough, without the interference of the Dewan's agents. With the spring thaw, huge boulders tumbled down into the valleys, there were swarms of insects, the undergrowth (especially along the routes suggested by the 'guides') was almost impenetrable, and then there were the leeches. Hooker wrote to his mother that:

I go dressed nearly as I did in Scotland, with the addition of an umbrella to keep off the sun as much as the rain, & I use a linen coat in the hot weather. I always wear long worsted stockings, & my trousers tucked up to the knees, on account of [the] leeches which get all over one's person, & of which I have sometimes taken off a hundred in a day: & they work quite through the clothes.

Although no part of the body was safe from the attentions of the leeches, small ones, Hooker later wrote, used to form clusters in the instep of each foot. What he did not tell his mother at the time was that when travelling at lower altitudes 'we daily [arrive] at our camping-ground streaming with blood, and mottled with the bites of peepsas, gnats, midges, and mosquitoes, besides being infested with ticks'. In his published *Himalayan Journals*, he elaborated further:

Leeches swarmed in incredible profusion in the streams and damp grass, and among the bushes: they got into my hair, hung on my eyelids, and crawled up my legs and down my back. I repeatedly took upwards of a hundred from my legs, where the small ones used to collect in clusters on the instep; the sores which they produced were not healed for five months afterwards, and I retain the scars to the present day.

But at least he only encountered a dozen or so species of snake in Sikkim, and just seven of them were venomous.

In spite of the difficulties, the collecting was superb, and included *Rhododendron niveum*, many other rhododendrons, and the 'magnificent yellow cowslip' *Primula sikkimensis*. More than any other individual, Hooker, thanks to the specimens he sent back to Kew, was responsible for the rhododendron craze that swept Victorian Britain. His own collection from Sikkim and India, combined with that of another botanical explorer, Thomas Thomson, who had collected in Tibet and the North West area of the Himalayas, eventually included nearly 7,000 species.

After retracing his steps from the high plateau down through the tropical discomforts to obtain supplies at the village of Choongtam, where he arrived on 5 August and stayed for ten days, Hooker set off up a more easterly valley for the Donkia pass, at an altitude of 18,466 feet; he reached it on 9 September. It was on this leg of his travels that he lost his dog, Kinchin, who rushed ahead of the party onto one of the fragile bamboo bridges, slipped, and fell into the raging torrent below.

At the Donkia pass, in order to get a better view across the Tibetan plateau, Hooker ascended Mount Donkia itself, reaching an altitude of more than 19,300 feet, which was at that time a record for any European explorer:

I was greatly pleased with finding my most Antarctic plant, *Lecanora miniata*, at the top of the Pass, and to-day I saw stony hills at 19,000 feet stained wholly orange-red with it, exactly as the rocks of Cockburn Island were in 64° South;

is not this most curious and interesting? To find the identical plant forming the only vegetation at the two extreme limits of vegetable life is always interesting; but to find it absolutely in both instances painting a landscape, so as to render its colour conspicuous in each case five miles off, is wonderful.

This was, of course, one of the key features of the Himalayas for the botanist explorer—climbing from the valleys to the Tibetan plateau provided the same range of habitats and plants as travelling all the way from the tropics to the Antarctic. But it was still a surprise to find exactly the same plant (a kind of lichen) in the mountains as in the Antarctic.

After a few days exploring, surveying, and botanizing around the pass, Hooker received news that Campbell was once again on a mission to improve relations with the Rajah, and to look into the way Hooker had been treated by the Dewan; he planned to join Hooker at Choongtam. Hooker hurried back down the valley, and they met up on 4 October 1849. Campbell was shocked to learn how badly Hooker had been treated by the Dewan's agents, and instead of opposing any action which might lead to a border incident he eagerly accepted Hooker's suggestion that they should return to the Kongra Lama pass, where Hooker had been in July, before visiting the Rajah. The senior representative of the Rajah who accompanied them was the Tchebu Lama, Sikkim's representative to the British, who was already out of favour with his Rajah and the Dewan for his friendship with Campbell. In a letter to Sir William, Hooker recounts what happened when they reached the border and met up with Tibetan border guards who objected forcefully to their presence:

The Lama...got frightened and implored us to stop for a conference, to which Campbell properly acceded, and I put spurs to my pony and galloped ahead on to the sandy plains of Thibet, determined to stay away all day and see what I could, for there was no good I could do by waiting with C., who could make no retrograde motion whilst I was ahead.

Hooker's impulsive action saw him racing ahead of the two border guards sent after him, round a spur of Kanchenjunga to Lake Chola-moo, fifteen miles from the pass, where the exhausted pony and Hooker, himself suffering from dizziness in the high altitude, both took a rest. He arrived at about 1 p.m., and stayed for only half an hour, aware of the bitter cold setting in as the afternoon wore on. At 3 p.m. he rejoined the main party, 'determined to stay a day or two where we were'. But thanks to the negotiating skills of the Tchebu Lama, the commanding officer of the Tibetan border guards agreed to escort Hooker's party round the mountain so that they could leave Tibet by the Donkia pass. This gave them four days in Tibet, where Hooker climbed to the peak of Mount Bhomtso at 15,900 feet, where the only botanical samples to be gathered were lichens. 'The transparency of the pale-blue atmosphere', he wrote, 'can hardly be described, nor the clearness and precision with which most distant objects are projected against the sky.'

Flushed with the success of this excursion, and restored by a rest at Singtam, where supplies had arrived from Darjeeling and he was able to indulge in mince pies and sherry before dinner, Hooker decided to try his luck at the eastern passes linking Sikkim with Tibet. But there his luck ran out.

Although Hooker, Campbell, and his party reached the Chola pass on 7 November, they were politely but firmly turned back by the Tibetan border guards, who claimed that there was no road beyond the frontier. It was on 10 November, on their way back down into Sikkim, at a hut used by travellers, that they met up with a gang of ruffians commanded by the governor of Singtam, the Singtam Sou-bah. Campbell was seized, beaten up, and tortured by having his hands tied behind his back, 'the wrist of the right hand being bound to the left arm above the elbow', and the cords holding them twisted;[11] but the only force used on Hooker was to restrain him from going to Campbell's aid. It was all part of a plan by the Dewan to use Campbell as a hostage and force concessions from the British; when Hooker made it clear that this would not work, the story was changed to a charge that by crossing into Tibet without permission Campbell, an official representative of the British, had endangered the relationship between Sikkim and its powerful neighbour.

Hooker was free to go, but determined to stay with his friend. 'My durance here', he wrote to his fiancée of the experience, 'has been somewhat of the vilest'. But even while being marched off with Campbell to imprisonment, Hooker took the opportunity of 'quietly gathering rhododendron-seeds by the way'. The Dewan had made a serious (from his point of view) misjudgement, and when Lord Dalhousie heard of the situation he ordered a regiment and three guns to the border with Sikkim. Campbell and Hooker were quickly released, on 7 December 1849, but with the Dewan reluctant to face the music, were then taken extremely slowly back to Darjeeling, where they arrived on Christmas Eve. Although there was some feeling in official British circles that Campbell had indeed acted unwisely in crossing the border into Tibet with Hooker, nobody could be allowed to cock a snook at the British Empire; as a punishment the Rajah of Sikkim lost his British pension and the fertile land in the south of his country, which soon turned out to be good for growing *Cinchona* and tea.[12] Some 75,000 acres were given to the Tchebu Lama, who had burned his boats back home by his support for Campbell. So Hooker's four-day excursion into Tibet literally resulted in the redrawing of the map of India, as well as providing the first maps of the regions he visited in the high country. But there would be no more adventures on that scale, and no more visits to the high Himalaya.

It should now have been time for Hooker to make his arrangements to join up with the Royal Navy expedition to the Malay archipelago— but that had been cancelled following the death of Lord Auckland in 1849. So Hooker was given permission to stay on in India without his full Navy pay for a further year, which proved much more relaxing and enjoyable, though not providing as much material of interest to us. He spent a couple of months putting his journals in order, completing his map of the region he had travelled through (this became the basis of an official map produced by the Indian Trigonometrical Survey), and sorting his collections and seeing them despatched from Calcutta. He was helped in this by Thomas Thomson, a friend from his student days in Glasgow (they both graduated in the same year, 1839). Thomson was in India as a surgeon with the army, and had some leave due to him, which he took in order to go botanizing with Hooker. After considering the options open to them, the two men set out at the beginning of May 1850 on a trip through the hills of Assam, which lasted for nine months. It was on this trip that Hooker met Thomas Lobb, at Myrung. The region was so rich in flora that even though Hooker and Thomson were by no means the first European botanists to go there, and their efforts should be described as plant collecting rather than exploring, they still managed to send back to Kew a profusion of plants, including virtually all the remaining 'undiscovered' rhododendrons and the valuable blue orchid, *Vanda caerulea.*

In a dig at the Thomas Lobbs of the botanical world, and at the parsimony of the holders of the official purse strings, Hooker commented that if he had been paid for his plants he would have made '£1500 by Rhododendron seed and seedlings alone'. If anything this was an underestimate. The rhododendron craze in Victorian Britain reached such a frenzy following Hooker's introductions that it has been estimated that the amount spent on the plants over the next thirty years could have paid off the country's National Debt.[13] But Hooker himself was left out of pocket by his activities in India. He returned home after the Assam excursion, sailing from India on 7 February and arriving in London on 25 March 1851.[14] In the Preface to his *Himalayan Journals* he wrote that:

The total expense of my Indian journey, including outfit, three years and a half travelling, and the sending of my collections to Calcutta, was under £2,000 (of which £1,200 were defrayed by the Government) ... This sum does not include the purchase of books and instruments, with which I supplied myself, and which cost about £200 . . .

There were, though, financial advantages to being an official collector which did not appear in the ledgers. As Hooker acknowledged, he had free passage between England and India, the cost of sending plants back to England from Calcutta was covered by the Government, and P&O carried parcels to and from Hooker without charge.

Back home, Hooker's first priority was to marry the patient Frances Henslow; the ceremony took place on 15 August 1851. Professionally speaking, his long-term future was still uncertain (a year earlier, he wrote to a friend, 'expectations I have none but a wife to maintain and expensive appearances to keep up'), but he was offered £400 a year by the Government until 1854 to put the Indian material in order, and allowed to keep his appointment as a Royal Navy surgeon on half-pay while writing up his book on the botany of Antarctica. This also enabled him to prepare for publication his *Himalayan Journals*, first published in 1854 and dedicated to Charles Darwin by 'his affectionate friend'. Longer term, he hoped to follow in his father's footsteps, for, as he had written to George Bentham back in May 1849, 'a position like my father's is the only thing I am cut out for except travelling'. He got his wish in May 1855, when after considerable lobbying he was appointed as Assistant Director at Kew with a salary of £400 a year and a house on Kew Green. Although never enthusiastic about his administrative duties, which cut into the time available for his botanical studies, Hooker stayed there for the rest of his career, succeeding his father as Director when Sir William died in 1865 and retiring only at the end of November 1885, at the age of 68. He was succeeded by his own Assistant Director, William Thiselton-Dyer, who by that time was also Hooker's son-in-law.

Although his duties at Kew left him little scope for further exploring,[15] Hooker did manage to take time out in the autumn of 1860 for a visit to Syria and Lebanon, accompanying a Royal Navy hydrographer, Captain John Washington, to seek out the famous cedars of Mount Lebanon. The grove was found in a moraine (debris deposited by an old glacier) at 6,000 feet. The party was also able to visit Damascus and Jerusalem, ignoring (as the British did in those days) the inconvenience of a local civil war, before returning to England. In 1871, Hooker, now in his mid-fifties and with deteriorating eyesight, fulfilled a childhood dream by travelling to Morocco with two friends, George Maw and John Ball. This was much more of an adventure in the style of Hooker's travels in Sikkim, with a large caravan of servants and guides, and hostile local rulers obstructing their activities in regions of the Atlas Mountains where visitors from north of the Mediterranean were virtually unknown. Their way was smoothed by Hooker's medical skills, which not only made him popular with the villagers they met, but also provided an explanation they could accept for the presence of the travellers and their botanical activities—the word was that they were doctors who were in search of medicinal plants.

Hooker's last foreign excursion was to America, meeting up with Asa Gray to travel as guests of the US Geological and Geographical Survey in the Rockies. The 60-year-old Hooker left England on 28 June 1877, placing Kew in the hands of his capable Assistant Thiselton-Dyer, who had just married Hooker's daughter Harriet; the couple actually postponed their honeymoon to enable Hooker to make the American trip. During the time he was in the United States, Hooker travelled 8,000 miles by train and wagon, studied the geographical distribution of North American plants,[16] saw the giant Redwoods of California, and geologized in the Rocky Mountains; but, he wrote to his friend Brian Hodgson, 'as to the mountain scenery it is a bagatelle compared with any little bit of the Himalaya or Alps'. He was even more dismissive of the teaching of Brigham Young, whom he met in Salt Lake City:

In person and conversation he is less of a Yankee than $^9/_{10}$ of the gentlemen I have been introduced to. Of course he is an arrant impostor, but nothing in speech, look or manner differs from those of a quiet well-bred English gentleman... All the school children are brought up to believe in him and in a lot of Scripture history as useless and idle as that taught in our schools, and the religious teaching is altogether contemptible. The Gentile ladies hold no intercourse with their Mormonite sisters; nor is it likely they should. Educated U.S. ladies would not care to associate with the ignorant class to which the Mormonite ladies belong. In short as far as I can make out, the system of polygamy is that of making young female servants your wives. They are servants without pay who cannot run away![17]

In October 1877 Hooker was back in England and his travelling days were behind him. By now, he was a pillar of the scientific establishment (he served as President of the Royal Society from 1873 to 1878) with honours heaped upon him. But there is no doubt which honour he cared about most. Just before he had sailed for North America, Hooker had been made a Knight Commander of the Order of the Star of India, something that he had wanted so much that he had previously (twice!) turned down an 'ordinary' knighthood for fear that it would undermine his chances of obtaining the Indian honour, which was limited to twenty-five Europeans who had been in the Indian Service. Strictly speaking, he was not eligible for the honour, but an exception was made for Hooker, who happily wrote to Darwin that:

It has a flavor of hard work under difficulties, of obstacles overcome, and of brilliant deeds that is very attractive. Assuredly I would rather go down to posterity as one of the 'Star of India' than as of any other dignity whatever that the Crown can offer... Is this not a jolly strain of self-gratulation and glorification?

Poor Darwin never received a knighthood of any kind, but was genuinely pleased for his friend.

Hooker's most important achievement since returning from India had, of course, been his role as a sounding-board for Darwin's ideas on evolution, and along with Charles Lyell, his part in persuading Darwin to publish his work at the end of the 1850s, when news came from Alfred Russel Wallace, by then botanizing in the Malay Archipelago, of his own independent discovery of the principle of natural selection. It is not always appreciated that Hooker's unrivalled experience of the geographical distribution of plants, from the tropics to Antarctica and from the Indian plains to the high Himalaya, was of great value in helping Darwin to formulate his ideas on natural selection. In 1882, Hooker was one of the pallbearers at Darwin's funeral.

Like Darwin's, Hooker's personal life was a mixture of happiness and heartbreak. Darwin had lost his favourite daughter, Annie, in 1851, when she was only 10 years old. On 28 September 1863, Hooker's daughter Minnie died at the age of 6, and he poured out his grief to Darwin, who was not only a friend but had experienced the same kind of loss. On 1 October he wrote:

I have just buried my darling little girl and read your kind note. I tried hard to make no difference between her and the other children, but she was my very own, the flower of my flock in every one's eyes, the companion of my walks, the first of my children who has shown any love for music and flowers, and the sweetest tempered, affectionate little thing that ever I knew. It will be long before I cease to hear her voice in my ears, or feel her little hand stealing into mine; by the fireside and in the Garden, wherever I go she is there.

Also like Darwin, Hooker had the consolation of a happy marriage and, as he put it, a 'flock' of other children. Apart from Minnie, Frances gave him four sons (William, Charles, Brian, and Reginald) and another two daughters (Harriet and Grace) who survived infancy. But Frances herself died suddenly in November 1874, after twenty-three years of marriage. On the morning of 13 November, Hooker set off at eleven in the morning leaving her in normal good health, and returned at four in the afternoon to learn she was dead. She was 49 years old; Hooker was 57. In a letter to Thomas Henry Huxley, Hooker said: 'My memory of the immediate past is blurred, and I have difficulty recalling her features. I think of her mostly as the girl I so long and so dearly loved 25 years ago, and feel as if I had never returned from the East to marry her—and never shall now.' Like so many men placed in a similar position in those days, however, Hooker was not alone in his grief, and had a young family to look after. 'No one can have an idea who has not experienced it, what a house of six children is without a female guide—let the children behave ever so well!'

There was only one solution to the problem. In August 1876 Hooker married for a second time. His second wife, Hyacinth, was a 34-year-old widow who had been a friend of the Hookers for more than ten years, and she shared many of Joseph's interests—her father, William Symonds, the Rector of Pendock, in Worcestershire, was a keen geologist, and her late husband Sir William Jardine (who also died in 1874) had been a respected ornithologist. Hooker's second marriage produced two more sons (Joseph and Richard), the younger born in January 1885, when Hooker was 67, thirty-two years to the month after the birth of his first child. This new young family must have been taxing as well as rewarding for Hooker, who was by that time 'exceedingly shortsighted'; his health was declining and according to Thistleton-Dyer 'he got excited over trifles'. As well as family pressures Hooker was also constantly under pressure of work from Kew.

1885 also saw a revival of British interest in Antarctic exploration, with Hooker now the last surviving officer of the Ross expedition and the grand old man of British polar explorers. The British Association for the Advancement of Science set up a committee to look into the case for a new Antarctic expedition, and naturally Hooker was asked to contribute to its report, which appeared in 1887. The Government was not impressed, but the idea gradually gathered momentum in the scientific community. Following a discussion at a meeting of the Royal Geographical Society in 1893, Sir Clements Markham (by then President of the RGS) formed another Antarctic committee, on which he invited Hooker to serve. With Markham's intense lobbying, pressure for an Antarctic expedition built up over the 1890s, and the possibilities were discussed again at a meeting of the Royal Society in 1898. At that meeting Hooker, who remembered how the towering ice cliffs of Antarctica had prevented the members of the Ross expedition getting a view of the interior, suggested that a tethered man-carrying balloon could be used to see whether there was indeed a land mass, a true Antarctic continent, beyond the ice. He became increasingly involved in the preparations for such an expedition, and although now in his eighties was chairman of a Biological Subcommittee set up by a new Antarctic Committee formed jointly by the RGS and the Royal Society in 1898.[18]

All this pressure eventually gained the approval and financial support of the Government. A ship, the *Discovery*, was specially built for Antarctic exploration, and Robert Scott was chosen to lead the expedition. Markham and Scott were easily persuaded of the wisdom of Hooker's balloon suggestion, and between them they managed to extract funds for not one but two such balloons to be carried on the ship. The *Discovery* expedition sailed in 1901 and returned in 1904; on 4 February 1902, Scott himself became the first balloonist in the Antarctic, ascending to 800 feet above the ship and observing that the Ross ice sheet, far from being flat, consisted of a series of long undulations.

Hooker's active retirement continued into the twentieth century, marked by the award of the Order of Merit in 1907, when he was 90; although his physical strength slowly declined he remained mentally alert and continued to write scientific papers to the end. In 1910, Scott was planning his second expedition to the Antarctic, in the ship *Terra Nova*; he wrote to Hooker to ask if the old man would like to carry out the ceremony of hoisting the ship's white ensign on the formal occasion of her being commissioned by the Admiralty; but Hooker was too weak to travel, and had to decline 'an honour which would have been the crowning one of my long life'. He died peacefully in his sleep, aged 94, in the middle of the night of 10 December 1911. An offer for his remains to lie alongside those of Darwin and Lyell in Westminster Abbey was declined by his family (Hyacinth survived him by almost exactly ten years), who respected Hooker's wish to be buried alongside his father at St Anne's, Kew. With his passing the great era of the botanical explorers came to an end, not least because of the advent of air travel, the value of which Hooker had been among the first to appreciate. Travel by railway and steamship, ballooning in Antarctica—all part of Hooker's life, and all a far cry indeed from John Ray's pioneering travels in Europe.

IN THE GARDEN

A huge feature of any Joseph Dalton Hooker garden would have to be Rhododendrons and of course the first place to look for inspiration is his book *Rhododendrons of Sikkim-Himalaya* (1849–51). His introductions triggered the planting of Rhododendron groves and alpine gardens throughout the estates and gardens of Victorian and Edwardian England and America that can still be seen today. One of the most beautiful is *Rhododendron argenteum,* a white-bloomed Rhododendron from Sikkim whose showy blooms and long shiny leaves rise magnificently from bushes that can reach heights of over twelve metres. Hooker had a charming habit of naming plants in honour of those who had helped him on the way. The stunning deep pink to reddish purple *Rhododendron hodgsonii* he named for Brian Hodgson, his host in Darjeeling, and the deep red *Rhodendron thomsonii* he named after his old college friend from Glasgow Dr Thomas

Thomson. *Magnolia campbellia,* which is an equally lovely pink, was named after the wife of Dr Archibald Campbell, who was Superintendent of Darjeeling and Political Agent for Sikkim.

Joseph Hooker also had a particular affection for *Grevilleas* of which he wrote: 'Amongst the most graceful of ornamental plants is *Grevillea robusta* which is perhaps the most widely used foliage plant for table decoration that ever was introduced into Europe', and he described *Grevillea rosmarinifolia* (then known as *Grevillea ericfolia*) as 'a very attractive ornament in both conservatory and temperate garden'. He was keen to introduce *Proteas* into European gardening, but this never took off and very few Australian *Protoceae* are grown in Europe today.

NOTES

Prologue

1. The forerunner of St Catharine's College; when founded in 1473, the college was actually called Katharine Hall.

2. A Greek physician of the first century AD who published a list detailing some 600 plants.

3. Ray wrote most of his books in Latin, but we shall generally give the English versions of their titles.

4. On 28 November, the day before Ray's 33rd birthday.

5. Samuel Pepys mentioned the debate in his diary entry for 21 March 1661, because at that time the year changed on 25 March, but we have modernized all dates given in this book.

6. Willughby had been one of the original Fellows of the Royal Society at its foundation. He was not a great scientist, but like many of his contemporaries he played an invaluable role in helping to fund the society through his subscription, and through witnessing the experiments carried out at the Royal. It was a fundamental feature of the scientific revolution led by the Royal that nothing was taken for granted, and all experiments had to be corroborated by reasonably expert witnesses. As one of the founding Fellows quipped, their patron saint should have been Doubting Thomas!

7. Published in 1746 in the sixth volume of *A Collection of Voyages and Travels*, edited by A. and J. Churchill.

Chapter 1

1. So the name Linnaeus was never–a 'Latinized version of Linné', as some biographies claim.

2. According to Linnaeus himself, if it hadn't been for this intervention by his teachers, Carl's father would have had him apprenticed to a shoemaker.

3. The students were mostly nothing special either, either academically or in their dress and habits; they were described by E. D. Clarke, a Cambridge academic who visited Uppsala a little later, as having an 'appearance not unlike the effigies which the rabble in England dress up to represent Guy Fawkes upon the Fifth of November'.

4. There were two medical professorships at Uppsala at that time. Rudbeck's involved more theory and botany; the other, held by Lars Roberg, was more practical and clinical.

5. Curiously, when Anders Celsius (1701–44) came up with his temperature scale, he originally set 0° as the temperature of boiling water and 100° as the temperature of freezing water; it was reputedly Linnaeus who suggested switching the numbers around, although credit is usually given to Celsius's pupil Martin Strömer. The truth is probably that the idea was discussed by Linnaeus, Celsius, and their contemporaries before Celsius formally proposed his scale to the Swedish Academy of Sciences in 1742. Linnaeus being Linnaeus, this was enough for him later to claim that he invented the whole scale.

6. Apparently, Linnaeus wore his Sami clothing when paying formal visits as a suitor to Sara and her family.

7. At that time, the Netherlands was a confederation of seven states, Friesland, Gelderland, Groningen, Holland, Overijssel, Utrecht, and Zeeland.

8. Another was Petrus Artedi, whom he met up with, by chance, in Leiden on this visit. Artedi had come to the Netherlands to study medicine after visiting London to study fish. But the reunion was brief; Artedi died on 27 September.

9. He was, of course, the Sloane after whom the eponymous square in London was named.

10. Jussiae, the Primrose Willow, was named in their honour.

11. The common treatment in those days involved an ointment containing mercury, hence the topical quip 'a night with Venus; a lifetime with Mercury'.

12. All such classification schemes are, of course, no more than cataloguing systems invented by scientists to help them in their work; none of them necessarily reveals any evolutionary truth about the relationships between species and their origins, but they provide a framework for debate about the origins of species as well as their present-day relationships.

13. There were, though, sound scientific reasons to criticize the system even in those days. Any system based on only one feature of plants is bound to be inadequate, and even more artificial than other systems which take account of a wider range of properties.

14. Charles Darwin's Big Idea was not evolution, which was already being widely discussed by the mid-nineteenth century, but natural selection, which provides a mechanism to *explain* evolution.

15. See Blunt.

16. For the record, she never did remarry, and lived until 1806, when she was 90.

17. Though not conventionally religious by the standards of his time and place. His theological colleagues at Uppsala complained that he equated God and nature a little too closely, and he seems not to have believed that Jesus Christ rose from the dead.

18. The modern interpretation of the evidence is that these strata used to be much lower, and have been uplifted by tectonic forces operating on time scales much longer than anything even Linnaeus imagined.

19. For the detailed reasons for this including DNA evidence, see Gribbin and Cherfas.

20. This was a bad year all round, with severe food shortages in Sweden and the start of the Seven Years War, fought between the power blocs of Austria, France, Russia, Sweden, and Saxony on one side, with Prussia, Britain, and Portugal on the other. One of the main outcomes of the war was that Britain gained large amounts of territory in North America from France.

21. See Blunt.

22. See Blunt.

23. Banks had, in fact, offered to buy the collection on the death of the elder Carl Linnaeus, but in the intervening years circumstances had changed and he knew Smith had a wealthy father who could afford the purchase.

Chapter 2

1. The most recent transit of Venus occurred in 2004; the second in this pair will be visible in 2012.

2. The story didn't end there. All the data from both transits were not fully analysed until 1807, when they yielded a measurement for the distance from Earth to the sun (known as the Astronomical Unit) of 153 million kilometres. The best modern measurement gives 149.6 million kilometres.

3. We use modern names throughout.

4. But it was about to be adopted; Cook carried chronometers based on Harrison's design on his second voyage of discovery, which left England in 1772, and finally proved their value to navigation. The voyage of the *Endeavour* was therefore unique in being the only major voyage of discovery on which longitude was determined solely using the lunar technique.

5. We give the date 'New Style', although the Gregorian calendar was not adopted in Britain until 1752. Some sources give the date of birth as 13 December 1743, but the evidence favours the February date; see Cameron.

6. See Banks, *The Endeavour Journal.*

7. One of the native words he learned was 'tapu', which entered the English language as 'taboo.'

8. The first European to set foot on Australia was Isaac Smith, the 18-year-old cousin of Cook's wife.

9. With the names 'New England', 'New Scotland' (Nova Scotia), and 'New Britain' already used up by geographers, Cook named the entire eastern part of Australia New South Wales (not just 'New Wales', obviously,

because it is in the southern hemisphere). The name stuck to a rather smaller portion of the land.

10. This was before the term 'homesickness' had been coined—it was invented by the poet Coleridge in 1798.

11. See Cameron.

12. The second ship, slightly smaller than the *Endeavour*, was the *Adventure*.

13. After whom, incidentally, the Sandwich Islands were named, as well as the sandwich.

14. Young midshipmen, officers in training, were not flogged but beaten, like schoolboys, with a cane.

15. The post had originally been offered to Mungo Park, who turned it down.

16. Flinders was one of the first people (possibly *the* first) to use the name in official communications.

17. One of Banks's pet unfulfilled ambitions was to see Iceland incorporated into the British Isles.

Chapter 3

1. This brief account of Thunberg's life draws on an unpublished manuscript by Catharina Blomberg, of Stockholm University: *The Botanist in the Police State: Carl Peter Thunberg in Tokugawa Japan 1775–1776.*

2. In the language of the day a factor was a business agent and a factory was a place where the business of buying and selling went on.

3. One morning Masson woke to find a poisonous snake, attracted by the warmth of his body, had coiled itself round his leg while he was asleep. Fortunately, in the morning chill the snake was too lethargic to pose much of a threat.

Chapter 4

1. The exact border was still disputed in 1823, and Canada had nowhere near taken on its present identity, but Douglas stepped ashore into what is now recognized as the Province of Ontario.

2. The name is hyphenated because the tree is not a true fir—that is, not a member of the genus *Abies*—and the name had already stuck before this was recognized.

3. 'Pseudo' because it isn't a *Tsuga*, or Hemlock, although it resembles the true North American Hemlock. So both the Douglas-fir's names are flags of convenience.

4. Two Hudson's Bay Company people.

5. A couple of times, this meant he was reduced to eating his horse.

6. Published as a Companion to the *Botanical Magazine*, 2 (1836), 79–182.

7. Quoted by Lindsay and House.

8. It was purchased by the United States in 1867, but only became a state, the largest but least populous in the Union, in 1959.

9. In Britain, Christmas trees were popularized by Prince Albert, the Consort of Queen Victoria. She would come to the throne only in 1837, after Douglas had died.

10. At this time, California was still controlled by Mexico, which had become independent from Spain in 1821. It was only in the 1840s that settlement from the United States led to rebellion and war, which resulted in California becoming the thirty-first State of the Union in 1850.

11. As in sealing wax; not the marine mammal.

12. The tsar, Nicholas I, was a Fellow of the Horticultural Society and a keen follower of Douglas's adventures.

13. There were many Fort Georges, named in honour of the succession of English kings with that name.

14. Probably the first person ever to climb all three peaks, let alone in a month.

Chapter 5

1. One reason for the rise of the English flower garden at this time was the invention of the lawnmower, patented in 1832. These machines could easily be manoeuvred around the now-fashionable flower beds, cutting strips of grass that would have been hard to tend with a scythe.

2. The tree received its common name when a visitor to the gardens at Pencarrow, Sir William Molesworth's garden in Cornwall, commented that the outward-pointing spikes of the leaves would make a real puzzle for any monkey that tried to climb it.

3. *Hindsia* were named in honour of Richard Brinsley Hinds, a surgeon in the Royal Navy who had been the naturalist on *HMS Sulfur* between 1836 and 1842.

4. One of James Junior's brothers, William, also worked in the nursery, at his father's insistence, but he had no real love for the work, and had wanted to be an architect.

5. The British wanted to sell opium to the Chinese; the Chinese authorities sought to prevent this drug-trafficking.

6. It is perhaps worth mentioning that following the break-up of the Spanish Empire in South America, between 1810 and 1831 what are now Venezuela, Colombia, and Ecuador formed a single country, the Republic of Colombia. They then became separate republics: Venezuela, Nueva Granada, and Ecuador. It was only in 1861 that the name Nueva Granada was changed, first to the United States of Colombia and then, in 1886, to the Republic of Colombia. We use the term 'Colombia' where Lobb would have referred to 'Nueva Granada'.

7. Quoted by Musgrave *et al.*

8. Quoted by Shephard.

9. Part of the reason for the booming interest in hothouse plants was that the Glass Tax had been repealed in 1845; this, coupled with improved technology for glass manufacture, reduced the cost of glass for green-houses and conservatories by four-fifths over the next twenty years.

10. Quoted by Ewan.

11. From a description in the *Gardener's Chronicle* dated 24 Dec. 1853, written by John Lindley.

12. Sequoyah was the son of an English fur trader and a Cherokee woman, who was raised as a Cherokee. He invented a written version of the Cherokee language in the second decade of the 19th c., and became a leader of the Cherokee people. He died in 1843.

Chapter 6

1. So he would have been 7 when Joseph Banks died.

2. Fortune himself tells us that in order to make friends 'during my travels in the interior, I often found the benefit of having a joke with the natives'.

3. In the words of Fortune's contract, he was to take any opportunity of 'selling [the firearms] to advantage', or failing that to 'restore' them to the Society on his return.

4. Near the end of his first book, Fortune laments that the British chose Hong Kong as their base rather than Chusan, an island he grew to love, which is farther north and 'commands the central and most important parts of [the Chinese] empire. That we committed a blunder and made a bad bargain is quite certain.'

5. We shall often follow Fortune's spelling of Chinese names from here on, rather than cluttering the text with every modern equivalent—for example, Ningbo for Ningpo.

6. It is said that the tree was 'planted' by Victoria herself, in the sense that when it was placed in its hole she threw the first trowel of earth onto its roots.

7. The reference to the 'Northern Provinces' in the title of Fortune's first book is something of an exaggeration!

8. Early in 1845, he also visited the Philippines, to collect orchids.

9. 'Fortune's Double Yellow.'

10. Curiously, the evidence suggests that although tea has been important in China for at least three thousand years, the camellia plant, whose tips are used in making tea, was probably first used for this purpose in the mountainous region between Assam and Burma. The tea habit (and plant) probably originally spread from there into China, although by the 19th c. China was producing by far the best tea, in by far the largest quantities.

11. His companions would introduce him as an important visitor from a land 'beyond the Great Wall', which wasn't so far from the truth!

12. He also, of course, took every opportunity to obtain specimens of other interesting plants.

13. Fortune later estimated that nearly 20,000 plants eventually made it into the soil of India.

14. Hong Xiuquan was a former village schoolteacher who had a grudge against the government after failing the civil service examinations several times. He began to have visions, adopted his own version of Christianity, told his followers that he was the younger brother of Jesus Christ, styled himself 'Heavenly King', and aimed to set up a 'kingdom of heavenly peace' on Earth. The cost of this was a death toll in the civil war estimated at between 20 million and 50 million, out of a population of some 400 million, making it arguably the bloodiest civil war in human history. Along with an estimated 100,000 of his followers, Hong committed suicide rather than face capture when Nanking fell in 1864.

Chapter 7

1. And later famous for his homosexual writings.

2. But she was related to this Lord North, who was a descendant of one of the brothers of Roger North, Marianne's ancestor.

3. Edward Sabine (1788–1883) was the brother of Joseph Sabine. In a long and distinguished career, he was, among other things, the official astronomer on the first Arctic expedition of John Ross in search of the Northwest Passage.

4. Introduction to *A Vision of Eden*.

Chapter 8

1. In 1859, to George Bentham; the letter is now in the Kew Archives.

2. The botanist George Bentham, an influential figure in his own right and Secretary of the Linnean Society, was the nephew of Jeremy Bentham (1748–1832), founder of University College, London.

3. Known as the *Journal of Researches*.

4. Little more is heard of King, who doesn't seem to have found the wilds of the Amazon as tolerable as he had expected. By the time he got down to serious exploring, Spruce was on his own.

5. Alas, the impact 'Western' civilization has made on the rainforest is another matter.

6. There are four different kinds of malaria parasite, but they all operate the same way. A thread-like parasite injected into the blood while the mosquito is feasting settles in the liver and produces a cyst in which the parasites reproduce. When the cysts burst, the next phase of the parasite's life cycle invades red blood corpuscles, causing the severe chills and fevers associated with the disease. Parasites get back into mosquitoes, of course, when they feast on an infected person. Quinine cures the disease by binding to haemoglobin in the red blood cells and nullifying the attack by the parasites.

7. Seasons don't mean the same in the Amazon basin as in a temperate region like Europe, but for the record at this time Spruce was just north of the equator, so we mean 'northern hemisphere summer'.

8. There were other, unsuccessful, attempts; but their story belongs in another book.

9. This uprising against British rule started in Meerut in May 1857 and spread through northern India, with Delhi falling to the rebels. The British regained control only in the summer of 1858, and more sporadic violence continued into 1859.

10. For an accessible popular account of Markham's contribution, and more on Spruce's contribution to the quinine story, see Honigsbaum, *The Fever Trail*.

11. Weir and Cross were chosen as 'good practical working gardeners'.

12. Spruce described his time there as 'the most agreeably placed...in my South American wanderings'.

13. The collections obtained on the journey went back down river with the traders.

14. Spruce was a superb linguist.

15. Wallace described Spruce himself, whom he visited both in Sussex and Yorkshire, as 'tall and dark, with fine features of a somewhat southern cast, courteous and dignified in manner, but with a fund of quiet humour which made him a most delightful companion'.

Chapter 9

1. The botanical Hookers were, incidentally, related to the 16th-c. Anglican theologian Richard Hooker (1554–1600).

2. Joseph later commented that the particular value of his father's teaching was that 'it taught the art of exact observation and reasoning therefrom, a schooling of inestimable value'.

3. *Nature*, 60 (1899), 187.

4. None of the saplings survived on the windswept islands.

5. Named after the Scot James Weddell, the master of a sealing ship which reached 74 °S in 1823.

6. Where Hooker received news that his sister Mary Harriet, whom he called 'that little favourite of us all', had died of tuberculosis in June 1841, at the age of 15.

7. Even in the 1840s, the *fact* of evolution was widely recognized; the puzzle was *how* evolution works, which is where natural selection comes in.

8. As we shall see, in the end the Navy expedition was cancelled, but by then Hooker was already in the Himalayas.

9. Such curious hybrids were seldom successful, being neither one thing nor the other, and Hooker wrote to his fiancée that 'despite her size and terribly grand look, [she] is a very poor steamer or sailor'.

10. The cooking was important to Hooker, who found Indian cookery 'in every respect villainous and atrocious. Your stews, pilaffs and curries I abhor and eschew.'

11. Try holding your arms in this position and you will see how painful it is.

12. The Dewan, hardly surprisingly, lost his job.

13. The estimate, originally by Shirley Hibberd, is quoted by Musgrave, Gardner, and Musgrave.

14. This was just ten days after Robert Fortune arrived in Calcutta with his tea plants. The two botanical explorers missed overlapping in India by eight days.

15. Although he did visit both Paris and Moscow on scientific business, these trips gave no opportunity for botanizing.

16. In a letter to Daniel Oliver, Professor of Botany at London University, he commented 'I cannot fancy any route over which a European would get more accessible Botany new to him than a railroad trip across N. America. The Flora of the E. and W. are of two continents!'

17. Letter to Frances Hooker.

18. This was just two years after the publication of Joseph Banks's *Journal*, which Hooker had edited.

SOURCES AND FURTHER READING

ALLEN, J. L., *Lewis and Clark* (New York: Dover, 1975).

ALLEN, MEA, *The Hookers of Kew* (London: Michael Joseph, 1967).

AUGHTON, PETER, *Endeavour* (Moreton-in-Marsh: Windrush Press, 1999).

BABINGTON, CHARLES, *Flora of Cambridgeshire* (London: John van Voorst, 1860).

BANKS, JOSEPH, *The Endeavour Journal*, 2 vols., ed. J. C. Beaglehole (Sydney: Angus & Robertson, 1962).

BATES, HENRY WALTER, *Naturalist on the River Amazon* (London: John Murray, 1863).

BEECHING, JACK, *The Chinese Opium Wars* (London: Hutchinson, 1975).

BLUNT, WILFRID (with William Stearn), *The Compleat Naturalist* (London: Collins, 1971).

BROWNE, JANET, *The Secular Ark* (New Haven: Yale University Press, 1983).

BRYAN, MALCOLM, *John Ray* (Braintree: The John Ray Trust, 2005).

CAMERON, HECTOR, *Sir Joseph Banks* (London: Batchworth, 1952).

CARTER, HAROLD, *Sir Joseph Banks* (London: British Museum (Natural History), 1988).

COOK, JAMES, *The Journals of Captain James Cook on his Voyages of Discovery*, i: *The Voyage of the Endeavour 1768–1771*, ed. J. C. Beaglehole (London: Hakluyt Society, 1955).

COX, E. H. M., *Plant-Hunting in China* (London: Collins, 1945).

DARWIN, CHARLES, *Journal of Researches into the Geology and Natural History of the Various Countries Visited during the Voyage of HMS Beagle round the World* (London: Henry Colburn, 1839).

—— *The Life and Letters of Charles Darwin*, ed. Francis Darwin (London: John Murray, 1887).

DAVIES, JOHN, *Douglas of the Forests* (Edinburgh: Harris, 1980).

DESMOND, RAY, *Joseph Hooker* (Kew: Antique Collectors' Club with Royal Botanic Gardens, 1999).

DOUGLAS, DAVID, *Journal kept by David Douglas during his Travels in North America 1823–1827* (New York: Antiquarian Press, 1959 (reprint of 1914 edition published by William Wesley & Son, London).

DURAN-REYNOLDS, M. L., *The Fever Bark Tree* (New York: Doubleday, 1946).

EWAN, JOSEPH, *William Lobb, Plant Hunter for Veitch and Messenger of the Big Tree* (Berkeley: University of California Press, 1973).

FORTUNE, ROBERT, *Three Years' Wanderings in the Northern Provinces of China* (London: John Murray, 1847).

—— *A Journey to the Tea Countries of China* (London: John Murray, 1852).

FRÄNGSMYR, TORE (ed.), *Linnaeus: The Man and his Work* (Berkeley: University of California Press, 1983).

GASCOIGNE, JOHN, *Joseph Banks and the English Enlightenment* (Cambridge: Cambridge University Press, 1994).

—— *Science in the Service of Empire* (Cambridge: Cambridge University Press, 1998).

GOURLIE, NORAH, *The Prince of Botanists: Carl Linnaeus* (London: Witherby, 1953).

GRAY, ASA, *The Letters of Asa Gray*, ed. J. Gray (Boston: Houghton Mifflin, 1893).

GRIBBIN, JOHN, *Science: A History* (London: Allen Lane, 2002).

—— *The Fellowship: The Story of a Revolution* (London: Allen Lane, 2005).

GRIBBIN, JOHN AND CHERFAS, JEREMY, *The First Chimpanzee* (London: Penguin, 2001).

—— AND GRIBBIN, MARY, *FitzRoy* (London: Review, 2003).

HAGEN, VICTOR VON, *South America Called Them* (London: Robert Hale, 1949).

HARVEY, A. G., *Douglas of the Fir* (Cambridge, Mass.: Harvard University Press, 1947).

HEPPER, NIGEL (ed.), *Kew* (London: HMSO, 1982).

HONIGSBAUM, MARK, *The Fever Trail* (London: Macmillan, 2001).

HOOKE, ROBERT, *The Diary of Robert Hooke*, ed. Henry Robinson and Walter Adams (London: Taylor & Francis, 1935).

HOOKER, J. D., *Himalayan Journals* (2nd edn., London: J. Murray, 1855; repr. London: Ward, Lock, Bowden & Co., 1891).

HUXLEY, LEONARD, *Life and Letters of Sir Joseph Dalton Hooker*, 2 vols. (London: John Murray, 1918).

JACKSON, B. D., *Linnaeus* (London: Witherby, 1923) (English adaptation of Swedish book by Theodor Fries).

KENT, ADOLPHUS, *Veitch's Manual of the Conifer* (2nd edn., London: James Veitch & Sons, 1900).

KEYNES, GEOFFREY, *John Ray: A Bibliography, 1660–1970* (2nd edn., Amsterdam: Van Heusden, 1976) (first edition published London: Faber & Faber, 1951).

KILLIP, ELLSWORTH, *The Botanical Collections of William Lobb in Colombia* (Washington, DC: Smithsonian Institution, 1932).

KOERNER, LISBET, *Linnaeus* (Cambridge, Mass.: Harvard University Press, 1999).

LAMB, CHRISTIAN, *From the Ends of the Earth* (Honiton, Devon: Bene Factum Publishing, 2004).

LEE, JAMES, *An Introduction to Botany* (London: J. & R. Tonson, 1765).

LINDSAY, ANN AND HOUSE, SYD, *The Tree Collector* (London: Arum Press, 2005).

LYTE, CHARLES, *The Plant Hunters* (London: Orbis, 1983).

MARKHAM, ALBERT, *The Life of Sir Clements R. Markham* (London: John Murray, 1917).

MARKHAM, CLEMENTS, *Peruvian Bark* (London: John Murray, 1880).

—— *Travels in Peru and India* (London: John Murray, 1862).

MASSON, FRANCIS, *An Account of Three Journeys from Cape Town in to the Southern Parts of Africa* (Kew: Royal Botanic Gardens, 1775).

—— *Francis Masson's Account of Three Journeys at the Cape of Good Hope, 1772–1775*, ed. F. R. Bradlow (Cape Town: Tablecloth Press, 1994).

MORWOOD, W., *Traveller in a Vanished Landscape* (London: Gentry, 1973).

MUSGRAVE, TOBY, GARDENER, CHRIS, AND MUSGRAVE, WILL, *The Plant Hunters* (London: Ward Lock, 1998).

NORTH, MARIANNE, *Recollections of a Happy Life*, 2 vols., ed. Catherine Symonds (London: Macmillan, 1892); a third volume, *Further Recollections of a Happy Life*, appeared in 1893; an accessible condensation of North's books was published in one volume under the title *A Vision of Eden* by the Royal Botanical Gardens, Kew, 1993.

O'BRIAN, PATRICK, *Joseph Banks* (London: Collins Harvill, 1988).

RAVEN, CHARLES, *John Ray* (Cambridge: Cambridge University Press, 1942).

RAY, JOHN, *Correspondence of John Ray*, ed. Edwin Lankester (London: Ray Society, 1848).

—— *Further Correspondence of John Ray*, ed. R. W. T. Gunther (London: Ray Society, 1928).

ROCCO, FIAMMETTA, *The Miraculous Fever-Tree* (London: Harper Collins, 2003).

SCOURSE, N., *The Victorians and their Flowers* (London: Croom Helm, 1983).

A Selection of the Correspondence of Linnaeus and Other Naturalists, ed. J. E. Smith (London: Longman, 1821).

SHEPHARD, SUE, *Seeds of Fortune* (London: Bloomsbury, 2003).

SHORT, PHILIP, *In Pursuit of Plants* (Portland, Ore.: Timber Press, 2004).

SMITH, A., *Explorers of the Amazon* (New York: Viking, 1990).

SMITH, EDWARD, *The Life of Sir Joseph Banks* (London: John Lane/ Bodley Head, 1911).

SPRUCE, RICHARD, *Notes of a Botanist on the Amazon and the Andes*, ed. Alfred Russel Wallace (London: Macmillan, 1908).

STAFLEU, FRANS, *Linnaeus and the Linnaeans* (Utrecht: Oosthoek, 1971).

TAYLOR, NORMAN, *Cinchona in Java: The Story of Quinine* (New York: Greenberg, 1945).

STEARN, WILLIAM, *Stearn's Dictionary of Plant Names for Gardeners* (London: Cassell, 1972).

THUNBERG, CARL PETER, *Resa uti Europa, Africa, Asia* (Uppsala, 1789; English translation, *Travels in Europe, Africa and Asia* published by F. & C. Rivington, London, 1795).

—— *Travels at the Cape of Good Hope, 1772–1775*, ed. Vernon Forbes (Cape Town: Van Riebeeck Society, 1986) (based on the original English version published in London between 1793 and 1795).

TURRILL, W. B., *The Royal Botanic Gardens, Kew, Past and Present* (London: H. Jenkins, 1959).

—— *Joseph Dalton Hooker* (London: Nelson & Sons, 1963).

VEITCH, JAMES HERBERT, *Hortus Veitchii*, published privately by James Veitch & Sons, 1906.

WALLACE, ALFRED RUSSEL, *A Narrative of Travels on the Amazon and Rio Negro* (London: Reeve, 1853).

WARD, NATHANIEL, *On the Growth of Plants in Closely Glazed Cases* (London: John Van Voorst, 1842).

WHITTLE, TYLER, *The Plant Hunters* (Philadelphia: Chilton, 1970).

WILSON, ERNEST, *Plant Hunting* (Boston: Harvard University Press, 1927).

INDEX